THE WORKS OF SRI CHINMOY

PRAYERS

VOLUME I

THE WORKS OF SRI CHINMOY

PRAYERS

VOLUME I

★

MY MORNING SOUL-BODY PRAYERS

LYON · OXFORD
GANAPATI PRESS
LXXXIX

© 2019 THE SRI CHINMOY CENTRE

ISBN 978-1-911319-20-7

See appendix for notice regarding this edition.

FIRST EDITION WENT TO PRESS ON 7 FEBRUARY 2019

PRAYERS

VOLUME I

MY MORNING SOUL-BODY PRAYERS

1. AUTHOR'S INTRODUCTION

Every day, with folded hands, I give these prayers for you, for humanity. I do this not for myself. I do it for all my spiritual children. I do not think about what I am going to say on any particular day. I just throw myself into the Universal Consciousness and identify myself with this person or that person. It is like plucking a flower from a garden. The flower that I like most, I take. I see that one particular prayer is most appropriate for that person on that day. Tomorrow I will identify with someone else. It is all oneness, oneness, oneness. Where my spiritual children are, I also am there. If you take me to hell, even there I will go, but with the hope that one day I will be able to bring you to Heaven.

–Sri Chinmoy

SRI CHINMOY

30 SEPTEMBER 1998

2

My Supreme, my Supreme, my Supreme,
I do not know what I am doing,
But I do know that You know
What You are doing
In and through me
For Your own Manifestation-Light
Here on earth
And for Your own Satisfaction-Delight
There in Heaven.
My Supreme, my Supreme, my Supreme!

MY MORNING SOUL-BODY PRAYERS

1 OCTOBER 1998

3

My Supreme, my Supreme, my Supreme,
When I cry for You,
The Beauty of Your Eye
Embraces my heart.
When I smile at You,
The Fragrance of Your Heart
Pilots my life-boat
To Your own Golden Shore
Of the ever-transcending Beyond.
My Supreme, my Supreme, my Supreme!

4

My Supreme, my Supreme, my Supreme!
My prayer to God tells me
How far away my mind is
From God.
My meditation on God tells me
How close my heart is
To God.
My Supreme, my Supreme, my Supreme!

2 OCTOBER 1998

5

My Supreme, my Supreme, my Supreme,
May my self-giving
Remain ever-increasing
To see Your creation smiling
And Your Heartbeats dancing.
My Supreme, my Supreme, my Supreme!

6

My Supreme, my Supreme, my Supreme,
Your Compassion-Eye
Spoke a Nectar-Word
To my aspiration-heart
And changed my life entirely.
My Supreme, my Supreme, my Supreme!

MY MORNING SOUL-BODY PRAYERS

3 OCTOBER 1998

7

My Supreme, my Supreme, my Supreme,
May I prayerfully breathe in Love
From Your Heart
And soulfully breathe out peace
To all my brothers and sisters
Of the world.
My Supreme, my Supreme, my Supreme!

5 OCTOBER 1998

8

My Supreme, my Supreme, my Supreme!
O God-faith-heart-telescope,
I love you, I love you, I love you.
O God-doubt-mind-microscope,
I detest you, I detest you, I detest you.
My Supreme, my Supreme, my Supreme!

9

My Supreme, my Supreme, my Supreme!
O greatness-mind,
You are a part-time God-worshipper.
O goodness-heart,
You are a full-time God-worshipper,
God-lover, God-server
And God-fulfiller
Here on earth and there in Heaven.
My Supreme, my Supreme, my Supreme!

10

My Supreme, my Supreme, my Supreme!
My mind tells God that it wants to be
A great leader of mankind.
God says to my mind,
"My son, wait, wait.
When the time arrives,
I shall inform you."

My heart tells God that it wishes to be
A humble server of mankind.
God says to my heart,
"My child, My child, come!
Come and sit with Me
On My Golden Throne;
Embrace Me, embrace Me,
I am all yours.
I have so many things, My child,
For you to do for Me.
You may begin here and now."
My Supreme, my Supreme, my Supreme!

6 OCTOBER 1998

11

My Supreme, my Supreme, my Supreme,
May my heart love You
Exactly the way my soul loves You.
May my life need You
Exactly the way my heart needs You.
My Supreme, my Supreme, my Supreme!

12

My Supreme, my Supreme, my Supreme,
May my past life
Not remain in me as a thorn.
May my present life
Be the beauty of my heart.
May my future life
Be the fragrance of my soul.
My Supreme, my Supreme, my Supreme!

13

My Supreme, my Supreme, my Supreme,
Do stop my mind's
Wild interruptions
When You and I enjoy
Our heart-to-heart
Power-conversations.
My Supreme, my Supreme, my Supreme!

14

My Supreme, my Supreme, my Supreme,
My dear Supreme, My Lord Supreme,
My Beloved Supreme,
My Absolute Lord Beloved Supreme,
To You I bow,
To You I bow,
To You I bow,
To You I bow.
My prayer
Is my God-search.
My meditation
Is my God-discovery.
My prayer
Is my God-love-infancy-cry.
My meditation
Is my God-oneness-intimacy-smile.
My Supreme, my Supreme, my Supreme!

10 OCTOBER 1998

15

My Supreme, my Supreme, my Supreme,
Do transform my heart, my mind,
My vital and my body
In the Compassion-Flames
Of Your Love-Sun.
My Supreme, my Supreme, my Supreme!

16

My Supreme, my Supreme, my Supreme!
O humanity's mind,
Love God, love God, love God.
If you love God,
You will never run the risk
Of entering into the darkness-abyss.
My Supreme, my Supreme, my Supreme!

17

My Supreme, my Supreme, my Supreme,
Out of Your infinite Bounty,
You have freed my soul
From all weaknesses.
Can You not do the same
For my heart, mind, vital and body?
My Supreme, my Supreme, my Supreme!

MY MORNING SOUL-BODY PRAYERS

15 OCTOBER 1998

18

My Supreme, my Supreme, my Supreme,
Many, many difficulties I have
In every aspect of my life.
That does not mean
That I shall doubt You
Or I shall doubt myself.
No, I shall just take shelter
Under Your Protection-Canopy,
And with the help
Of Your Compassion-flooded Eye,
I shall conquer all my difficulties
Within and without.
My Supreme, my Supreme, my Supreme!

19

My Supreme, my Supreme, my Supreme,
You are far beyond my clasp,
Yet You have chosen
To be within my easy clasp.

My Supreme, my Supreme, my Supreme,
I do not dare to claim You,
Yet You have chosen me to claim You
As my own, very own.
My Supreme, my Supreme, my Supreme!

20

My Supreme, my Supreme, my Supreme,
There is only one real failure in my life,
And that failure is
When I do not come to You
Lovingly, cheerfully and self-givingly.
My Supreme, my Supreme, my Supreme!

MY MORNING SOUL-BODY PRAYERS

16 OCTOBER 1998

21

My Supreme, my Supreme, my Supreme,
May the doubting mind of the world
Accept the all-illumining Light
Of the world's Inner Pilot,
And that Inner Pilot is You
And You
And nobody else.
My Supreme, my Supreme, my Supreme!

18 OCTOBER 1998

22

My Supreme, my Supreme, my Supreme,
Every morning You stand before me
With Your infinite Compassion-Light.
Alas, alas, I do not know how
To receive Your Light.
Please, my Lord,
Since You take the trouble
Of coming to me every morning
With Your infinite Light,
Will You not teach me how to receive
Even an iota of Your Light
To transform my nature
And fulfil You inside my life?
My Supreme, my Supreme, my Supreme!

23

My Supreme, my Supreme, my Supreme,
My Beloved Supreme,
Only when Your unconditional Grace
Descends,
My heart, my life
And everything that I have and am
Can ascend.
My Supreme, my Supreme, my Supreme!

24

My Supreme, my Supreme, my Supreme,
My happiness is the creation
Of Your Feet.
My happiness is the inspiration
Of Your Eye.
My happiness is the manifestation
Of Your Life.
My Supreme, my Supreme, my Supreme!

(AFTER COMPLETING THE LIFTS)

My Lord, I have made a new record. Your unconditional Grace has enabled me to make a new record in my bodyweight lift.

25

My Supreme, my Supreme, my Supreme,
The closer my heart and I come to You,
The harder my mind and vital strike You.
Why? Why? Why?
Why do You not stop my mind and vital
From this wild insolence-behaviour?
My Supreme, my Supreme, my Supreme!

26

My Supreme, my Supreme, my Supreme,
You are telling me that it is Your task
To hide my mind's ignorance-night,
And it is my task to bring to the fore
My heart's wisdom-light.
My Supreme, I am all gratitude to You,
All gratitude to You.
My Supreme, my Supreme, my Supreme!

27

My Supreme, my Supreme, my Supreme,
My soul has placed its victory-crown
At Your Lotus-Feet
Lovingly, prayerfully and self-givingly.
May my heart, mind, vital and body
Do exactly the same.
My Supreme, my Supreme, my Supreme!

MY MORNING SOUL-BODY PRAYERS

(AFTER COMPLETING THE LIFT)

My Supreme, at long last I have done it, with Your boundless Grace. It is not my capacity, it is Your Compassion that has enabled me to lift up 120 pounds. It is Your Compassion, Your Compassion, Your Compassion and not my capacity.

21 OCTOBER 1998

28

My Supreme, my Supreme, my Supreme,
Do give me what You have:
Your Infinity's Compassion-Power,
And do receive from me what I am:
My mortality's surrender-strength.
My Supreme, my Supreme, my Supreme!

29

My Supreme, my Supreme, my Supreme,
Please do not allow me to pray to You
For the removal of my sufferings.
Please allow me to pray to You
Only to conquer all my sufferings.
My Supreme, my Supreme, my Supreme!

MY MORNING SOUL-BODY PRAYERS

23 OCTOBER 1998

30

My Supreme, my Supreme, my Supreme,
May this be my last prayerful promise:
I shall never, never, never
Lose faith in You.
My Supreme, my Supreme, my Supreme!

31

My Supreme, my Supreme, my Supreme,
The world cannot see You,
But You can see the world.
May this Blessing
Be enough for the world.
My Supreme, my Supreme, my Supreme!

32

My Supreme, my Supreme, my Supreme!
We do not realise
That in order to be perfect
In our outer life,
We must be perfect
In our inner heart first.
My Supreme, my Supreme, my Supreme!

24 OCTOBER 1998

33

My Supreme, my Supreme, my Supreme,
Voices I hear, inner and outer,
That lead me nowhere.
Yours is the only Voice,
My Lord Supreme,
That is carrying me
To Your Golden Shore.
My Supreme, my Supreme, my Supreme!

34

My Supreme, my Supreme, my Supreme,
Please tell me when I am going to learn
That I am nothing,
I can do nothing.
Everything is done in and through me
By You.
My Supreme, my Supreme, my Supreme!

35

My Supreme, my Supreme, my Supreme,
Although the world does not love me,
The world does not need me,
My Supreme,
I want to love the world,
I want to need the world.
If I can love the world
And if I can need the world,
Then I shall be able to blossom
In my heart-garden
With the purity of a lotus
And the beauty of a rose.
My Supreme, my Supreme, my Supreme!

36

My Supreme, my Supreme, my Supreme,
No dream of mine will ever be lost,
For I know that Your choice Hour
Will fulfil all my soulful dreams.
My Supreme, my Supreme, my Supreme!

37

My Supreme, my Supreme, my Supreme!
O pleasures and pains,
You are not of me.
Therefore, how do you dare
To claim me as your own,
Very own?
My Supreme, my Supreme, my Supreme!

27 OCTOBER 1998

38

My Supreme, my Supreme, my Supreme,
My prayer waits for Your Arrival.
My meditation opens my life-door
For You.
My contemplation begs You to occupy
My heart-seat.
My Supreme, my Supreme, my Supreme!

MY MORNING SOUL-BODY PRAYERS

28 OCTOBER 1998

39

My Supreme, my Supreme, my Supreme,
No more ingratitude in my thoughts.
No more ingratitude in my words.
No more ingratitude in my actions.
My Supreme, my Supreme, my Supreme!

30 OCTOBER 1998

40

My Supreme, my Supreme, my Supreme,
I am fulfilling three supreme Commands
Of Yours:
I am loving my prayer-life.
I am loving my temple-heart.
I am loving my shrine-breath.
My Supreme, my Supreme, my Supreme!

MY MORNING SOUL-BODY PRAYERS

1 NOVEMBER 1998

41

My Supreme, my Supreme, my Supreme,
Marathon I run, marathon I run,
Marathon –
To be the smile of Your Infinity's Dawn.
My Supreme, my Supreme, my Supreme!

SRI CHINMOY

2 NOVEMBER 1998

42

My Supreme, my Supreme, my Supreme,
May Your Light dispel my mind's
Darkness number one: ignorance.
May Your Oneness dispel my life's
Weakness number one: ingratitude.
My Supreme, my Supreme, my Supreme!

MY MORNING SOUL-BODY PRAYERS

3 NOVEMBER 1998

43

My Supreme, my Supreme, my Supreme,
Where is my ultimate victory?
My victory is inside
My heart's God-gratitude-tears;
My victory is inside
My life's God-surrender-smiles.
My Supreme, my Supreme, my Supreme!

4 NOVEMBER 1998

44

My Supreme, my Supreme, my Supreme,
Every day I pray to You
Only for one thing:
May today be the last day
Of my desire-life.
My Supreme, my Supreme, my Supreme!

6 NOVEMBER 1998

45

My Supreme, my Supreme, my Supreme,
My Lord Beloved Supreme,
Do break me into millions of pieces
Before, long before,
My ego plans to break me.
My Supreme, my Supreme, my Supreme!

7 NOVEMBER 1998

46

My Supreme, my Supreme, my Supreme,
May my life-boat ply
Between my singleness-mind
And
My oneness-heart
Every day.
My Supreme, my Supreme, my Supreme!

MY MORNING SOUL-BODY PRAYERS

8 NOVEMBER 1998

47

My Supreme, my Supreme, my Supreme,
My heart's inner conviction-power
Is my life's outer manifestation-delight.
My Supreme, my Supreme, my Supreme!

9 NOVEMBER 1998

48

My Supreme, my Supreme, my Supreme,
The material poverty of the human life
Pitifully cries.
The spiritual poverty of the human heart
Profusely bleeds.
My Supreme, my Supreme, my Supreme!

49

My Supreme, my Supreme, my Supreme,
How can a true peace-dreamer
Be a stranger to me?
No, he is my friend,
He is my brother,
He is my oneness-heart.
My Supreme, my Supreme, my Supreme!

50

My Supreme, my Supreme, my Supreme,
I am extremely, extremely, extremely
Grateful to You,
For You have chosen my heart
To be Your keynote speaker
All the time,
And not my confusing
And confused mind —
Never!
My Supreme, my Supreme, my Supreme!

MY MORNING SOUL-BODY PRAYERS

51

My Supreme, my Supreme, my Supreme,
My mind teaches me
How to forget You easily.
My heart teaches me
How to get You immediately.
My Supreme, my Supreme, my Supreme!

15 NOVEMBER 1998

52

My Supreme, my Supreme, my Supreme!
God, when I call You
My Lord Supreme,
I happily run faster than the fastest.
God, when I call You
My Lord Beloved Supreme,
I proudly fly higher than the highest.
God, when I call You
My Lord Beloved Absolute Supreme,
I self-givingly dive
Deeper than the deepest.
God, when I just call You
My Supreme, my Supreme, my Supreme,
We immediately claim each other
For Eternity
In the heart of Your Infinity's Home.
My Supreme, my Supreme, my Supreme!

53

My Supreme, my Supreme, my Supreme,
My heart-door is wide open.
Please do not stay outside like a dream,
But do come in and become a reality
In my life-breath.
My Supreme, my Supreme, my Supreme!

54

My Supreme, my Supreme, my Supreme,
My mind did not help me at all
To realise You.
My heart helped me in every way
To realise You.
And now my heart is the only one
That is helping me
And will forever help me
To manifest You completely
Here on earth.
Therefore, I have found my true friend
In my heart,
And my heart has found a true friend
In my life.
And my heart, my life and I
Know that there is only one Friend
To please,
And that Friend is You, my Lord —
You, with Your Compassion-Eye,
You, with Your Forgiveness-Heart.
My Supreme, my Supreme, my Supreme!

55

My Supreme, my Supreme, my Supreme,
I am not perfectly happy
When I love You.
I am not perfectly happy
When I serve You.
I am not perfectly happy
When I make my complete surrender
To Your Will.
I am completely happy
Only when I sleeplessly
And breathlessly claim You
As my own, very own.
My Supreme, my Supreme, my Supreme!

56

My Supreme, my Supreme, my Supreme,
My mind wants to enjoy
Itself only.
My heart wants to enjoy
Only You —
Your Compassion-Eye,
Your Forgiveness-Feet
And
Your Satisfaction-Heart.
My Supreme, my Supreme, my Supreme!

57

My Supreme, my Supreme, my Supreme,
I am asking You to bless me
With satisfaction.
You are telling me that right now
What I need from You
Is instruction,
And not satisfaction.
Satisfaction will come in its own way
At the right time.
My Supreme, my Supreme, my Supreme!

58

My Supreme, my Supreme, my Supreme,
I am so grateful to You for allowing me
To watch the hide-and-seek game
That is being played by my purity-mind
And my sweetness-heart.
My Supreme, my Supreme, my Supreme!

MY MORNING SOUL-BODY PRAYERS

16 NOVEMBER 1998

59

My Supreme, my Supreme, my Supreme,
According to my mind,
My perfection is suspicion.
According to my heart,
My perfection is hesitation.
According to my soul,
My perfection is satisfaction.
According to me,
My perfection is Compassion –
Your Compassion,
Your unreserved Compassion,
Your unconditional Compassion.
My Supreme, my Supreme, my Supreme!

60

My Supreme, my Supreme, my Supreme,
You are asking me to tell
The whole world
That the aspiration-barrenness-sickness
Is definitely curable, curable, curable.
My Supreme, my Supreme, my Supreme!

61

My Supreme, my Supreme, my Supreme,
May my mind always remain
Wide awake, anxious and eager
To run towards You
To make You happy.
My Supreme, my Supreme, my Supreme!

62

My Supreme, my Supreme, my Supreme,
When I touched the God-realisation
Finish line,
You said to me, "My child,
I am extremely happy with you;
I am extremely proud of you.
But if you want Me to be
Infinitely more pleased with you
And infinitely more proud of you,
Then you must continue running
And reach the God-manifestation
Finish line."
My Supreme, my Supreme, my Supreme!

MY MORNING SOUL-BODY PRAYERS

17 NOVEMBER 1998

63

My Supreme, my Supreme, my Supreme,
I know, I know, I know,
No volcano-mind-determination,
No success-life-glory.
My Supreme, my Supreme, my Supreme!

64

My Supreme, my Supreme, my Supreme,
I know, I know, I know,
No mountain-heart-aspiration,
No progress-life-happiness.
My Supreme, my Supreme, my Supreme!

65

My Supreme, my Supreme, my Supreme,
Alas, why do we allow our body's fear
And our mind's doubt
To weaken our heart's faith in You?
My Supreme, my Supreme, my Supreme!

66

My Supreme, my Supreme, my Supreme,
What is the meaning of disobedience?
"My child, My child,
Disobedience means an unavoidable
Disaster-life."
My Supreme, my Supreme, my Supreme!

18 NOVEMBER 1998

67

My Supreme, my Supreme, my Supreme,
I am happy
When You guide my heart.
I am more happy
When You govern my mind.
I am infinitely more happy
When You enslave my life.
My Supreme, my Supreme, my Supreme!

68

My Supreme, my Supreme, my Supreme,
I do not learn my age
From the earthly calendar.
I learn my age
From my life-surrender to the Will
Of Your Compassion-Eye.
My Supreme, my Supreme, my Supreme!

69

My Supreme, my Supreme, my Supreme,
I do not need and I do not want
An exciting mind and an exciting vital.
My Supreme, I need from You
Only an inspiring mind
And an energising vital.
My Supreme, my Supreme, my Supreme!

70

My Supreme, my Supreme, my Supreme,
An ocean-vast fact-knowledge
Cannot properly guide my life,
But an iota of wisdom-delight
Can guide my life properly,
And it is doing so.
My Supreme, my Supreme, my Supreme!

21 NOVEMBER 1998

71

My Supreme, my Supreme, my Supreme,
Please, please promise to me
That You will never allow
My aspiration-lotus-heart
To wither.
"Never, My child, never!
Your aspiration-lotus-heart
Shall blossom and blossom and blossom."
My Supreme, my Supreme, my Supreme!

72

My Supreme, my Supreme, my Supreme,
My Heaven
Is inside Your Compassion-Eye.
My Heaven's Heaven
Is at Your Forgiveness-Feet.
My Supreme, my Supreme, my Supreme!

73

My Supreme, my Supreme, my Supreme,
Everything else can be separated,
But two things can never, never
Be separated:
Your Compassion-Eye
And
Your Forgiveness-Heart.
These two abide eternally together.
My Supreme, my Supreme, my Supreme!

74

My Supreme, my Supreme, my Supreme,
May my heart aspire
To Your complete Satisfaction.
May my life serve
To Your complete Satisfaction.
My Supreme, my Supreme, my Supreme!

22 NOVEMBER 1998

75

My Supreme, my Supreme, my Supreme,
I know, I know, I know,
Far above
All human punishment-laws
Is Your Forgiveness-Heart.
My Supreme, my Supreme, my Supreme!

76

My Supreme, my Supreme, my Supreme,
For me, the only way of living
Is my prayerful, soulful
And self-giving life.
My Supreme, my Supreme, my Supreme!

77

My Supreme, my Supreme, my Supreme,
With Your infinite Grace
I am discovering
My yesterday's weaknesses
To uncover
My tomorrow's strengths.
My Supreme, my Supreme, my Supreme!

78

My Supreme, my Supreme, my Supreme,
Every day
I prayerfully and gratefully watch
My full God-manifestation-hope
Blossoming
At Your Compassion-flooded Feet.
My Supreme, my Supreme, my Supreme!

MY MORNING SOUL-BODY PRAYERS

23 NOVEMBER 1998

79

My Supreme, my Supreme, my Supreme,
You do not allow impossibility-plant
To grow in my life's service-garden.
Such is Your Compassion for me!
My Supreme, my Supreme, my Supreme!

80

My Supreme, my Supreme, my Supreme,
Do give me the strength of self-giving.
In self-giving alone lies
My peace of mind
And
My heart of fulfilment.
My Supreme, my Supreme, my Supreme!

81

My Supreme, my Supreme, my Supreme!
The mind
Secretly and openly enjoys
Scattering disobedience-thoughts.
The heart
Prayerfully and self-givingly enjoys
The beauty and fragrance of obedience.
My Supreme, my Supreme, my Supreme!

82

My Supreme, my Supreme, my Supreme,
Smile, smile, smile,
So that my heart and I can feel
That You still love us.
My Supreme, my Supreme, my Supreme!

My Supreme, my Supreme, my Supreme,
Smile, smile, smile,
So that my life and I can know
That You still need us.
My Supreme, my Supreme, my Supreme!

MY MORNING SOUL-BODY PRAYERS

24 NOVEMBER 1998

83

My Supreme, my Supreme, my Supreme,
Why is it
That You are more pleased with me
When I play with You
Than when I pray to You?
"My child, just because
When you play with Me
You are more sincere
Than when you pray to Me.
A very difficult question,
But a very simple answer!"
My Supreme, my Supreme, my Supreme!

84

My Supreme, my Supreme, my Supreme,
You want me to offer You
Pure devotion at every moment.
My Supreme, I am all ready.
My heart is ready,
My mind is ready,
My vital is ready
And
My body is ready
To offer You devotion
At every moment.
My Supreme, my Supreme, my Supreme!

85

My Supreme, my Supreme, my Supreme,
My outer failure
Is my inner eye-opener.
My outer success
Is the beginning
Of my life's new dream.
My Supreme, my Supreme, my Supreme!

86

My Supreme, my Supreme, my Supreme,
God-doubt is the most ruthless
Self-torture.
God-faith is Infinity's
Self-rapture.
My Supreme, my Supreme, my Supreme!

MY MORNING SOUL-BODY PRAYERS

25 NOVEMBER 1998

87

My Supreme, my Supreme, my Supreme,
Please tell me how I can free myself
From my earth-bound limited self.
"My child, just go and stay
All the time
With your Heaven-free unlimited Self.
Your earth-bound limited self
Will not dare to follow you."
My Supreme, my Supreme, my Supreme!

88

My Supreme, my Supreme, my Supreme,
I am extremely grateful to You
For telling me that
I need more sincerity
In my aspiration
And more faithfulness
In my devotion,
So that I can have a peaceful mind
And a blissful heart
Beyond measure.
My Supreme, my Supreme, my Supreme!

89

My Supreme, my Supreme, my Supreme,
You are compassionately asking me
To correct and perfect
My unbelief and disbelief-mind,
So that I can be sleeplessly
And breathlessly happy.
My Supreme,
I shall fulfil Your kind Request.
I shall fulfil Your supreme Command.
My Supreme, my Supreme, my Supreme!

90

My Supreme, my Supreme, my Supreme,
I must choose only one thing:
Your Forgiveness-Delight,
Even though I do not know
When I shall experience it.
My Supreme, my Supreme, my Supreme!

MY MORNING SOUL-BODY PRAYERS

27 NOVEMBER 1998

91

My Supreme, my Supreme, my Supreme,
The more faith I have in You,
The sooner You claim me
As Your own, very own.
My Supreme, my Supreme, my Supreme!

92

My Supreme, my Supreme, my Supreme,
When I say that
Each and every human being is my friend,
I tell a lie.
When I say that
I have many, many friends,
It is another lie.
But when I say that
I have only one Friend,
And that Friend
Is my Lord Beloved Supreme,
Then I tell the Absolute Truth.
My Supreme, my Supreme, my Supreme!

93

My Supreme, my Supreme, my Supreme,
I have perfect faith in my faith.
The faith that has brought me to You
Will place me at Your Feet
And will keep me at Your Feet
Forever and forever and forever.
My Supreme, my Supreme, my Supreme!

SRI CHINMOY

30 NOVEMBER 1998

94

My Supreme, my Supreme, my Supreme,
Today marks
A new beginning of my life,
A new hope of my heart
And
A new promise of my soul.
My Supreme, my Supreme, my Supreme!

MY MORNING SOUL-BODY PRAYERS

1 DECEMBER 1998

95

My Supreme, my Supreme, my Supreme,
I do not need self-confidence.
I need only one thing:
Your Grace, Your Grace, Your Grace.
My Supreme, my Supreme, my Supreme!

2 DECEMBER 1998

96

My Supreme, my Supreme, my Supreme,
Since You are my Source
Of Infinity's Peace,
Infinity's Light
And
Infinity's Delight,
I must live inside my Source
And nowhere else, nowhere else.
My Supreme, my Supreme, my Supreme!

MY MORNING SOUL-BODY PRAYERS

5 DECEMBER 1998

97

My Supreme, my Supreme, my Supreme,
The human life is not for fun.
The human life is for a constant
And continuous run
Towards the Golden Shore.
My Supreme, my Supreme, my Supreme!

SRI CHINMOY

6 DECEMBER 1998

98

My Supreme, my Supreme, my Supreme,
My mind's outer battles
Shockingly weaken me.
My heart's inner battles
Astonishingly strengthen me,
Plus enlighten me.
My Supreme, my Supreme, my Supreme!

MY MORNING SOUL-BODY PRAYERS

7 DECEMBER 1998

99

My Supreme, my Supreme, my Supreme!
I have dispelled doubt from my mind.
I have invoked faith from my heart.
The Victory of my Lord's Compassion-Eye
I now am.
My Supreme, my Supreme, my Supreme!

8 DECEMBER 1998

100

My Supreme, my Supreme, my Supreme,
Your Newness does not satisfy me.
Your Oneness does not satisfy me.
Your Fulness does not satisfy me.
Only Your Forgiveness satisfies me.
Your Forgiveness satisfies me fully,
Integrally and eternally.
My Supreme, my Supreme, my Supreme!

MY MORNING SOUL-BODY PRAYERS

10 DECEMBER 1998

101

My Supreme, my Supreme, my Supreme,
Your Determination and Your Compassion
Will never mix
With my unwanted unwillingness.
My Supreme, my Supreme, my Supreme!

SRI CHINMOY

11 DECEMBER 1998

102

My Supreme, my Supreme, my Supreme,
I am crying for a new strength-discovery
Inside my body, vital, mind,
Heart and soul.
My Supreme, my Supreme, my Supreme!

MY MORNING SOUL-BODY PRAYERS

12 DECEMBER 1998

103

My Supreme, my Supreme, my Supreme,
May Thy supreme Victory be proclaimed
Even by my idle body, my restless vital,
My stupid mind and my weak heart.
My Supreme, my Supreme, my Supreme!

13 DECEMBER 1998

104

My Supreme, my Supreme, my Supreme,
Every day You perform countless miracles
To make Your children happy.
My Supreme, for me
Your most significant miracle
Is Your Smile.
Your Smile brings my dead body,
Dead vital, dead mind, dead heart
And even my dead soul to life.
My Supreme, my Supreme, my Supreme!

MY MORNING SOUL-BODY PRAYERS

14 DECEMBER 1998

105

My Supreme, my Supreme, my Supreme,
You are telling me
That in our spiritual life
The physical must not be rejected,
Must not be neglected.
The physical has to be accepted,
The physical has to be respected.
And also You are telling me
That the physical has a very special role
To perform in Your Cosmic Play.
My Supreme, my Supreme, my Supreme!

18 DECEMBER 1998

106

My Supreme, my Supreme, my Supreme,
Onward my body marches,
Inward my heart dives,
Upward my soul flies
To be at Your Feet,
To be Your choice instrument,
To please You and fulfil You
In Your own Way,
In Your own Way,
In Your own Way.
My Supreme, my Supreme, my Supreme!

MY MORNING SOUL-BODY PRAYERS

19 DECEMBER 1998

107

My Supreme, my Supreme, my Supreme,
The doubt of the human mind
Darkens and blights
The aspiration-heart.
The faith of the human mind
Brightens and strengthens
The dedication-life.
My Supreme, my Supreme, my Supreme!

SRI CHINMOY

20 DECEMBER 1998

108

My Supreme, my Supreme, my Supreme!
In the inner world,
My Lord Beloved Supreme
Blessingfully and compassionately
Feeds my heart.
In the outer world,
I prayerfully and self-givingly
Feed my Lord Beloved Supreme.

In the inner world,
God the Creator feeds me
With His infinite Compassion.
In the outer world,
I feed God the creation
With my blossoming love, devotion,
Surrender and gratitude.
My Supreme, my Supreme, my Supreme!

MY MORNING SOUL-BODY PRAYERS

21 DECEMBER 1998

109

My Supreme, my Supreme, my Supreme!
My mind,
Come, come, come!
Be brave, be brave, be brave!
Be pure, be pure, be pure!
Be prayerful, be prayerful, be prayerful!
Be soulful, be soulful, be soulful!
Surrender, surrender, surrender!
This is the time to surrender, my mind.
My Lord's infinite Patience
Does not astonish you?
My Supreme, my Supreme, my Supreme!

SRI CHINMOY

22 DECEMBER 1998

110

My Supreme, my Supreme, my Supreme,
When You teach me
In front of Your Third Eye,
My mind becomes happy.
When You teach me
Inside Your Heart,
My heart becomes happy.
And when You teach me
At Your Feet,
My entire earth-existence becomes happy.
My Supreme, my Supreme, my Supreme!

111

My Supreme, my Supreme, my Supreme,
The moment I touch Your Feet
And place myself lovingly, devotedly
And self-givingly at Your Feet,
You immediately turn me into
Your Message-Light
To cover the length and breadth
Of the world.
My Supreme, my Supreme, my Supreme!

MY MORNING SOUL-BODY PRAYERS

23 DECEMBER 1998

112

My Supreme, my Supreme, my Supreme,
May my outer life be
Your own Success-Speed-Beauty.
May my inner life be
Your own Progress-Satisfaction-Fragrance.
My Supreme, my Supreme, my Supreme!

29 DECEMBER 1998

113

My Supreme, my Supreme, my Supreme,
My only happiness
Is in the fulfilment
Of Your Commands.
My Supreme, my Supreme, my Supreme!

114

My Supreme, my Supreme, my Supreme!
My self-assertion,
You are embarrassing me.
You are weakening my heart.
You are destroying my life.
You are taking me away
Farther than the farthest
From my own divinity.
You are taking me away
Far beyond my own imagination
From my All,
My Lord Beloved Supreme.
My Supreme, my Supreme, my Supreme!

MY MORNING SOUL-BODY PRAYERS

30 DECEMBER 1998

115

My Supreme, my Supreme, my Supreme!
The human in me
Makes deplorable mistakes
Frequently.
The divine in me
Corrects my mistakes
Occasionally.
The Supreme in me
Forgives them and illumines them.
My Supreme, my Supreme, my Supreme!

116

My Supreme, my Supreme, my Supreme!
O my past,
Away you go, away you go, away you go!
O my present,
You must always be with me,
In me and for me.
O my future,
I am preparing myself for you,
Lovingly, carefully and prayerfully,
Soulfully, powerfully and eagerly,
Enthusiastically and self-givingly.
My Supreme, my Supreme, my Supreme!

31 DECEMBER 1998

117

My Supreme, my Supreme, my Supreme,
My Lord Beloved Supreme,
Smile, smile, smile!
Do You not know, my Beloved Supreme,
That a fleeting Smile of Yours
Can win my crying and bleeding heart
A million times over?
My Supreme, my Supreme, my Supreme!

118

My Supreme, my Supreme, my Supreme,
The divine in me
Loftily and unreservedly
Appreciates, admires and adores
The divine in me.
The undivine in me
Ruthlessly and indefinitely
Fights against the undivine in me.
My Supreme, my Supreme, my Supreme!

MY MORNING SOUL-BODY PRAYERS

1 JANUARY 1999

119

My Supreme, my Supreme, my Supreme,
May my outer service-life
Be the beauty of the New Year.
May my inner aspiration-heart
Be the fragrance of the New Year.
My Supreme, my Supreme, my Supreme!

120

My Supreme, my Supreme, my Supreme!
My yesterday,
I am all gratitude to you.
My today,
I am extremely, extremely and extremely
Proud of you.
My tomorrow,
You and I together
Shall fulfil our Lord Beloved Supreme
Far beyond the flights of our imagination.
My Supreme, my Supreme, my Supreme!

2 JANUARY 1999

121

My Supreme, my Supreme, my Supreme,
Out of Your Heart's infinite Bounty,
You are telling me
To take my world-service-opportunity
As something divinely significant
And supremely sacred.
My Supreme, my Supreme, my Supreme!

122

My Supreme, my Supreme, my Supreme,
May my God-closeness be
An infallible
And
Ever-blossoming experience.

May my God-oneness be
An everlasting
And
Ever-transcending reality.
My Supreme, my Supreme, my Supreme!

MY MORNING SOUL-BODY PRAYERS

3 JANUARY 1999

123

My Supreme, my Supreme, my Supreme,
You are telling me
That our belief in You is not sufficient.
We must make You a living Reality
On earth
If we want to prove
That we love You only
And we need You only.
My Supreme, my Supreme, my Supreme!

124

My Supreme, my Supreme, my Supreme,
You have brought me into the world
To tell humanity what I know about You.
You have not brought me into the world
To teach humanity – no, never!
My Supreme, my Supreme, my Supreme!

5 JANUARY 1999

125

My Supreme, my Supreme, my Supreme,
I do not want to have a mind
That either ridicules me
Or extols me to the skies.
The opinion of the mind
Is of no consequence to me.
My Supreme, my Supreme, my Supreme,
I only need a heart
To love You and be loved by You.
My Supreme, my Supreme, my Supreme!

126

My Supreme, my Supreme, my Supreme,
My name is self-confidence
Only because my self-confidence
Is founded upon
My God-obedience and God-reliance.
When my God-obedience
And my God-reliance
Want me to have self-confidence,
I accept it.
Otherwise, I only want my life to be
God-obedience and God-reliance.
My Supreme, my Supreme, my Supreme!

MY MORNING SOUL-BODY PRAYERS

6 JANUARY 1999

127

My Supreme, my Supreme, my Supreme,
My heart's gratitude-attitude
Is
My life's plenitude-altitude.
My Supreme, my Supreme, my Supreme!

128

My Supreme, my Supreme, my Supreme,
I purposely forgot my lower self
To discover quickly my higher Self:
God, my Lord Beloved Supreme.
My Supreme, my Supreme, my Supreme!

7 JANUARY 1999

129

My Supreme, my Supreme, my Supreme,
Why do You not love me
Any more?
"My child, your question deserves
No answer."
My Supreme, my Supreme, my Supreme!

130

My Supreme, my Supreme, my Supreme,
Even if You do not love me
Any more,
Even if You do not speak to me
Any more,
I shall not leave You.

"My child, My child, My child,
You will not be able to leave Me.
You will not be able to run away
From Me.
You will not be able to escape
From My Infinity's Heart-Home,
My child, My child, My child!"
My Supreme, my Supreme, my Supreme!

MY MORNING SOUL-BODY PRAYERS

8 JANUARY 1999

131

My Supreme, my Supreme, my Supreme,
My heart is all gratitude to You
For telling me
That my tremendous concern
For humanity
Certifies my genuine love
For You.
My Supreme, my Supreme, my Supreme!

132

My Supreme, my Supreme, my Supreme,
You are telling me that spirituality
Is not a matter of
Rushing towards something.
Spirituality means self-giving
And God-becoming.
Deep within the fulness of time,
Each and every human being
Will realise God, reveal God
And manifest God.
This blessingful Message I am receiving
From You today.
My Supreme, my Supreme, my Supreme!

9 JANUARY 1999

133

My Supreme, my Supreme, my Supreme,
I am able to see You every day.
This is, indeed, not my highest privilege.
I am able to speak to You every day.
This is, indeed, not my highest privilege.
I am able to sit at Your Feet
Whenever I want to.
This is, indeed, not my highest privilege.
My Supreme, I am able to kiss
The dust of Your Feet
Every day to my heart's content.
This is, indeed, my highest,
Absolutely highest privilege.
My Supreme, my Supreme, my Supreme!

134

My Supreme, my Supreme, my Supreme,
You are asking me to be swift of foot
So that I can love You
Unreservedly and unconditionally.
You are asking me to be pure of heart
So that I can serve You
Sleeplessly and breathlessly.
My Supreme, my Supreme, my Supreme!

MY MORNING SOUL-BODY PRAYERS

10 JANUARY 1999

135

My Supreme, my Supreme, my Supreme,
Today my heart's God-revelation-hope
And
My life's God-manifestation-promise
Are so happily swimming together
In my soul's God-oneness-river.
My Supreme, my Supreme, my Supreme!

136

My Supreme, my Supreme, my Supreme,
Life is not
A tormenting fear-cloud.
Life is
A challenging, cheering, inspiring,
Illumining and fulfilling
Courage-sunburst.
My Supreme, my Supreme, my Supreme!

11 JANUARY 1999

137

My Supreme, my Supreme, my Supreme,
My life is made of excuses.
Your Heart is made of Forgiveness.
I give You what I have:
My nothingness.
You give me what You have:
Infinitude.
Plus, You give me what You are:
Your Eternity's Cry,
Your Infinity's Smile,
Your Immortality's Self-Transcendence-Dream-Reality.
My Supreme, my Supreme, my Supreme!

138

My Supreme, my Supreme, my Supreme,
You are so kind to me,
So compassionate to me.
You have given my gratitude-heart
And my surrender-life
Two front-row seats to watch,
Prayerfully and soulfully,
Your world-fulfilment-peace-performance.
My Supreme, my Supreme, my Supreme!

MY MORNING SOUL-BODY PRAYERS

12 JANUARY 1999

139

My Supreme, my Supreme, my Supreme,
I am piloting my heart-boat
To my surrender-harbour,
Where You are so indulgently,
Compassionately and proudly
Waiting for my prayerful
And soulful arrival.
My Supreme, my Supreme, my Supreme!

140

My Supreme, my Supreme, my Supreme,
No longer shall I remain
Blinded by the dust
Of my endlessly long desire-road.
My Supreme, my Supreme, my Supreme!

14 JANUARY 1999

141

My Supreme, my Supreme, my Supreme,
How is it possible for me
To hurt the ones
That I love deeply?
"My child, here is the proof
That you do not actually love them."

My Supreme, my Supreme, my Supreme,
Now tell me,
Do I not sincerely and deeply
Love You, my Supreme?
Why do You then hurt me so often,
If not always?
"My child, My child,
Go beyond, far beyond,
The boundaries of your futile mind.
Then you will have the answer
From Me."
My Supreme, my Supreme, my Supreme!

142

My Supreme, my Supreme, my Supreme,
Am I correct when I say
That each human being
Is a winner in his own way
In the desire-hunger-race?
"Yes, My child, you are correct,
Absolutely correct."
My Supreme, my Supreme, my Supreme!

MY MORNING SOUL-BODY PRAYERS

15 JANUARY 1999

143

My Supreme, my Supreme, my Supreme,
I must not stop halfway,
I must not!
I must reach the Golden Shore,
I must!
I must arrive
At the ever-transcending Beyond,
I must, I must, I must!
My Supreme, my Supreme, my Supreme!

144

My Supreme, my Supreme, my Supreme,
In vain I pray to God the Creator
And
In vain I meditate on God the Creator
If I do not love God the creation
And
If I do not serve God the creation.
My Supreme, my Supreme, my Supreme!

16 JANUARY 1999

145

My Supreme, my Supreme, my Supreme,
The self-made man proudly thinks
That he can do and he can become.
The God-made man devotedly
And unmistakably sees
That God has already done
Everything for him
And
God Himself has chosen him
To be God's choicest instrument.
My Supreme, my Supreme, my Supreme!

146

My Supreme, my Supreme, my Supreme,
The divine within
Welcomes and embraces
The divine without.
The undivine within
Challenges
The undivine without,
And they fight and destroy each other.
My Supreme, my Supreme, my Supreme!

MY MORNING SOUL-BODY PRAYERS

17 JANUARY 1999

147

My Supreme, my Supreme, my Supreme,
Finally, I have come to realise
That the supremely divine way
Of living here on earth
Is to live
The God-surrender-determination-
Fulfilment-way.
My Supreme, my Supreme, my Supreme!

148

My Supreme, my Supreme, my Supreme,
Finally, I have come to realise
That to be happy and remain happy
We must forget the past,
We must!
To be happy and remain happy
We must love and serve the present,
We must!
To be happy and remain happy
We must prepare ourselves for the future,
We must, we must!
My Supreme, my Supreme, my Supreme!

19 JANUARY 1999

149

My Supreme, my Supreme, my Supreme,
My soul's
Perfection-freedom-delight
Is my divinity.
My life's
Imperfection-bondage-unhappiness
Is my humanity.
My Supreme, my Supreme, my Supreme!

150

My Supreme, my Supreme, my Supreme,
With my mind's courage-sword,
I go forward.
With my life's patience-shield,
I dive inward.
With my heart's compassion-flute,
I soar upward.
My Supreme, my Supreme, my Supreme!

MY MORNING SOUL-BODY PRAYERS

20 JANUARY 1999

151

My Supreme, my Supreme, my Supreme,
I live in this world
Neither to possess the world
Nor to be possessed by the world.
I live in this world
To love the world,
To serve the world
And
To become the world —
The beautiful and breathtaking
Creation of God.
My Supreme, my Supreme, my Supreme!

152

My Supreme, my Supreme, my Supreme,
My love readily and willingly
Climbs high
To look at Your Eye.
My devotion intensely and eagerly
Climbs higher
To feel Your Heart.
My surrender sleeplessly and breathlessly
Climbs highest
To sit at Your Feet
And
Wait for Your Commands.
My Supreme, my Supreme, my Supreme!

22 JANUARY 1999

153

My Supreme, my Supreme, my Supreme,
I must climb beyond
All obstacle-mountains
To reach Your Life's Pride-Fountain
And
Your Heart's Satisfaction-Fountain.
My Supreme, my Supreme, my Supreme!

154

My Supreme, my Supreme, my Supreme,
May my aspiration-heart
And my dedication-life
Be both firmly rooted
In my surrender-soil.
My Supreme, my Supreme, my Supreme!

MY MORNING SOUL-BODY PRAYERS

23 JANUARY 1999

155

My Supreme, my Supreme, my Supreme,
My searching eyes desperately desire
Your outer Concern-Presence.
My crying heart breathlessly desires
Your inner Compassion-Presence.
My Supreme, my Supreme, my Supreme!

156

My Supreme, my Supreme, my Supreme,
Your Nearness-Presence
Is unimaginably blissful.
Your Remoteness-Presence
Is unforgettably painful.
My Supreme, my Supreme, my Supreme!

24 JANUARY 1999

157

My Supreme, my Supreme, my Supreme,
May I worship You sleeplessly
And breathlessly
In my love-devotion-surrender-delight-
Temple-heart.
My Supreme, my Supreme, my Supreme!

158

My Supreme, my Supreme, my Supreme,
Today I am determined
To smash asunder
My mind's long and strong
Desire-train-chain.
My Supreme, my Supreme, my Supreme!

MY MORNING SOUL-BODY PRAYERS

5 FEBRUARY 1999

159

My Supreme, my Supreme, my Supreme!
I must always remain
Inside my temple-heart
To become
A supremely choice instrument
Of Yours.
My Supreme, my Supreme, my Supreme!

160

My Supreme, my Supreme, my Supreme!
I am praying to You
Not for a shorter destination-road,
But for two bright eyes
And
Two stronger legs.
My Supreme, my Supreme, my Supreme!

6 FEBRUARY 1999

161

My Supreme, my Supreme, my Supreme!
My heart, my God-seeker-heart,
My God-dreamer-heart, my God-lover-heart,
True, you have a few unfortunate critics,
But certainly you have no equal,
And you do not have even one worthy rival.
My heart, my heart, my heart!
My Supreme, my Supreme, my Supreme!

162

My Supreme, my Supreme, my Supreme!
Your unconditional Grace
Has made my sleeplessly self-giving heart
A God-discovery-delight.
My Supreme, my Supreme, my Supreme!

MY MORNING SOUL-BODY PRAYERS

8 FEBRUARY 1999

163

My Supreme, my Supreme, my Supreme!
I know, I know, I know,
My physical ability, my vital ability
And my mental ability
Entirely depend on
My spiritual dependability,
And my spiritual dependability
Is all Your unconditional Compassion.
My Supreme, my Supreme, my Supreme!

164

My Supreme, my Supreme, my Supreme!
I shall not give up, I shall not give up!
I shall continue, I shall continue!
No matter how many times I have failed,
I shall continue.
Regret is worthless, regret is useless,
Regret is totally futile.
I shall keep on!
I must reach my destination, I must!
My goal is beckoning me.
My Supreme, my Supreme, my Supreme!

9 FEBRUARY 1999

165

My Supreme, my Supreme, my Supreme!
The ambition of my vital and my mind
To become another Julius Caesar
Or Napoleon or Akbar
Compels You to swim in the sea
Of sorrows.

The aspiration of my heart
To become a sleeplessly self-giving
Child of Yours
Inspires You to swim in the sea
Of ecstasy.
My Supreme, my Supreme, my Supreme!

166

My Supreme, my Supreme, my Supreme!
I must not choose joys.
I must not choose sorrows.
I must choose You,
Only You, only You, only You.
My Supreme, my Supreme, my Supreme!

167

My Supreme, my Supreme, my Supreme!
I shall no more compel You
To play the role of a fool
In me, through me and for me.
My Supreme, my Supreme, my Supreme!

168

My Supreme, my Supreme, my Supreme!
My heart's gratitude-offering to You
Is my immediate experience
Of Heaven's Delight.
My Supreme, my Supreme, my Supreme!

SRI CHINMOY

10 FEBRUARY 1999

169

My Supreme, my Supreme, my Supreme!
What I need is resolute faith
To love more sincerely
The Heart of God the Creator
And to serve most devotedly
The Feet of God the creation.
My Supreme, my Supreme, my Supreme!

170

My Supreme, my Supreme, my Supreme!
My world-opinion is the thickness
Of my mind's stupidity-night.
My world-union is the brightness
Of my heart's wisdom-light.
My Supreme, my Supreme, my Supreme!

171

My Supreme, my Supreme, my Supreme!
I must love You more,
I must value You more,
If I desperately need to arrive
At Your Golden Shore.
My Supreme, my Supreme, my Supreme!

MY MORNING SOUL-BODY PRAYERS

172

My Supreme, my Supreme, my Supreme!
My mind,
Today you must go out of your way
To love the world, to serve the world
And to become
The beauty and the fragrance
Of the world.
My Supreme, my Supreme, my Supreme!

15 FEBRUARY 1999

173

My Supreme, my Supreme, my Supreme!
May my life become
An ever-blossoming God-gratitude-heart.
My Supreme, my Supreme, my Supreme!

174

My Supreme, my Supreme, my Supreme!
The rose-beginning of the day
Is not my mind's emptiness-fantasy,
But my heart's fulness-ecstasy.
My Supreme, my Supreme, my Supreme!

175

My Supreme, my Supreme, my Supreme!
You want each and every human being
To be a God-manifestation-hero-warrior.
How I wish we could fulfil
Your blessingful Command
Lovingly, cheerfully, unreservedly
And unconditionally!
My Supreme, my Supreme, my Supreme!

176

My Supreme, my Supreme, my Supreme!
My mind, my mind, my mind,
It matters not how much you know.
For me to have joy and peace,
It only matters to what extent
You are ready, willing and eager
To unlearn.
My Supreme, my Supreme, my Supreme!

MY MORNING SOUL-BODY PRAYERS

16 FEBRUARY 1999

177

My Supreme, my Supreme, my Supreme!
Do tell me when I will be able
To need You desperately
The way a drowning man
Needs to catch a breath!
My Supreme, my Supreme, my Supreme!

178

My Supreme, my Supreme, my Supreme!
I need peace, I need peace,
I need peace.
Today I must put an end
To all my frustrations, irritations
And exasperations.
My Supreme, my Supreme, my Supreme!

179

My Supreme, my Supreme, my Supreme!
My soul has zero tolerance
For God-disobedience-seekers.
My Supreme, my Supreme, my Supreme!

180

My Supreme, my Supreme, my Supreme!
Today I must win
My love-devotion-surrender-trophy
From You.
My Supreme, my Supreme, my Supreme!

181

My Supreme, my Supreme, my Supreme!
I must run faster than the fastest
To my beckoning Goal
To fulfil my Lord's express Desire.
My Supreme, my Supreme, my Supreme!

182

My Supreme, my Supreme, my Supreme!
Please tell me what You want from me.
I shall immediately give it to You.

"My child, I need only one thing from you:
Your surrender-blossom-smile."

My Supreme, my surrender-blossom-smile
Is all Yours.
I place it at Your Feet.
Do make me Your own, very own.
My Supreme, my Supreme, my Supreme!

MY MORNING SOUL-BODY PRAYERS

21 FEBRUARY 1999

183

My Supreme, my Supreme, my Supreme!
Out of Your infinite Bounty,
Do bless me with a God-adoration-mind,
A God-devotion-heart
And a God-worship-breath.
My Supreme, my Supreme, my Supreme!

184

My Supreme, my Supreme, my Supreme!
I am avidly devouring
The golden dust of Your Feet.
My Supreme, please, please
Promise to me
That You will blessingfully feed
My life's devotion-tree
Whenever it is needed.
My Supreme, my Supreme, my Supreme!

185

My Supreme, my Supreme, my Supreme!
Every day, in the small hours
Of the morning,
I devotedly send You an express telegram
With a prayerful gratitude-message-cry.
My Supreme, do You ever read
My express telegrams?

"My child, not only do I read them,
But I love them and I treasure them."
My Supreme, my Supreme, my Supreme!

22 FEBRUARY 1999

186

My Supreme, my Supreme, my Supreme!
Please tell me how I can be
A choice instrument of Yours.

"My child, just try to be
A constant, sleepless server
Of Mine.
You can be not only a choice
But the choicest instrument of Mine
If you can become
My sleepless eagerness-server."
My Supreme, my Supreme, my Supreme!

187

My Supreme, my Supreme, my Supreme!
There was a time when I used to dream
Of having a world of my own.
But now, my Supreme, I wish to live
Most devotedly in Your own World,
And nowhere else.
My Supreme, my Supreme, my Supreme!

188

My Supreme, my Supreme, my Supreme!
Please bless me and my heart
With a confidence-umbrella
So that we can easily walk
Through our mind's doubt-storms.
My Supreme, my Supreme, my Supreme!

189

My Supreme, my Supreme, my Supreme!
You allow me to breathe with You
Simultaneously
Only when my life
Is sleepless self-giving.
My Supreme, my Supreme, my Supreme!

23 FEBRUARY 1999

190

My Supreme, my Supreme, my Supreme!
My God-oneness-life
Entirely depends on
My heart's God-devotion-tears.
My Supreme, my Supreme, my Supreme!

191

My Supreme, my Supreme, my Supreme!
The eye that sees beauty
In every human being
And in every creation of God's
Is, indeed, a very special pride of God.
My Supreme, my Supreme, my Supreme!

192

My Supreme, my Supreme, my Supreme!
O my aspiring heart, smile, smile, smile!
If you smile,
You will be able to transform
All the obstacles that the doubting mind
Is creating for you.
My Supreme, my Supreme, my Supreme!

MY MORNING SOUL-BODY PRAYERS

24 FEBRUARY 1999

193

My Supreme, my Supreme, my Supreme!
I shall make all my golden dreams
Come true
By sleeplessly serving God the creation.
My Supreme, my Supreme, my Supreme!

194

My Supreme, my Supreme, my Supreme!
May I cry for You every day,
Every hour, every minute
And every second
With my heart's pure sincerity-tears.
My Supreme, my Supreme, my Supreme!

26 FEBRUARY 1999

195

My Supreme, my Supreme, my Supreme!
I feed my intense God-hunger
With my streaming
Devotion-heart-tears.
My Supreme, my Supreme, my Supreme!

196

My Supreme, my Supreme, my Supreme!
I am extremely grateful to You
For telling me
That my climbing heart-cries
Gladden Your Heart immensely.
My Supreme, my Supreme, my Supreme!

197

My Supreme, my Supreme, my Supreme!
To place myself at Your Lotus-Feet
My tearful heart cries and cries
And my soulful eyes smile and smile.
My Supreme, my Supreme, my Supreme!

MY MORNING SOUL-BODY PRAYERS

15 MARCH 1999

198

My Supreme, my Supreme, my Supreme!
I know, I know,
If I do not feed my God-hunger
With my devotion-heart,
Then my spiritual life will,
Without fail,
End in vain.
My Supreme, my Supreme, my Supreme!

199

My Supreme, my Supreme, my Supreme!
My Lord happily and immediately hires
The God-readiness, God-willingness
And God-eagerness-server.
My Supreme, my Supreme, my Supreme!

200

My Supreme, my Supreme, my Supreme!
May all human beings live
Smiling, singing and dancing
Their Heavenly oneness-life
Here on earth.
My Supreme, my Supreme, my Supreme!

16 MARCH 1999

201

My Supreme, my Supreme, my Supreme!
I have come to realise
That in my spiritual life
My enthusiasm without my soulfulness
Is incomplete.
My Supreme, my Supreme, my Supreme!

202

My Supreme, my Supreme, my Supreme!
My Lord's Newness-Dream
Is my life's progress-reality.
My Supreme, my Supreme, my Supreme!

203

My Supreme, my Supreme, my Supreme!
Only one thing is indispensable
In my spiritual life
For God-realisation:
My obedience to my Master's will,
My obedience to my Master's will.
My Supreme, my Supreme, my Supreme!

MY MORNING SOUL-BODY PRAYERS

17 MARCH 1999

204

My Supreme, my Supreme, my Supreme!
When I am a humility-mind,
A sincerity-heart
And a purity-life,
I fly and fly and fly
In Infinity's Delight-Sky.
My Supreme, my Supreme, my Supreme!

205

My Supreme, my Supreme, my Supreme!
Your Forgiveness-Heart has changed
My inner life of aspiration
Completely.
Your Compassion-Eye has changed
My outer life of dedication
Amazingly.
My Supreme, my Supreme, my Supreme!

206

My Supreme, my Supreme, my Supreme!
I have discovered my God-oneness
In my heart's devotion-tears.
My Supreme, my Supreme, my Supreme!

18 MARCH 1999

207

My Supreme, my Supreme, my Supreme!
My heart's faith does not need God
To come and stand before me
When I pray and meditate,
But my mind's doubt not only expects
But also demands His Appearance.
My Supreme, my Supreme, my Supreme!

208

My Supreme, my Supreme, my Supreme!
My life will be flooded
With peace and bliss
Only when I say and do
Everything
With Your Kindness-Permission.
My Supreme, my Supreme, my Supreme!

209

My Supreme, my Supreme, my Supreme!
Only because of Your Heart's
All-fulfilling Blessing-Grace,
Today I am my life's
Smiling face.
My Supreme, my Supreme, my Supreme!

MY MORNING SOUL-BODY PRAYERS

19 MARCH 1999

210

My Supreme, my Supreme, my Supreme!
In my spiritual life,
My unconditional surrender
To Your Will
Far surpasses everything else
In beauty and divinity.
My Supreme, my Supreme, my Supreme!

211

My Supreme, my Supreme, my Supreme!
There was a time
When I had countless desires
For You to fulfil.
Now, my Supreme,
I have only one desire,
Only one,
And that desire is to sit
At Your Compassion-Feet
For the rest of my life.
My Supreme, my Supreme, my Supreme!

212

My Supreme, my Supreme, my Supreme!
My dear Supreme, my sweet Supreme,
My Lord Supreme, my Beloved Supreme,
My Absolute Supreme,
Your Compassion-Eye
Has taken away my empty mind,
My empty heart
And my empty life.
Now my mind can smile,
My heart can sing
And my life can dance.
My Supreme, my Supreme, my Supreme!

MY MORNING SOUL-BODY PRAYERS

21 MARCH 1999

213

My Supreme, my Supreme, my Supreme!
The mind does not want
To surrender to You.
Therefore, the mind cannot enjoy
The delight of oneness-freedom.
My Supreme, my Supreme, my Supreme!

214

My Supreme, my Supreme, my Supreme!
My implicit faith in You
Is the smile-beauty
Of my heart-garden.
My Supreme, my Supreme, my Supreme!

215

My Supreme, my Supreme, my Supreme!
The very start of a new adventure
Is giving me tremendous joy.
My Supreme, my Supreme, my Supreme!

(AFTER THE PRAYER)

I have never attempted 180 lbs – never, never, never! So this will be my first attempt, and it is my new adventure.

22 MARCH 1999

216

My Supreme, my Supreme, my Supreme!
I love You only, only, only.
I need You only, only, only.

"My child, come, come, come!
Come to Me.
You and I shall fly together
In My Heart's Ecstasy-Sky."
My Supreme, my Supreme, my Supreme!

217

My Supreme, my Supreme, my Supreme!
You only ask me to do
What I must do.
My Supreme, I am telling You
That I shall do everything
You ask me to do
Immediately, happily, cheerfully,
Soulfully, self-givingly
And unconditionally.
My Supreme, my Supreme, my Supreme!

MY MORNING SOUL-BODY PRAYERS

218

My Supreme, my Supreme, my Supreme!
My dear Supreme, my sweet Supreme,
My Lord Supreme, my Beloved Supreme,
My Absolute Supreme,
My only, only Supreme,
Out of Your Heart's infinite Bounty,
You are making my heart
A new dream of Your own Heart;
You are making my life
A new reality of Your own Vision-Eye.
My Supreme, my Supreme, my Supreme!

26 MARCH 1999

219

My Supreme, my Supreme, my Supreme!
My Supreme,
You are telling me
That my purity-heart
Is a very special child
Of Yours.
My Supreme, my Supreme, my Supreme!

220

My Supreme, my Supreme, my Supreme!
Each desire-fulfilment
Is immediately followed
By heavy taxes!
My Supreme, my Supreme, my Supreme!

221

My Supreme, my Supreme, my Supreme!
Please bless me
With some divine capacities
So You can put them to use
Smilingly, lovingly
And compassionately.
My Supreme, my Supreme, my Supreme!

MY MORNING SOUL-BODY PRAYERS

28 MARCH 1999

222

My Supreme, my Supreme, my Supreme!
Every day,
In the small hours of the morning,
I speedily run to my shrine
To measure my devotion-heart
And treasure Your Compassion-Eye.
My Supreme, my Supreme, my Supreme!

223

My Supreme, my Supreme, my Supreme!
Out of Your infinite Bounty,
You are asking me not to worry.
You will transform my mind-jungle
Into a rose-blossom garden
Before long.
My Supreme, my Supreme, my Supreme!

224

My Supreme, my Supreme, my Supreme!
You love me now,
But You will love me
Infinitely, infinitely, infinitely more
If I love You only
And if I do not beg You
To tell me who You truly are.
My Supreme, my Supreme, my Supreme!

31 MARCH 1999

225

My Supreme, my Supreme, my Supreme!
My prayer is my oneness
With Your Transcendental Eye.
My meditation is my fulness
Inside Your Universal Heart.
My Supreme, my Supreme, my Supreme!

226

My Supreme, my Supreme, my Supreme!
I become the tower of strength
Only when I remain seated
At Your Compassion-Feet.
My Supreme, my Supreme, my Supreme!

227

My Supreme, my Supreme, my Supreme!
May my life's unconditional surrender
To Your Will
Be as beautiful as my heart
And as fragrant as my soul.
My Supreme, my Supreme, my Supreme!

MY MORNING SOUL-BODY PRAYERS

1 APRIL 1999

228

My Supreme, my Supreme, my Supreme!
I am all gratitude to You
For keeping Your Ear wide open
To my heart's cries
And Your Eye wide open
To my soul's smiles.
My Supreme, my Supreme, my Supreme!

229

My Supreme, my Supreme, my Supreme!
To my greatest joy,
You are much closer to me
Than I thought.
You are doing much more for me
Than I ever expected.
My Supreme, my Supreme, my Supreme!

230

My Supreme, my Supreme, my Supreme!
I am my heart's
Infancy-prayer.
You are Your Heart's
Intimacy-sower
And intimacy-grower.
My Supreme, my Supreme, my Supreme!

2 APRIL 1999

231

My Supreme, my Supreme, my Supreme!
Only a heart of true God-devotion
Can escape the snares of temptations,
Frustrations and destructions.
My Supreme, my Supreme, my Supreme!

232

My Supreme, my Supreme, my Supreme!
A heart of true God-devotion
Is the fastest speed
In the world of aspiration
And in the world of dedication.
My Supreme, my Supreme, my Supreme!

233

My Supreme, my Supreme, my Supreme!
A heart of true God-devotion
Is the pride-treasure of God.
My Supreme, my Supreme, my Supreme!

MY MORNING SOUL-BODY PRAYERS

3 APRIL 1999

234

My Supreme, my Supreme, my Supreme!
I have only one prayer:
Please use me
Only in Your own Way.
My Supreme, my Supreme, my Supreme!

5 APRIL 1999

235

My Supreme, my Supreme, my Supreme!
I must be committed,
Solely and sleeplessly,
Only to Your Compassion-Eye
And Forgiveness-Heart.
My Supreme, my Supreme, my Supreme!

236

My Supreme, my Supreme, my Supreme!
I must realise
That if I do not forgive
My enemies,
Then I shall lose You
As my Friend,
Specially as my only Friend.
My Supreme, my Supreme, my Supreme!

237

My Supreme, my Supreme, my Supreme!
My heart is all gratitude to You
For giving me the opportunity
To enjoy immensely
The nectar-delight
Of forgiveness-light.
My Supreme, my Supreme, my Supreme!

238

My Supreme, my Supreme, my Supreme!
I am offering
The smiles of my heart
To Your Eye unreservedly.

I am offering
The tears of my breath
To Your Heart unconditionally.
My Supreme, my Supreme, my Supreme!

6 APRIL 1999

239

My Supreme, my Supreme, my Supreme!
Today my life and I
Are completely surrendering
To Your Will
So that our love for You
Can take infinitely deeper root
In our heart.
My Supreme, my Supreme, my Supreme!

240

My Supreme, my Supreme, my Supreme!
To establish my inseparable oneness
With suffering humanity,
I must learn the art
Of being humble.
My Supreme, my Supreme, my Supreme!

241

My Supreme, my Supreme, my Supreme!
I know, I know,
Possession has no peace.
But oneness has peace,
And fulness founded upon oneness
Is bliss.
My Supreme, my Supreme, my Supreme!

242

My Supreme, my Supreme, my Supreme!
You are so kind to me.
You are so compassionate to me.
Do allow the tears of my devotion-heart
To flow
Only towards Your Compassion-Sea.
My Supreme, my Supreme, my Supreme!

7 APRIL 1999

243

My Supreme, my Supreme, my Supreme!
Smiling and smiling
You go before me.
Blessingfully and compassionately
You keep the path ready for me.
Yet my mind is so unmindful
And my heart is so ungrateful,
Alas, alas!
My Supreme, my Supreme, my Supreme!

244

My Supreme, my Supreme, my Supreme!
Please tell me, what actually happens
When I lose imagination?
"My child, when you lose imagination,
You become spiritually sick."

My Supreme, what happens
When I lose inspiration?
"My child, your case becomes
Extremely critical."

My Supreme, and when I lose
Aspiration?
"My child, you spiritually die."

My Supreme, when I have imagination
In my spiritual life, what happens?
"My child, you become My joy."

My Supreme, when I have inspiration,
What happens?
"My child, you become My pride."

My Supreme, when I have aspiration,
What happens?
"My child, you become
An exact prototype
Of My Transcendental Dream
And My Universal Reality."
My Supreme, my Supreme, my Supreme!

245

My Supreme, my Supreme, my Supreme!
You are telling me not to be afraid
Of anything undivine.
You are also telling me to continue doing
Only things divine,
Sleeplessly and unconditionally.
My Supreme, my Supreme, my Supreme!

246

My Supreme, my Supreme, my Supreme!
I am placing my life's progress-smiles
And my heart's gratitude-tears
At Your Feet
Lovingly, prayerfully,
Soulfully and self-givingly.
My Supreme, my Supreme, my Supreme!

MY MORNING SOUL-BODY PRAYERS

8 APRIL 1999

247

My Supreme, my Supreme, my Supreme!
True, You do not respond
To each and every call of mine,
But You do respond
To my every tear-heart-call.
My Supreme, my Supreme, my Supreme!

248

My Supreme, my Supreme, my Supreme!
My heart's newness
Inspires my life
To run fast, faster, fastest
Towards You.
My Supreme, my Supreme, my Supreme!

249

My Supreme, my Supreme, my Supreme!
I do not want to find a way.
I want You to find me a way –
The Way –
To reach You and sit at Your Feet.
My Supreme, my Supreme, my Supreme!

9 APRIL 1999

250

My Supreme, my Supreme, my Supreme!
You are telling me
That You will leave an indelible mark
On my heart's shrine
When I am eager to become
A constant self-giver to humanity.
My Supreme, my Supreme, my Supreme!

251

My Supreme, my Supreme, my Supreme!
When will You accept
The leadership of my life?

"My child, I shall accept
The leadership of your life
Only after you have established
Your devotional friendship
With Me and My Heart."
My Supreme, my Supreme, my Supreme!

252

My Supreme, my Supreme, my Supreme!
You are telling me
That if I want to become
A joy-giver to humanity,
Then I must first become
A dreamer
Of Your Compassion-Eye
And Your Forgiveness-Feet.
My Supreme, my Supreme, my Supreme!

253

My Supreme, my Supreme, my Supreme!
My heart and I
Are missing You terribly!

"My child,
You and your heart will never miss Me,
Even for a fleeting second,
If you give Me your unconditionally
Self-giving breath."
My Supreme, my Supreme, my Supreme!

SRI CHINMOY

10 APRIL 1999

254

My Supreme, my Supreme, my Supreme!
Please bless me
With an ever-blossoming
Devotion-heart.
My Supreme, my Supreme, my Supreme!

255

My Supreme, my Supreme, my Supreme!
Please bless me
With an ever-growing
Surrender-life.
My Supreme, my Supreme, my Supreme!

256

My Supreme, my Supreme, my Supreme!
You love to examine
My aspiration-heart.
You love to examine
My dedication-life.
But You never, never care to examine
My qualification-mind!
My Supreme, my Supreme, my Supreme!

257

My Supreme, my Supreme, my Supreme!
You disarm me
With Your Heart's untiring Love.
I disarm You
With my heart's streaming tears.
My Supreme, my Supreme, my Supreme!

MY MORNING SOUL-BODY PRAYERS

12 APRIL 1999

258

My Supreme, my Supreme, my Supreme!
Today You have given my heart
A new name: joy,
And I am giving my life
A new name: gratitude.
I am placing my heart's immensity-joy
And my life's intensity-gratitude
At Your Compassion-flooded Feet.
My Supreme, my Supreme, my Supreme!

259

My Supreme, my Supreme, my Supreme!
I know, I know, I know,
If in the morning I offer You
A sincere prayer
And a deep meditation,
Then You will undoubtedly bless me
With a beautiful and fruitful day.
My Supreme, my Supreme, my Supreme!

260

My Supreme, my Supreme, my Supreme!
I am a constantly changing mind.
You are a sleeplessly unchanging
Heart.
My Supreme, my Supreme, my Supreme!

261

My Supreme, my Supreme, my Supreme!
May my faith
In my aspiration-heart,
In my dedication-life
And in Your Manifestation-Smile
Every day, every hour,
Every minute, every second
Increase.
My Supreme, my Supreme, my Supreme!

MY MORNING SOUL-BODY PRAYERS

13 APRIL 1999

262

My Supreme, my Supreme, my Supreme!
Thirty-five years ago
I came from India – the Old World –
To America – the New World.
Before I left,
I prayed to the soul of India
To bless me.
The soul of India compassionately
And tearfully
Fulfilled my desire.
On my arrival here in America,
I prayed to the heart of America
To embrace me.
The heart of America smilingly
And unreservedly embraced me.
My Supreme, my Supreme, my Supreme!

263

My Supreme, my Supreme, my Supreme!
Thirty-five years ago
I stoically wanted
To change the world,
But now I am desperately trying
To change myself.
My Supreme, my Supreme, my Supreme!

264

My Supreme, my Supreme, my Supreme!
Thirty-five years ago
I thought that the world
Belonged to the strong,
Both inwardly and outwardly.
But now I see that the world
Belongs to the morally sick
And spiritually weak.
My Supreme, my Supreme, my Supreme!

265

My Supreme, my Supreme, my Supreme!
Thirty-five years ago
This world of ours
Was clear, pure and certain.
But now, alas, alas,
This world of ours
Is confused, blind and greedy.
My Supreme, my Supreme, my Supreme!

MY MORNING SOUL-BODY PRAYERS

18 APRIL 1999

266

My Supreme, my Supreme, my Supreme!
Do give my devotion-heart
A handkerchief
To wipe Your Tears.
My Supreme, my Supreme, my Supreme!

(AFTER THE PRAYER)

The whole morning I had nothing but tears, tears for what is happening in Yugoslavia. God is so sad at what is happening there.

267

My Supreme, my Supreme, my Supreme!
Who can console You,
If not Your own Eternity's
Blue-gold Dreams?
My Supreme, my Supreme, my Supreme!

268

My Supreme, my Supreme, my Supreme!
Who can console You,
If not Your smiling,
Singing, dancing
And perfection-dreaming
Children?
My Supreme, my Supreme, my Supreme!

269

My Supreme, my Supreme, my Supreme!
Who can inspire You
And encourage You,
If not my heart's absolutely sincere
And pure promises?
My Supreme, my Supreme, my Supreme!

MY MORNING SOUL-BODY PRAYERS

21 APRIL 1999

270

My Supreme, my Supreme, my Supreme!
Only the sacred dust-worship
Of Your Feet
I need, I need.
My Supreme, my Supreme, my Supreme!

271

My Supreme, my Supreme, my Supreme!
What I need is more intensity
In my aspiring heart.
What I need is more immensity
In my God-searching mind.
What I need is more humility
In my God-serving life.
My Supreme, my Supreme, my Supreme!

272

My Supreme, my Supreme, my Supreme!
Your compassionate Heart
Responds immediately
Only to those who need You
Only, only, only.
My Supreme, my Supreme, my Supreme!

273

My Supreme, my Supreme, my Supreme!
How often I do things
And tell the world
That I am doing everything
For You,
When actually I am doing everything
For my own fulfilment!
My Supreme, my Supreme, my Supreme!

MY MORNING SOUL-BODY PRAYERS

22 APRIL 1999

274

My Supreme, my Supreme, my Supreme!
You have opened my heart-eye
So I can see and feel
How much You love me,
Care for me and need me –
And not so I can see
How many weaknesses I have
Or how insignificant I am.
My Supreme, my Supreme, my Supreme!

275

My Supreme, my Supreme, my Supreme!
Today do bless my mind
With a new inspiration-joy,
Do bless my heart
With a new aspiration-joy
And do bless my life
With a new dedication-joy.
My Supreme, my Supreme, my Supreme!

276

My Supreme, my Supreme, my Supreme!
Mine are the self-giving dreams
To manifest You in Your own Way.
My Supreme, my Supreme, my Supreme!

25 APRIL 1999

277

My Supreme, my Supreme, my Supreme!
No devotion,
No destination.
No destination,
No God-realisation.
No God-realisation,
No God-Satisfaction.
My Supreme, my Supreme, my Supreme!

278

My Supreme, my Supreme, my Supreme!
You are telling me
That a seeker does not need
Strict spiritual disciplines.
He does not need austerities.
He does not need the highest
And deepest meditation.
What he needs to realise You
Is only pure, pure, pure devotion.
You are also telling me
That all are equal in Your Sight,
But those who have sincere
Devotion to You
Have a very, very special place
In Your Heart,
And their hearts
Are Your choicest homes.
My Supreme, my Supreme, my Supreme!

279

My Supreme, my Supreme, my Supreme!
Your Command is
My golden opportunity
To become all Yours
In the twinkling of an eye!
My Supreme, my Supreme, my Supreme!

280

My Supreme, my Supreme, my Supreme!
O my stupidity-flooded mind,
Do not try to understand God.
You will never, never, never succeed.
Just try to love God.
Lo, you have already succeeded.
You have become
A truly choice instrument of God.
My Supreme, my Supreme, my Supreme!

SRI CHINMOY

27 APRIL 1999

281

My Supreme, my Supreme, my Supreme!
My heart's soulful smile
Is my God-satisfying
Sacred secret.
My Supreme, my Supreme, my Supreme!

282

My Supreme, my Supreme, my Supreme!
My heart's streaming tears
Shorten
My God-Destination-distance.
My Supreme, my Supreme, my Supreme!

283

My Supreme, my Supreme, my Supreme!
I need Your blessingful,
Infinite Grace
To change my inner life
Completely
And my outer life
Immediately.
My Supreme, my Supreme, my Supreme!

284

My Supreme, my Supreme, my Supreme!
Your Forgiveness-Heart
And Your Compassion-Eye
Do not allow You to remember
How long You have been waiting for me.
My Supreme, my Supreme, my Supreme!

285

My Supreme, my Supreme, my Supreme!
When I breathe in,
Do allow me to breathe in
Gratitude-tears.
When I breathe out,
Do allow me to breathe out
Surrender-smiles.
My Supreme, my Supreme, my Supreme!

286

My Supreme, my Supreme, my Supreme!
My prayerful and soulful determination
Has a special name given by You:
You call my determination
Your Heart-hero.
My Supreme, my Supreme, my Supreme!

287

My Supreme, my Supreme, my Supreme!
My faith-life
You have lovingly, compassionately
And unconditionally
Kept inside Your very Breath.
My Supreme, my Supreme, my Supreme!

29 APRIL 1999

288

My Supreme, my Supreme, my Supreme!
Alas, alas, early in the morning
Why do I forget
To fold my hands devotedly?
Why do I forget
To bow to You prayerfully?
My Supreme, my Supreme, my Supreme!

289

My Supreme, my Supreme, my Supreme!
Do give me the capacity
To bind You inwardly,
Prayerfully, soulfully
And self-givingly
Only with my devotion
In my inner life of aspiration.
My Supreme, my Supreme, my Supreme!

MY MORNING SOUL-BODY PRAYERS

1 MAY 1999

290

My Supreme, my Supreme, my Supreme!
May all my God-dreams
Blossom
In my aspiring heart-garden.
My Supreme, my Supreme, my Supreme!

291

My Supreme, my Supreme, my Supreme!
Please, please give me
Sincerity and intensity
In my prayers
So that when I pray to You,
All my worries and anxieties
Disappear
In the infinite vastness of the sky.
My Supreme, my Supreme, my Supreme!

292

My Supreme, my Supreme, my Supreme!
My joy knows no bounds
To see Your Golden Chariot
On my world-oneness-heart-path.
My Supreme, my Supreme, my Supreme!

3 MAY 1999

293

My Supreme, my Supreme, my Supreme!
May my gratitude-heart-flight
Every day transcend itself
Most surprisingly.
My Supreme, my Supreme, my Supreme!

294

My Supreme, my Supreme, my Supreme!
Please tell me how I can fly
Far beyond
My life's problem-mountains.
My Supreme, my Supreme, my Supreme!

295

My Supreme, my Supreme, my Supreme!
May I become every morning
A new gratitude-heart-flower
And place myself
At Your Golden Feet.
My Supreme, my Supreme, my Supreme!

MY MORNING SOUL-BODY PRAYERS

4 MAY 1999

296

My Supreme, my Supreme, my Supreme!
Please bless my heart
With a new name.
"My child, your heart's new name
Will be:
The purity of silver tears."
My Supreme, my Supreme, my Supreme!

297

My Supreme, my Supreme, my Supreme!
Please, please, do bless my mind
With a new name.
"My child, your mind's new name
Will be:
The purity of golden smiles."
My Supreme, my Supreme, my Supreme!

298

My Supreme, my Supreme, my Supreme!
Please, please, open my heart-door
Wide
With the Light
Of Your Compassion-Eye.
My Supreme, my Supreme, my Supreme!

299

My Supreme, my Supreme, my Supreme!
Please, please, open my mind-door
Wide
With the Light
Of Your Forgiveness-Heart.
My Supreme, my Supreme, my Supreme!

MY MORNING SOUL-BODY PRAYERS

5 MAY 1999

300

My Supreme, my Supreme, my Supreme!
Please, please tell me
If I should consult You
Every time
Before I do anything.

"My sweet child,
If you truly love Me,
If you truly need Me,
If you truly value My Advice
And
If you consider yourself
To be a true child of My Heart,
Then it is not only necessary,
But also obligatory."
My Supreme, my Supreme, my Supreme!

301

My Supreme, my Supreme, my Supreme!
You have a very special Love
For the God-dreamer in me.
You have a very, very special Love
For the God-seeker in me.
You have a very, very, very special Love
For the God-lover in me.
My Supreme, my Supreme, my Supreme!

302

My Supreme, my Supreme, my Supreme!
I must sincerely admit
That I am a member
Of God's inner circle
Not because my aspiration-hunger
Is very deep,
But because God's Compassion-Meal
Is unconditional.
My Supreme, my Supreme, my Supreme!

MY MORNING SOUL-BODY PRAYERS

7 MAY 1999

303

My Supreme, my Supreme, my Supreme!
May my heart's silver songs
Carry me
To the highest height of Heaven
And place me
At Your Compassion-Feet.
My Supreme, my Supreme, my Supreme!

304

My Supreme, my Supreme, my Supreme!
My heart and I are all gratitude to You
For taking us to live at a new place,
Which is extremely far away
From the negativity-neighbourhood.
My Supreme, my Supreme, my Supreme!

305

My Supreme, my Supreme, my Supreme!
My morning prayers give my mind
The beauty of newness.
My morning prayers give my heart
The fragrance of fulness.
My Supreme, my Supreme, my Supreme!

9 MAY 1999

306

My Supreme, my Supreme, my Supreme!
May my heart be a most beautiful
Morning sunrise-smile.
My Supreme, my Supreme, my Supreme!

307

My Supreme, my Supreme, my Supreme!
May my life be a most peaceful
Evening sunset-song.
My Supreme, my Supreme, my Supreme!

308

My Supreme, my Supreme, my Supreme!
I shall not mind
If my life's outer glories
Fade away like the stars.
But please, please, my Supreme,
Keep my heart's inner songs
Inside Your Heart
To serve You, to please You
And to fulfil You in Your own Way.
My Supreme, my Supreme, my Supreme!

10 MAY 1999

309

My Supreme, my Supreme, my Supreme!
Today I must conquer
My God-manifestation-
Unwillingness-mind.
My Supreme, my Supreme, my Supreme!

310

My Supreme, my Supreme, my Supreme!
Do give me the capacity
To vehemently reject
My desire-life-slavery.
My Supreme, my Supreme, my Supreme!

11 MAY 1999

311

My Supreme, my Supreme, my Supreme!
My desire is for
The immediate extinction
Of my desire-life.
My Supreme, my Supreme, my Supreme!

312

My Supreme, my Supreme, my Supreme!
My aspiration is for
Constant God-satisfaction
In my dedication-life.
My Supreme, my Supreme, my Supreme!

313

My Supreme, my Supreme, my Supreme!
Do give my heart
The most sincere hunger
To fulfil immediately
Every Wish of Yours.
My Supreme, my Supreme, my Supreme!

MY MORNING SOUL-BODY PRAYERS

12 MAY 1999

314

My Supreme, my Supreme, my Supreme!
Please, please bind me,
Bind me, bind me!
The more You bind me
With Your Compassion-Eye
And Forgiveness-Heart,
The sooner I will get
My liberation-life.
My Supreme, my Supreme, my Supreme!

315

My Supreme, my Supreme, my Supreme!
Please, please, kick my mind
As hard as possible
So that I can receive from You
The humility-virtue.
My Supreme, my Supreme, my Supreme!

316

My Supreme, my Supreme, my Supreme!
I shall never allow my life
To start the day
With my confusion-mind-clouds.
I shall every day
Start my life
With my faith-heart-illumination-sun.
My Supreme, my Supreme, my Supreme!

13 MAY 1999

317

My Supreme, my Supreme, my Supreme!
May my heart be
Eternity's
God-aspiration-cry.
My Supreme, my Supreme, my Supreme!

318

My Supreme, my Supreme, my Supreme!
May my life be
Infinity's
God-manifestation-smile.
My Supreme, my Supreme, my Supreme!

319

My Supreme, my Supreme, my Supreme!
My heart is swimming
In the sea of tears
Because my sister Lily
Is suffering so much.
She is helpless in India
And I am helpless here in America.
My Supreme, my Supreme, my Supreme!

MY MORNING SOUL-BODY PRAYERS

14 MAY 1999

320

My Supreme, my Supreme, my Supreme!
Today I am sending my soul's joy,
My heart's love and my life's concern
Into the world unreservedly.
My Supreme, my Supreme, my Supreme!

321

My Supreme, my Supreme, my Supreme!
Today I must illumine
My outer life-tree
With my inner heart's purity.
My Supreme, my Supreme, my Supreme!

322

My Supreme, my Supreme, my Supreme!
I am extremely, extremely
Grateful to You
For allowing my life to be near You.

I am extremely, extremely
Grateful to You
For giving me the capacity
To live only for You,
Only for You.
My Supreme, my Supreme, my Supreme!

16 MAY 1999

323

My Supreme, my Supreme, my Supreme!
Please, please bless me
With an ever-blossoming
Gratitude-heart.
My Supreme, my Supreme, my Supreme!

324

My Supreme, my Supreme, my Supreme!
Please bless me
With a sleeplessly unconditional
World-service-life.
My Supreme, my Supreme, my Supreme!

325

My Supreme, my Supreme, my Supreme!
May my heart love
Each and every human being
In the world
The way You love my heart.
My Supreme, my Supreme, my Supreme!

MY MORNING SOUL-BODY PRAYERS

17 MAY 1999

326

My Supreme, my Supreme, my Supreme!
Your Compassion-Eye
Is the only sweetness
In my aspiration-heart.
My Supreme, my Supreme, my Supreme!

327

My Supreme, my Supreme, my Supreme!
Your Encouragement-Heart
Is the only fulness
In my dedication-life.
My Supreme, my Supreme, my Supreme!

18 MAY 1999

328

My Supreme, my Supreme, my Supreme!
I have four special desires:
May I have a God-searching mind,
May I have a God-aspiring heart,
May I have a God-serving life,
May I be a God-manifesting seeker.
My Supreme, my Supreme, my Supreme!

329

My Supreme, my Supreme, my Supreme!
May my heart sing
A sweetness-oneness-song with You.
May my life dance
A oneness-fulness-dance with You.
My Supreme, my Supreme, my Supreme!

330

My Supreme, my Supreme, my Supreme!
I must come back to Your Feet,
To Your Lotus-Feet,
To Your Nectar-Feet.
I must come back immediately,
I must come back breathlessly,
I must come back unconditionally.
My Supreme, my Supreme, my Supreme!

19 MAY 1999

331

My Supreme, my Supreme, my Supreme!
The human in me
Is the flickering of an eye.
The divine in me
Is Eternity's aspiration,
Infinity's vision
And
Immortality's manifestation.
My Supreme, my Supreme, my Supreme!

332

My Supreme, my Supreme, my Supreme!
May each human life be
A divinely manifested
Dream of God.
My Supreme, my Supreme, my Supreme!

333

My Supreme, my Supreme, my Supreme!
May my life reject
Once and for all
The slavery of endless desires.
My Supreme, my Supreme, my Supreme!

334

My Supreme, my Supreme, my Supreme!
My gratitude-heart has nothing to do
With fleeting time.
My gratitude-heart has everything to do
With Eternity.
My Supreme, my Supreme, my Supreme!

21 MAY 1999

335

My Supreme, my Supreme, my Supreme!
I have climbed the mountain
In search of You,
But You are not to be found.
Where are You, my Supreme,
Where are You?

I have crossed the desert
In search of You,
But You are not to be found.
Where are You, my Supreme,
Where are You?
My Supreme, my Supreme, my Supreme!

336

My Supreme, my Supreme, my Supreme!
I do not believe in my ability
At all.
I believe only in
My God-dependability.
My Supreme, my Supreme, my Supreme!

MY MORNING SOUL-BODY PRAYERS

23 MAY 1999

337

My Supreme, my Supreme, my Supreme!
May my surrender to Your Will
Be without even an iota
Of expectation.
My Supreme, my Supreme, my Supreme!

338

My Supreme, my Supreme, my Supreme!
May I offer to You
My failure-life
Exactly the same way I offer
My success-life –
Happily, happily, happily.
My Supreme, my Supreme, my Supreme!

339

My Supreme, my Supreme, my Supreme!
Every breath
Of my gratitude-heart
May I offer to You consciously.
My Supreme, my Supreme, my Supreme!

340

My Supreme, my Supreme, my Supreme!
I know, I know,
For the God-obedience-seeker
God's Heart-Door
Always remains wide open.
My Supreme, my Supreme, my Supreme!

341

My Supreme, my Supreme, my Supreme!
If I feel Your Presence inside my heart,
Nothing else do I need,
Either from this world
Or from any other world.
My Supreme, my Supreme, my Supreme!

342

My Supreme, my Supreme, my Supreme!
A moment without my God-oneness
Is the worst possible crisis
In my life.
My Supreme, my Supreme, my Supreme!

343

My Supreme, my Supreme, my Supreme!
May my love for You
Grow into
An ever-increasing hunger.
My Supreme, my Supreme, my Supreme!

MY MORNING SOUL-BODY PRAYERS

25 MAY 1999

344

My Supreme, my Supreme, my Supreme!
May my heart-shrine-candle
Steadily glow,
And may I sleeplessly aspire.
My Supreme, my Supreme, my Supreme!

345

My Supreme, my Supreme, my Supreme!
Please be the real and only
Owner and leader
Of my life, my heart and my breath.
My Supreme, my Supreme, my Supreme!

346

My Supreme, my Supreme, my Supreme!
When my life is without
God-devotion,
My heart becomes a sea of tears.
My Supreme, my Supreme, my Supreme!

347

My Supreme, my Supreme, my Supreme!
Do give me the capacity
To sail my heart's aspiration-boat
Much faster
Towards the Golden Shore.
My Supreme, my Supreme, my Supreme!

SRI CHINMOY

26 MAY 1999

348

My Supreme, my Supreme, my Supreme!
May You desire my soul, my heart,
My mind, my vital, my body,
Everything that I have
And everything that I am
Every day
Only for Your personal use.
My Supreme, my Supreme, my Supreme!

349

My Supreme, my Supreme, my Supreme!
Do give me a soul of forgiveness,
A heart of compassion
And a life of tolerance
And patience.
My Supreme, my Supreme, my Supreme!

MY MORNING SOUL-BODY PRAYERS

27 MAY 1999

350

My Supreme, my Supreme, my Supreme!
I must immediately stop
My ceaseless desire-hunger,
I must.
My Supreme, my Supreme, my Supreme!

351

My Supreme, my Supreme, my Supreme!
Each time I sing my heart-songs
Prayerfully and soulfully,
I am allowed to go to Heaven
And enjoy Heaven's Bliss.
My Supreme, my Supreme, my Supreme!

352

My Supreme, my Supreme, my Supreme!
My fortitude-heart
Must triumphantly fight
Against my life's failures.
My Supreme, my Supreme, my Supreme!

28 MAY 1999

353

My Supreme, my Supreme, my Supreme!
To forget You is to fail
In the examination
Of my life's very existence on earth.
My Supreme, my Supreme, my Supreme!

354

My Supreme, my Supreme, my Supreme!
I must awaken the divine lion
That is sleeping inside my heart.
My Supreme, my Supreme, my Supreme!

355

My Supreme, my Supreme, my Supreme!
May Your supreme Will,
May Your absolute Will
Work faster than the fastest
In and through my life
For Your full manifestation
Here on earth.
My Supreme, my Supreme, my Supreme!

356

My Supreme, my Supreme, my Supreme!
The deeper
My God-discovery is,
The higher
Is God's Pride in me.
My Supreme, my Supreme, my Supreme!

MY MORNING SOUL-BODY PRAYERS

29 MAY 1999

357

My Supreme, my Supreme, my Supreme!
I must live my life in such a way
That everyone can receive You
Inside my heart-garden.
My Supreme, my Supreme, my Supreme!

31 MAY 1999

358

My Supreme, my Supreme, my Supreme!
What a fool I am!
I try to test Your Will
Instead of tasting and devouring
Your Will.
My Supreme, my Supreme, my Supreme!

359

My Supreme, my Supreme, my Supreme!
You are telling me that my way
Has to be the way of aspiration
And dedication,
Not the way of resignation
And renunciation.
My Supreme, my Supreme, my Supreme!

360

My Supreme, my Supreme, my Supreme!
The 20th Century and the world
Gave each other the message
Of desire-enjoyment.
The 21st Century and the world
Will give each other the message
Of aspiration-enlightenment.
My Supreme, my Supreme, my Supreme!

361

My Supreme, my Supreme, my Supreme!
When my life becomes
A desire-beggar,
I would like You to immediately be
A denial-emperor.
My Supreme, my Supreme, my Supreme!

1 JUNE 1999

362

My Supreme, my Supreme, my Supreme!
Please, please bless me
With a new heart, new mind,
New vital, new body
And new life.
I shall not allow my new heart,
New mind, new vital, new body
And new life
To drown in expectation-ocean.
My Supreme, my Supreme, my Supreme!

363

My Supreme, my Supreme, my Supreme!
Today we shall all invite You
To come and watch
Our world-oneness-exhibit-art.
My Supreme, my Supreme, my Supreme!

364

My Supreme, my Supreme, my Supreme!
May my ever-blossoming faith-heart
Always remain inaccessible
To my doubting mind.
My Supreme, my Supreme, my Supreme!

MY MORNING SOUL-BODY PRAYERS

2 JUNE 1999

365

My Supreme, my Supreme, my Supreme!
My God-obedience must never be
Fearful and regretful.
My God-obedience has to be always
Prayerful, soulful, cheerful
And peaceful.
My Supreme, my Supreme, my Supreme!

366

My Supreme, my Supreme, my Supreme!
Without Your Compassion-Eye,
Your Protection-Feet
And Your Forgiveness-Heart,
My life is artificial, superficial,
Meaningless and useless.

My Supreme, with Your Compassion-Eye,
Your Protection-Feet
And Your Forgiveness-Heart,
My life is beautiful, prayerful,
Meaningful and fruitful.
My Supreme, my Supreme, my Supreme!

3 JUNE 1999

367

My Supreme, my Supreme, my Supreme!
Yesterday I was a most devoted slave
Of the desire-world.
Today, out of Your infinite Bounty,
You have made me a choice child
Of Your Heart.
My Supreme, my Supreme, my Supreme!

368

My Supreme, my Supreme, my Supreme!
Do turn my life into
A sleeplessly hungry heart
At Your Lotus-Feet.
My Supreme, my Supreme, my Supreme!

369

My Supreme, my Supreme, my Supreme!
I was born to be
A lover of Your Dreams
And a server of Your Realities.
My Supreme, my Supreme, my Supreme!

MY MORNING SOUL-BODY PRAYERS

4 JUNE 1999

370

My Supreme, my Supreme, my Supreme!
I shall never give up,
I shall never give up!
I must continue,
I must continue!
I know my Goal is ahead,
And I am destined to reach my Goal.
My Supreme, my Supreme, my Supreme!

371

My Supreme, my Supreme, my Supreme!
Today I must increase
My mind's simplicity,
My heart's sincerity,
My life's purity
And my God-necessity
In incredible measure.
My Supreme, my Supreme, my Supreme!

372

My Supreme, my Supreme, my Supreme!
May Your Victory supreme
Be proclaimed
By my soul, my heart, my mind,
My vital and my body
At every moment
Lovingly, soulfully and self-givingly.
My Supreme, my Supreme, my Supreme!

373

My Supreme, my Supreme, my Supreme!
No matter how badly
Everything goes wrong in my life,
My soul and I shall smile.
My Supreme, my Supreme, my Supreme!

MY MORNING SOUL-BODY PRAYERS

15 JUNE 1999

374

My Supreme, my Supreme, my Supreme!
The human law
Is very, very painful.
The divine Grace
Is extremely, extremely beautiful,
Fruitful and blissful.
My Supreme, my Supreme, my Supreme!

375

My Supreme, my Supreme, my Supreme!
The earthly arrival of a soul
Is an experience-beauty.
The Heavenly departure of a soul
Is a realisation-fragrance.
My Supreme, my Supreme, my Supreme!

376

My Supreme, my Supreme, my Supreme!
The human birth
Is an unknown journey.
The divine death
Is an unknowable Goal.
My Supreme, my Supreme, my Supreme!

377

My Supreme, my Supreme, my Supreme!
The human in us
Cries and cries and cries
Because it does not know
Who God is
And where God is.

Who is God?
He who is at once
Knowable and unknowable.
Where is God?
God is everywhere,
But in a seeker's aspiration-heart
He is infinitely more visible.
My Supreme, my Supreme, my Supreme!

378

My Supreme, my Supreme, my Supreme!
My God is not
In my Heavenly Home.
My God is only
In my aspiration-heart.
My Supreme, my Supreme, my Supreme!

MY MORNING SOUL-BODY PRAYERS

17 JUNE 1999

379

My Supreme, my Supreme, my Supreme!
O my heart-breaking disappointments,
Today I shall deal with you,
Today I shall fight against you,
Today I shall conquer you!
If I do not conquer you,
How can I ever have
A God-appointment?
My Supreme, my Supreme, my Supreme!

380

My Supreme, my Supreme, my Supreme!
I must keep
All my God-fulfilment-promises,
I must!
My Supreme, my Supreme, my Supreme!

381

My Supreme, my Supreme, my Supreme!
From today on I shall live
Only by Your Standards
And not by man-made standards.
My Supreme, my Supreme, my Supreme!

382

My Supreme, my Supreme, my Supreme!
Today my heart, my mind and my life
Have very special prayers for You.
Please fulfil their soulful prayers.
My heart is begging You
To protect me.
My mind is begging You
To guide me.
My life is begging You
To lead me.
My Supreme, my Supreme, my Supreme!

MY MORNING SOUL-BODY PRAYERS

19 JUNE 1999

383

My Supreme, my Supreme, my Supreme!
My heart's ever-blossoming
Faith in You
Is my life's most precious treasure.
My Supreme, my Supreme, my Supreme!

384

My Supreme, my Supreme, my Supreme!
The songs
Of my God-devotion-heart
Are my only real friends.
My Supreme, my Supreme, my Supreme!

385

My Supreme, my Supreme, my Supreme!
Do give me
The light of patience
And the delight of patience.
My Supreme, my Supreme, my Supreme!

386

My Supreme, my Supreme, my Supreme!
I must value my life's
God-love, God-devotion
And God-surrender-exercises
Infinitely more
Than anything else.
My Supreme, my Supreme, my Supreme!

21 JUNE 1999

387

My Supreme, my Supreme, my Supreme!
The dark bitterness of the mind
Has to be conquered by
The bright sweetness of the heart.
My Supreme, my Supreme, my Supreme!

388

My Supreme, my Supreme, my Supreme!
The bright sweetness of the heart
Has to be increased
In infinite measure by
The immortal forgiveness of the soul.
My Supreme, my Supreme, my Supreme!

389

My Supreme, my Supreme, my Supreme!
May I live far beyond the domain
Of success and failure-life.
My Supreme, my Supreme, my Supreme!

390

My Supreme, my Supreme, my Supreme!
You are telling me
That You are with me and for me.
Therefore, I must not be afraid of
Saying what I am supposed to say,
Doing what I am supposed to do
And becoming
What I am supposed to become.
My Supreme, my Supreme, my Supreme!

MY MORNING SOUL-BODY PRAYERS

22 JUNE 1999

391

My Supreme, my Supreme, my Supreme!
Your Compassion-Smiles
Are the fulfilment
Of all my heart-dreams.
My Supreme, my Supreme, my Supreme!

392

My Supreme, my Supreme, my Supreme!
Your express Commands
Are the fulfilment
Of all my life-desires.
My Supreme, my Supreme, my Supreme!

393

My Supreme, my Supreme, my Supreme!
Today I am making a solemn promise
To You
That my heart, my mind, my vital
And my body
Will not keep You waiting
Any more.
My Supreme, my Supreme, my Supreme!

394

My Supreme, my Supreme, my Supreme!
May each and every prayer of mine
Be more sincere, more pure, more soulful
And more self-giving
Than the previous one.
My Supreme, my Supreme, my Supreme!

MY MORNING SOUL-BODY PRAYERS

23 JUNE 1999

395

My Supreme, my Supreme, my Supreme!
My soul was born
To be Your dreamer,
My heart was born
To be Your lover,
My mind, my vital and my body were born
To be Your servers,
And my life was born
To be Your messenger.
My Supreme, my Supreme, my Supreme!

396

My Supreme, my Supreme, my Supreme!
You come and go,
You come and go,
You come and go.
But this time when You come, I shall,
On the strength of my heart-tears,
Not allow You to go.
I shall keep You permanently
Inside my heart, my mind, my vital
And my body
Without fail!
My Supreme, my Supreme, my Supreme!

397

My Supreme, my Supreme, my Supreme!
I shall deeply value
Even a blade of grass
If it helps me increase
My love for You,
My devotion to You
And my surrender to You.
My Supreme, my Supreme, my Supreme!

MY MORNING SOUL-BODY PRAYERS

24 JUNE 1999

398

My Supreme, my Supreme, my Supreme!
From now on
I shall soulfully pray to You
For my heart's progress
And no more pitifully cry to You
For my life's success.
My Supreme, my Supreme, my Supreme!

399

My Supreme, my Supreme, my Supreme!
Please, please save me from my mind.
My mind every day, every hour,
Every minute, every second
Forces me to run with it
Wherever it goes.
I am already so tired,
Extremely tired!
My Supreme, my Supreme, my Supreme!

400

My Supreme, my Supreme, my Supreme!
I have come to realise
That my mind's humility
Comes from my heart's
Indomitable will-power.
My Supreme, my Supreme, my Supreme!

25 JUNE 1999

401

My Supreme, my Supreme, my Supreme!
Somebody has to reach
The Transcendental Beyond.
What is wrong with me?
What is wrong with my heart,
My mind, my vital and my body?
Let me try.
Let us try together
To reach the Transcendental Beyond.
We must succeed, we must!
My Supreme, my Supreme, my Supreme!

402

My Supreme, my Supreme, my Supreme!
Somebody has to make
His love, devotion and surrender
Unconditional.
What is wrong with me?
What is wrong with my heart,
My mind, my vital and my body?
I shall try.
We shall try together
To become unconditional.
We must succeed, we must!
My Supreme, my Supreme, my Supreme!

403

My Supreme, my Supreme, my Supreme!
I am telling the whole world
What my faith in You
Is doing now.
My faith in You is laughing
At my mind's stupid and feeble,
Feeble and stupid
Boasting.
My Supreme, my Supreme, my Supreme!

26 JUNE 1999

404

My Supreme, my Supreme, my Supreme!
My soul's God-blessed and God-given
Peace
Is immensely increasing
The beauty of my outer life
And the fragrance of my inner life.
My Supreme, my Supreme, my Supreme!

405

My Supreme, my Supreme, my Supreme!
Today I must challenge
The strength of my life's
Bondage-chains
With my soul's indomitable will.
My Supreme, my Supreme, my Supreme!

406

My Supreme, my Supreme, my Supreme!
Out of Your infinite Bounty,
Centuries ago You blessed me
With the God-realisation
That far transcended
Heaven's Summits.
My Supreme, my Supreme, my Supreme!

MY MORNING SOUL-BODY PRAYERS

28 JUNE 1999

407

My Supreme, my Supreme, my Supreme!
My life's God-surrender-songs
Are the most favourite songs
Of my aspiration-heart.
My Supreme, my Supreme, my Supreme!

408

My Supreme, my Supreme, my Supreme!
From life to death,
From death to life
I travel,
Carrying the message
Of Your universal Victory.
My Supreme, my Supreme, my Supreme!

409

My Supreme, my Supreme, my Supreme!
Every morning during my meditation,
You play Your Compassion-Flute
For my aspiration-heart
And You play Your Concern-Violin
For my dedication-life.
My Supreme, I am all gratitude to You.
My Supreme, my Supreme, my Supreme!

30 JUNE 1999

410

My Supreme, my Supreme, my Supreme!
I wish to regain
My happiness-heart.
Do allow me to sit at Your Feet
And pray and meditate
Day and night
To regain my childhood happiness-heart.
My Supreme, my Supreme, my Supreme!

411

My Supreme, my Supreme, my Supreme!
You are telling me
That if I start laughing,
Then You will start smashing
One by one
All my problems.
My Supreme, my Supreme, my Supreme!

412

My Supreme, my Supreme, my Supreme!
I need only two things
In this life:
I need the Beauty
Of Your Compassion-Eye;
I need the Fragrance
Of Your Forgiveness-Heart.
My Supreme, my Supreme, my Supreme!

MY MORNING SOUL-BODY PRAYERS

1 JULY 1999

413

My Supreme, my Supreme!
I do not want to be blinded
By my success-life.
I want my life to be illumined
By my progress-heart.
My Supreme, my Supreme!

414

My Supreme, my Supreme!
You are asking me
Not to discourage the world
And at the same time
Not to be discouraged by the world.
You are asking me
To encourage the world
And at the same time
To be encouraged by the world.
If I do this, then I shall please You
In Your own Way.
My Supreme, I shall fulfil
Your express Command.
My Supreme, my Supreme!

415

My Supreme, my Supreme!
I shall obey Your Eye
At every moment
To illumine my mind.
I shall obey Your Feet
At every moment
To liberate my life.
My Supreme, my Supreme!

5 JULY 1999

416

My Supreme, my Supreme!
My life's sorrows tell me
That I can do nothing special
Here on earth.
My heart's joys tell me
That anything inspiring,
Illumining and fulfilling
I can do if I want to.
My Supreme, my Lord Supreme,
My Beloved Supreme,
You tell me that I must do
Only one thing:
I must love each and every
Creation of Yours
Unreservedly and unconditionally.
My Supreme, only Your Wish,
Your Request, Your Command
I shall gladly and proudly fulfil.
My Supreme, my Supreme!

417

My Supreme, my Supreme!
If I am not for You only,
Sleeplessly and breathlessly,
Then why am I here on earth?
No reason for me
Even to stay for a second!
My Supreme, do give me the capacity
To live only for You.
My Supreme, my Supreme!

418

My Supreme, my Supreme!
I must devotedly practise
More and more and more and more.
Only then shall I be able
To accomplish my goals.
My Supreme, my Supreme!

6 JULY 1999

419

My Supreme, my Supreme!
Please, please awaken my heart.
Please, please brighten my smile.
Please, please enlighten my life.
My Supreme, my Supreme!

420

My Supreme, my Supreme!
I need inspiration every day
To feed my mind.
I need aspiration every hour
To feed my heart.
I need illumination every moment
To feed my soul.
My Supreme, my Supreme!

421

My Supreme, my Supreme!
Sincerity I need at every moment
In my mind
To please You only in Your own Way.
Purity I need at every moment
In my heart
To please You only in Your own Way.
Simplicity I need at every moment
In my life
To please You only in Your own Way.
My Supreme, my Supreme!

MY MORNING SOUL-BODY PRAYERS

7 JULY 1999

422

My Supreme, my Supreme!
Today I shall keep only one thing
In my aspiring heart:
Hope.
Today I shall keep only one thing
In my serving life:
Promise.
My Supreme, my Supreme!

423

My Supreme, my Supreme!
May my heart obey Your Eye.
May my life obey Your Heart.
May my breath obey Your Feet.
My Supreme, my Supreme!

424

My Supreme, my Supreme!
My Lord Beloved Supreme,
I feel Your Presence inside my heart
Even when I do not
Pray and meditate.
But, my Lord Beloved Supreme,
Your Presence I feel inside my mind
Only when I do pray and meditate.
My Supreme, my Supreme!

8 JULY 1999

425

My Supreme, my Supreme!
I must face all my life's problems
With my mind's determination,
My heart's aspiration
And
My life's dedication.
My Supreme, my Supreme!

426

My Supreme, my Supreme!
Today I am soulfully taking time
To appreciate and admire
Everything that I see
And
Everyone that I meet
On the way.
My Supreme, my Supreme!

427

My Supreme, my Supreme!
I have looked far beyond the clouds,
And I wish to tell You
What I have discovered.
I have discovered
Tomorrow's brightest sunshine.
My Supreme, my Supreme!

MY MORNING SOUL-BODY PRAYERS

9 JULY 1999

428

My Supreme, my Supreme!
Do give my heart the capacity
And opportunity
To completely surrender to Your Will.
Do cast aside
My world-supremacy-desiring mind.
My Supreme, my Supreme!

429

My Supreme, my Supreme!
May my heart grow into
An ever-blossoming devotion
To worship
Your Golden Feet.
My Supreme, my Supreme!

430

My Supreme, my Supreme!
I am extremely, extremely, extremely
Grateful to You
For giving me the opportunity
To decorate every day
A new heart-home for You.
My Supreme, my Supreme!

SRI CHINMOY

10 JULY 1999

431

My Supreme, my Supreme!
I shall pray to You,
I shall meditate on You,
I shall love You
And I shall serve You
Even long after I have made
My surrender complete.
My Supreme, my Supreme!

432

My Supreme, my Supreme!
My Lord Beloved Supreme,
My sleepless devotion to You
Is my mind's newness,
My heart's sweetness
And my life's fulness.
My Supreme, my Supreme!

433

My Supreme, my Supreme!
To realise You,
What I need is inner wealth:
Aspiration, and nothing else.
The outer wealth
Is infinitely worse than useless.
My Supreme, my Supreme!

MY MORNING SOUL-BODY PRAYERS

434

My Supreme, my Supreme!
Today I am receiving
Your divine Message of beauty
And Your supreme Message of duty
From everything
That I am looking at.
My Supreme, my Supreme!

11 JULY 1999

435

My Supreme, my Supreme!
What we need is faith in our mind.
What we need is love in our heart.
Lo, God-realisation
Does not remain any more
An impossible task.
My Supreme, my Supreme!

436

My Supreme, my Supreme!
My Supreme, You are
My Lord Beloved Absolute Supreme.
This is my realisation,
And this realisation throughout Eternity
Shall remain with me.
My Supreme, my Supreme!

437

My Supreme, my Supreme!
There was a time when I was
A part-time God-seeker,
God-lover and God-server.
To my greatest joy, I have now become
A full-time God-seeker,
God-lover and God-server.
My Supreme, may my gratitude to You
Remain sleepless and breathless
Throughout Eternity.
My Supreme, my Supreme!

MY MORNING SOUL-BODY PRAYERS

12 JULY 1999

438

My Supreme, my Supreme!
Indeed, the smiles of my life
Are beautiful and inspiring,
But the tears of my heart
Are exquisite and perfect.
My Supreme, my Supreme!

439

My Supreme, my Supreme!
My heart, my faith and I
Shall be satisfied
Only after
You have illumined
Our unlit mind.
My Supreme, my Supreme!

440

My Supreme, my Supreme!
Your absolute Commands
Are my life's
Only true fulfilment.
My Supreme, my Supreme!

SRI CHINMOY

13 JULY 1999

441

My Supreme, my Supreme!
The very sight of Your Lotus-Feet
Thrills my soul, my heart,
My mind, my vital, my body
And my entire being.
My Supreme, my Supreme!

MY MORNING SOUL-BODY PRAYERS

14 JULY 1999

442

My Supreme, my Supreme!
Do inundate my entire life
With Your infinite Compassion
So that I can soften the sorrows
And decrease the sufferings
Of the world.
My Supreme, my Supreme!

443

My Supreme, my Supreme!
I am my heart's deep sorrow.
I am still unable to concentrate
Every second of my life
On Your Will.
My Supreme, my Supreme!

444

My Supreme, my Supreme!
Today my heart would like
To introduce my mind to You,
But my mind is terribly afraid of You.
My Supreme, my Supreme!

445

My Supreme, my Supreme!
I know, I know,
You are not in my earthly house.
You are not in my Heavenly Home.
You are only in the tears
Of my heart.
My Supreme, my Supreme!

15 JULY 1999

446

My Supreme, my Supreme!
My soul's patience-light
Is the peace-dreamer
Of my mind.
My Supreme, my Supreme!

447

My Supreme, my Supreme!
My soul's confidence-height
Is the peace-maker
Of my body, vital and mind.
My Supreme, my Supreme!

448

My Supreme, my Supreme!
Dire challenges from the outer world
Enter into my inner world.
My soul's indomitable will-power says,
"Get out! Get out!
I have no time
To pay any attention to you."
My Supreme, my Supreme!

MY MORNING SOUL-BODY PRAYERS

16 JULY 1999

449

My Supreme, my Supreme!
The moment I touch Your Lotus-Feet
Lovingly, prayerfully, soulfully,
Unreservedly and unconditionally,
My tiny heart-hut becomes
A larger than the largest
And mightier than the mightiest
Palace.
My Supreme, my Supreme!

450

My Supreme, my Supreme!
I am so fortunate.
The moment I was born,
Gratitude accompanied me.
Right from the very first breath
Of my life,
Gratitude has been living
Inside the very depth of my heart.
My Supreme, my Supreme!

451

My Supreme, my Supreme!
I do not have the eyes
To see You,
But I do have the heart
To feel Your Presence
Inside my heart.
My soul is telling me
That is what You actually
Need from me and want from me.
My Supreme, my Supreme!

17 JULY 1999

452

My Supreme, my Supreme!
Today I shall have purity
In my thoughts,
I shall have beauty
In my speech
And I shall have sincerity
In my actions.
My Supreme, my Supreme!

453

My Supreme, my Supreme!
Today I shall wait devotedly
And unconditionally
To hear from You
What I am supposed to do
To please You only
In Your own Way.
My Supreme, my Supreme!

454

My Supreme, my Supreme!
My appreciation of You is good,
My admiration of You is better,
My adoration of You is best,
But my devotion for You
Is infinitely, infinitely better
Than my appreciation, my admiration
And my adoration.
My Supreme, my Supreme!

MY MORNING SOUL-BODY PRAYERS

455

My Supreme, my Supreme!
Only my unconditional surrender
To Your Will
Will forever succeed.
Everyone else will fail me,
And I shall fail them as well.
My Supreme, my Supreme!

19 JULY 1999

456

My Supreme, my Supreme!
My heart shall keep dreaming,
My life shall keep smiling,
My soul shall keep promising
And
I shall keep fulfilling.
My Supreme, my Supreme!

457

My Supreme, my Supreme!
Do bless me and my life
With an indomitable spirit
Once more.
My Supreme, my Supreme!

458

My Supreme, my Supreme!
May my life be a life of duty.
May my mind be a mind of purity.
May my heart be a heart of beauty
And fragrance.
My Supreme, my Supreme!

MY MORNING SOUL-BODY PRAYERS

21 JULY 1999

459

My Supreme, my Supreme!
Your sustaining Grace
Is saving me
From danger's destructive face.
I am offering You
My prayerful and soulful
Gratitude-heart-tears.
My Supreme, my Supreme!

460

My Supreme, my Supreme!
Your surprising Grace
Is making me win
The heart-race.
I am offering You
My prayerful and soulful
Gratitude-heart-tears.
My Supreme, my Supreme!

461

My Supreme, my Supreme!
Your unending Grace
Is encouraging me to chase away
The darkest ignorance-night.
I am offering You
My prayerful and soulful
Gratitude-heart-tears.
My Supreme, my Supreme!

22 JULY 1999

462

My Supreme, my Supreme!
When I am in my soul,
I clearly see and deeply feel
That all human beings
Are my divine oneness-brothers
And sisters.
My Supreme, my Supreme!

463

My Supreme, my Supreme!
When I am in my heart,
I see and feel
That all human beings
Are my true friends.
My Supreme, my Supreme!

464

My Supreme, my Supreme!
When I am in my body,
I am utter helplessness,
Ceaseless failure.
My capsizing life-boat sees no shore,
No tomorrow's dawn.
My Supreme, my Supreme!

MY MORNING SOUL-BODY PRAYERS

23 JULY 1999

465

My Supreme, my Supreme!
No more the unaspiring mind!
No more the doubting mind!
No more the suspecting mind!
No more the judging mind!
No more! No more!
My Supreme, my Supreme!

466

My Supreme, my Supreme!
What I desperately needed
I now sleeplessly and sacredly have:
A heart of silence.
And to You, my Supreme, I offer
My breathless gratitude.
My Supreme, my Supreme!

467

My Supreme, my Supreme!
The more I offer myself to humanity,
The closer You come to me
And the more certain I am
Of Your Presence in my heart.
My Supreme, my Supreme!

24 JULY 1999

468

My Supreme, my Supreme!
A true God-lover
Does not have to see miracles
To realise God.
No, no, no!
He only needs God's urgent Grace
To realise God.
My Supreme, my Supreme!

469

My Supreme, my Supreme!
Those who are eager to watch
Miracle-performances
Are either consciously
Or unconsciously
God's Omnipresence-Power-doubters.
My Supreme, my Supreme!

470

My Supreme, my Supreme!
Those who do not believe
In Your infinite Compassion-Light
And Your infinite Forgiveness-Delight
Have not yet reached
The human life-consciousness-level.
My Supreme, my Supreme!

471

My Supreme, my Supreme!
Self-doubters are self-torturers
And self-destroyers.
God-doubters can bring
Unspeakable disgrace
To the ever-compassionate
Mother Earth.
My Supreme, my Supreme!

26 JULY 1999

472

My Supreme, my Supreme!
Your Compassion is
My mind's illumination.
Your Compassion is
My life's liberation.
Your Compassion is
My heart's God-realisation.
My Supreme, my Supreme!

473

My Supreme, my Supreme!
My prayers, my meditations,
My aspiration and my dedication –
Everything that I have
And everything that I am –
Grows only in Your
Forgiveness-Heart-Garden.
My Supreme, my Supreme!

474

My Supreme, my Supreme!
Do bless my mind
With humility-light.
Do bless my life
With patience-delight.
Do bless my heart
With satisfaction-perfection.
My Supreme, my Supreme!

MY MORNING SOUL-BODY PRAYERS

27 JULY 1999

475

My Supreme, my Supreme!
Please, please give me
A childlike heart
Full of simplicity, sincerity
And purity
To follow You wherever You go.
My Supreme, my Supreme!

476

My Supreme, my Supreme!
Please, please never allow me
To act like an unaspiring human being
Who is all the time rushing
And rushing and rushing
With no destination.
My Supreme, my Supreme!

477

My Supreme, my Supreme!
I have seen the head and face
Of greatness.
I am not at all satisfied.
My Supreme, my Supreme,
I wish to feel the heart and breath
Of goodness
To be fully satisfied.
My Supreme, please fulfil
My long-cherished desire.
My Supreme, my Supreme!

478

My Supreme, my Supreme!
I must meditate and meditate
And meditate
Either to illumine my mind
Or to conquer the disasters
That my mind creates.
My Supreme, my Supreme!

479

My Supreme, my Supreme!
A purity-flooded heart
Knows no obstructions,
Knows no ignorance-night.
My Supreme, my Supreme!

MY MORNING SOUL-BODY PRAYERS

28 JULY 1999

480

My Supreme, my Supreme!
May my life become
A happiness-flower
With abundant beauty and fragrance
To worship You around the clock.
My Supreme, my Supreme!

481

My Supreme, my Supreme!
I wish to have a private interview.
I would like to know from You
How I can please You
Infinitely more.
My Supreme, my Supreme!

482

My Supreme, my Supreme!
I am so grateful to You
For allowing me to hear
The Nectar-Voice
Of Your omnipotent Will.
My Supreme, my Supreme!

30 JULY 1999

483

My Supreme, my Supreme!
May my soul's divinity-light
Permeate each and every action
Of my daily life.
My Supreme, my Supreme!

484

My Supreme, my Supreme!
As long as I have You
As my Friend, only Friend,
I do not have to pay any attention
To hostile enemies.
My Supreme, my Supreme!

MY MORNING SOUL-BODY PRAYERS

31 JULY 1999

485

My Supreme, my Supreme!
Do remove the thick veil
Of misunderstanding
Between me and my dear ones.
Misunderstanding is the most serious
And painful experience that we get.
Therefore, please, please remove
The thick veil of misunderstanding.
My Supreme, my Supreme!

486

My Supreme, my Supreme!
May my life be made of
My heart's streaming tears
And my soul's soaring smiles.
My Supreme, my Supreme!

487

My Supreme, my Supreme!
May willingness be
My mind's constant companion.
May eagerness be
My heart's constant companion.
May surrender to Your Will be
My life's sleepless companion.
My Supreme, my Supreme!

1 AUGUST 1999

488

My Supreme, my Supreme, my Supreme!
I am safe, perfectly safe,
Only when I stay inside
My God-obedience-orbit.
My Supreme, my Supreme, my Supreme!

489

My Supreme, my Supreme, my Supreme!
May every second of my life
Be a rainbow-beauty, rainbow-joy
And rainbow-enthusiasm.
My Supreme, my Supreme, my Supreme!

MY MORNING SOUL-BODY PRAYERS

2 AUGUST 1999

490

My Supreme, my Supreme, my Supreme!
When I do something wrong,
Please, please scold me severely.
If You scold me severely,
Only then will I feel
That You truly love me
And Your Concern for me
Is genuine.
My Supreme, my Supreme,
Do scold me, do scold me.
My Supreme, my Supreme, my Supreme!

491

My Supreme, my Supreme, my Supreme!
May my eyes look at You
Smilingly
And may my heart place itself
At Your Feet
Tearfully.
My Supreme, my Supreme, my Supreme!

3 AUGUST 1999

492

My Supreme, my Supreme, my Supreme!
Today do make my surrender
Complete, constant and sleepless
So that I can become
A supremely choice instrument
Of Yours.
My Supreme, my Supreme, my Supreme!

493

My Supreme, my Supreme, my Supreme!
You are telling me
That the more concern I have
For humanity,
The more confidence You will have
In me.
My Supreme, my Supreme, my Supreme!

494

My Supreme, my Supreme, my Supreme!
Please, please always allow me
To succeed
In my self-giving life.
My Supreme, my Supreme, my Supreme!

495

My Supreme, my Supreme, my Supreme!
I know, I know, I know
That nothing can be as pure,
As beautiful, as powerful
And as fruitful
As my heart's aspiration-tears.
My Supreme, my Supreme, my Supreme!

496

My Supreme, my Supreme, my Supreme!
O my mind, vital and body,
Please join my heart
In serving
The life of humanity.
My Supreme, my Supreme, my Supreme!

SRI CHINMOY

6 AUGUST 1999

497

My Supreme, my Supreme, my Supreme!
Please, please accept
My heart's gratitude-tears,
For today You have given me
The key
To open my heart-temple-door
To pray and meditate
Every morning and every evening.
My Supreme, my Supreme, my Supreme!

498

My Supreme, my Supreme, my Supreme!
I wish to cling only
To Your Protection-Feet.
I wish to cling only
To Your Compassion-Eye.
I wish to cling only
To Your Forgiveness-Heart.
My Supreme, my Supreme, my Supreme!

499

My Supreme, my Supreme, my Supreme!
My soul, my heart and even my mind
Have only one dream:
A oneness-world-heart-blossoming
Dream.
My Supreme, my Supreme, my Supreme!

MY MORNING SOUL-BODY PRAYERS

10 AUGUST 1999

500

My Supreme, my Supreme, my Supreme!
My desire-prayer goes to You
And comes back crying.
My aspiration-prayer goes to You
And stays with You
And smiles and smiles and smiles.
My Supreme, my Supreme, my Supreme!

501

My Supreme, my Supreme, my Supreme!
With my prayer-mind
I always try to please myself.
With my meditation-heart
I always long to please You
In Your own Way.
My Supreme, my Supreme, my Supreme!

502

My Supreme, my Supreme, my Supreme!
My prayers are my human life's
Helpless cries.
My meditations are my divine life's
Giant smiles.
My Supreme, my Supreme, my Supreme!

503

My Supreme, my Supreme, my Supreme!
My prayer-tears
Make my mind divinely pure.
My meditation-smiles
Make my heart supremely self-giving.
My Supreme, my Supreme, my Supreme!

504

My Supreme, my Supreme, my Supreme!
When I pray soulfully,
You feed me.
When I meditate self-givingly,
You ask me to feed You.
My Supreme, my Supreme, my Supreme!

MY MORNING SOUL-BODY PRAYERS

11 AUGUST 1999

505

My Supreme, my Supreme, my Supreme!
I have come to realise
That only a serene mind
Is a true God-necessity.
My Supreme, my Supreme, my Supreme!

506

My Supreme, my Supreme, my Supreme!
I have come to realise
That only a pure heart
Is an absolute God-necessity.
My Supreme, my Supreme, my Supreme!

507

My Supreme, my Supreme, my Supreme!
What I need is not
World-renunciation-hunger.
What I need is
World-acceptance-wisdom
To serve You and please You
In each and every human being.
My Supreme, my Supreme, my Supreme!

12 AUGUST 1999

508

My Supreme, my Supreme, my Supreme!
Age is no barrier
To the enthusiasm-eagerness
God-worshipper, God-lover
And God-server.
My Supreme, my Supreme, my Supreme!

509

My Supreme, my Supreme, my Supreme!
Age pitifully cries and cries
When it foolishly and greedily
Lives for itself.
Age brightly and powerfully
Smiles and smiles
When it lives in God, with God
And for God.
My Supreme, my Supreme, my Supreme!

510

My Supreme, my Supreme, my Supreme!
Age without God
Is ignorance-night-accumulation.
Age with God, in God and for God
Is the harvest of wisdom-light.
My Supreme, my Supreme, my Supreme!

MY MORNING SOUL-BODY PRAYERS

14 AUGUST 1999

511

My Supreme, my Supreme, my Supreme!
Out of Your infinite Compassion,
You have blessed my gratitude-heart
With a rainbow-beauty-smile.
My Supreme, my Supreme, my Supreme!

512

My Supreme, my Supreme, my Supreme!
You start singing, dancing
And flying
The moment You see
My willingness-mind,
Eagerness-heart
And enthusiasm-life.
My Supreme, my Supreme, my Supreme!

513

My Supreme, my Supreme, my Supreme!
O my mind, it is true
That you have not pleased God.
But please make a brave, soulful
And prayerful attempt
To please God.
I am sure that you will succeed,
My mind,
You will succeed.
My Supreme, my Supreme, my Supreme!

514

My Supreme, my Supreme, my Supreme!
When I reach the top,
I cannot stop
And I do not stop
Because I clearly see
A new goal beckoning me.
My Supreme, my Supreme, my Supreme!

515

My Supreme, my Supreme, my Supreme!
I am sure
That my heart's peace-bird
Will not nest
In my mind's dense forest.
My Supreme, my Supreme, my Supreme!

MY MORNING SOUL-BODY PRAYERS

15 AUGUST 1999

516

My Supreme, my Supreme, my Supreme!
Only a God-gratitude-heart-seeker
With a sleeplessly
Unconditional surrender
Knows God's Will
In its totality.
My Supreme, my Supreme, my Supreme!

517

My Supreme, my Supreme, my Supreme!
Every sincere seeker
Has been blessed by You
With the capacity to please You
In Your own Way
Always.
My Supreme, my Supreme, my Supreme!

518

My Supreme, my Supreme, my Supreme!
May my mind be a ceaseless search
For Your divine Will.
My Supreme, my Supreme, my Supreme!

519

My Supreme, my Supreme, my Supreme!
May my heart be a sleepless hunger
For Your supreme Will.
My Supreme, my Supreme, my Supreme!

SRI CHINMOY

16 AUGUST 1999

520

My Supreme, my Supreme, my Supreme!
I need absolute faith
In everything
That is created by You.
My Supreme, my Supreme, my Supreme!

521

My Supreme, my Supreme, my Supreme!
I have received
Three inner educations from You:
An aspiration-heart,
A dedication-life
And
A surrender-breath.
My Supreme, my Supreme, my Supreme!

522

My Supreme, my Supreme, my Supreme!
My mind believes in You.
I am now happy with my mind.
My heart believes in You.
I am now happy with my heart.
My life believes in You.
I am now happy with my life.
My mind's new awakening,
My heart's new awakening,
My life's new awakening
I now place at Your Lotus-Feet.
My Supreme, my Supreme, my Supreme!

523

My Supreme, my Supreme, my Supreme!
You are telling me
Never to turn my spirituality
Into scientific research.
Spirituality is self-discovery.
Self-discovery is God-realisation.
My Supreme, my Supreme, my Supreme!

17 AUGUST 1999

524

My Supreme, my Supreme, my Supreme!
In my God-obedience
I see the smiling Eye
And the dancing Heart
Of my Lord Beloved Supreme.
My Supreme, my Supreme, my Supreme!

525

My Supreme, my Supreme, my Supreme!
In my God-obedience I see and feel
The infinite affection
And infinite pride
Of both Heaven and earth.
My Supreme, my Supreme, my Supreme!

526

My Supreme, my Supreme, my Supreme!
Because of my God-obedience
You have made me
Your Satisfaction-Heart-Pride-
Banner-bearer.
My Supreme, my Supreme, my Supreme!

527

My Supreme, my Supreme, my Supreme!
Because of my God-obedience
You have blessed me with
A happiness-rainbow-heart-sky.
My Supreme, my Supreme, my Supreme!

MY MORNING SOUL-BODY PRAYERS

18 AUGUST 1999

528

My Supreme, my Supreme, my Supreme!
I must keep my aspiration-heart-flames
Constantly climbing
And ever-transcending.
My Supreme, my Supreme, my Supreme!

529

My Supreme, my Supreme, my Supreme!
May my life be
My heart-temple-beauty
And my soul-shrine-fragrance.
My Supreme, my Supreme, my Supreme!

530

My Supreme, my Supreme, my Supreme!
I must never be caught
By the desire-temptation-snare.
My Supreme, my Supreme, my Supreme!

531

My Supreme, my Supreme, my Supreme!
May I develop a ceaseless hunger
For Your Forgiveness-Smile.
My Supreme, my Supreme, my Supreme!

532

My Supreme, my Supreme, my Supreme!
Today I must revive
All my God-satisfaction-memories
Of the remote past.
My Supreme, my Supreme, my Supreme!

533

My Supreme, my Supreme, my Supreme!
Do bless me with
A completely shattered
Pride-existence-life.
My Supreme, my Supreme, my Supreme!

534

My Supreme, my Supreme, my Supreme!
I must either destroy
Or give a determined chase to
All the ruthless and shameless doubts
That attack my poor mind.
My Supreme, my Supreme, my Supreme!

MY MORNING SOUL-BODY PRAYERS

20 AUGUST 1999

535

My Supreme, my Supreme, my Supreme!
The full awakening of my heart
Is the beauty
Of my aspiration-tears
And the fragrance
Of my dedication-smiles.
My Supreme, my Supreme, my Supreme!

536

My Supreme, my Supreme, my Supreme!
The sweet awakening
Of my heart-lotus
Is the glorious blossoming
Of my life.
My Supreme, my Supreme, my Supreme!

537

My Supreme, my Supreme, my Supreme!
I am my sleepless heart's
Aspiration-awakening tear.
My Supreme, my Supreme, my Supreme!

538

My Supreme, my Supreme, my Supreme!
I am prayerfully and soulfully offering
The breath of my heart-awakening
To You
For Your full manifestation
Here on earth.
My Supreme, my Supreme, my Supreme!

539

My Supreme, my Supreme, my Supreme!
You have been waiting for centuries
For an iota of my heart's awakening.
I promise I shall not delay You
Any longer.
My Supreme, my Supreme, my Supreme!

MY MORNING SOUL-BODY PRAYERS

21 AUGUST 1999

540

My Supreme, my Supreme, my Supreme!
My heart's eagerness
Is an absolute necessity
To satisfy my Lord Beloved Supreme
In His own Way
At every moment.
My Supreme, my Supreme, my Supreme!

541

My Supreme, my Supreme, my Supreme!
My eagerness-heart does not house
Even an iota
Of hesitation-negativity-mind.
My Supreme, my Supreme, my Supreme!

542

My Supreme, my Supreme, my Supreme!
My sleepless and God-pleasing
Eagerness
Is my closest association with God.
My Supreme, my Supreme, my Supreme!

SRI CHINMOY

23 AUGUST 1999

543

My Supreme, my Supreme, my Supreme!
I know, I know,
No pure heart-devotion,
No true God-satisfaction,
No, never!
My Supreme, my Supreme, my Supreme!

544

My Supreme, my Supreme, my Supreme!
When my ego-vital is
The winner,
My confusion-mind becomes
The ruler.
My Supreme, my Supreme, my Supreme!

545..

My Supreme, my Supreme, my Supreme!
My self-doubt immediately opens
The floodgates
Of my anxieties and worries.
My Supreme, my Supreme, my Supreme!

MY MORNING SOUL-BODY PRAYERS

24 AUGUST 1999

546

My Supreme, my Supreme, my Supreme!
May my life-boat every day
Ply time and again
Between
My mind's God-obedience-shore
And my heart's God-gratitude-shore.
My Supreme, my Supreme, my Supreme!

547

My Supreme, my Supreme, my Supreme!
I shall not allow my mind to remain
Even one minute more
In the land of God-oblivion.
My Supreme, my Supreme, my Supreme!

548

My Supreme, my Supreme, my Supreme!
Today, to my deepest joy
And greatest relief,
My mind said to God,
"My Lord,
Your Will is not only acceptable
And serviceable,
But also adorable and lovable."
My Supreme, my Supreme, my Supreme!

SRI CHINMOY

25 AUGUST 1999

549

My Supreme, my Supreme, my Supreme!
Instead of surrendering
To our ever-increasing
Shortcomings,
We must challenge them
And conquer them
Once and for all!
My Supreme, my Supreme, my Supreme!

550

My Supreme, my Supreme, my Supreme!
Instead of powerfully
Chastising ourselves
For doing the wrong things,
We must divinely
Energise ourselves
To do the right things.
My Supreme, my Supreme, my Supreme!

551

My Supreme, my Supreme, my Supreme!
Every day I must discover
New ways
To please You in Your own Way.
My Supreme, my Supreme, my Supreme!

552

My Supreme, my Supreme, my Supreme!
Do make me a child
Of today's divine newness
And tomorrow's supreme fulness.
My Supreme, my Supreme, my Supreme!

26 AUGUST 1999

553

My Supreme, my Supreme, my Supreme!
The newness-fulness-pioneer-discoverers
Are Your supremely chosen children.
My Supreme, my Supreme, my Supreme!

554

My Supreme, my Supreme, my Supreme!
Only those who self-givingly
And unconditionally
Try to please You
Succeed at Your choice Hour.
My Supreme, my Supreme, my Supreme!

555

My Supreme, my Supreme, my Supreme!
I must not try to improve
The mind of the past.
I must only try to build
My heart-temple of the present.
My Supreme, my Supreme, my Supreme!

556

My Supreme, my Supreme, my Supreme!
No hesitation-mind,
No suspicion-mind,
No God-doubt-mind
Will ever be able to arrive
At God's Palace.
My Supreme, my Supreme, my Supreme!

MY MORNING SOUL-BODY PRAYERS

28 AUGUST 1999

557

My Supreme, my Supreme, my Supreme!
What I prayerfully and soulfully
Do,
I powerfully and fruitfully
Become.
My Supreme, my Supreme, my Supreme!

558

My Supreme, my Supreme, my Supreme!
At every moment I wish to be
Cheerfully and totally obedient
To Your Marching Orders.
My Supreme, my Supreme, my Supreme!

559

My Supreme, my Supreme, my Supreme!
To the God-worshipper, God says,
"My child,
I have everything for you."
To the God-lover, God says,
"My child,
You are everything to Me."
My Supreme, my Supreme, my Supreme!

560

My Supreme, my Supreme, my Supreme!
Alas, my mind does not believe
In God-surrender.
Therefore, it is saddled
With untold worries and anxieties.
My Supreme, my Supreme, my Supreme!

29 AUGUST 1999

561

My Supreme, my Supreme, my Supreme!
Your earliest and mightiest
Promise to humanity
Is this:
The finite mortal
Shall grow into
Infinity's Immortality.
My Supreme, my Supreme, my Supreme!

562

My Supreme, my Supreme, my Supreme!
A soulful smile
Is a mind-purification-guarantee.
My Supreme, my Supreme, my Supreme!

563

My Supreme, my Supreme, my Supreme!
My Lord Beloved Supreme
Is extremely fond of my heart's
Unconditional love, devotion
And surrender-whispers.
My Supreme, my Supreme, my Supreme!

564

My Supreme, my Supreme, my Supreme!
An iota of insecurity-mind
Can easily create
An ocean vast of unhappiness.
My Supreme, my Supreme, my Supreme!

MY MORNING SOUL-BODY PRAYERS

30 AUGUST 1999

565

My Supreme, my Supreme, my Supreme!
May my mind be always
Dynamic and enthusiastic,
And may my heart be always
Pure and self-giving.
My Supreme, my Supreme, my Supreme!

566

My Supreme, my Supreme, my Supreme!
I am so happy that I never miss
My God-obedience-classes.
My Supreme, my Supreme, my Supreme!

567

My Supreme, my Supreme, my Supreme!
Do make me Your most perfect
Satisfaction-Smile-stamp.
My Supreme, my Supreme, my Supreme!

568

My Supreme, my Supreme, my Supreme!
By Your infinite Grace
I am paving my progress-road
By sprinting,
And not by walking or running.
My Supreme, my Supreme, my Supreme!

31 AUGUST 1999

569

My Supreme, my Supreme, my Supreme!
May my mind and I every day
Read my Lord's Forgiveness-Book.
May my heart and I every day
Read my Lord's Compassion-Book.
May my life and I every day
Read my Lord's Will-Book.
My Supreme, my Supreme, my Supreme!

570

My Supreme, my Supreme, my Supreme!
You are telling me
That my gratitude
Is my heart's purest tear
And my life's sweetest smile.
My Supreme, my Supreme, my Supreme!

571

My Supreme, my Supreme, my Supreme!
I must never go back.
My victory's gong
Is my tomorrow's song.
My Supreme, my Supreme, my Supreme!

572

My Supreme, my Supreme, my Supreme!
I would like my heart always to live
In the sweetness and openness
Of my tiny Indian village-life,
While my present life lives
In the newness and fulness
Of America's New York.
My Supreme, my Supreme, my Supreme!

1 SEPTEMBER 1999

573

My Supreme, my Supreme, my Supreme!
My pinnacle-height-experience
Tells me
That every human being is Your Heart.
My abysmal abyss-experience
Tells me
That I am Your only Heart.
My Supreme, my Supreme, my Supreme!

574

My Supreme, my Supreme, my Supreme!
Today I have put up
Welcome signs for You
Not only in my heart-garden,
But also in my mind-jungle.
My Supreme, my Supreme, my Supreme!

575

My Supreme, my Supreme, my Supreme!
When my heart surrenders to Your Will,
You smile at my heart
And You also ask my heart
To smile at You.
When my mind surrenders to Your Will,
You ask my mind
To come and sing with You.
When my entire life surrenders
To Your Will,
You ask my life
To come and dance with You.
My Supreme, my Supreme, my Supreme!

576

My Supreme, my Supreme, my Supreme!
I know, I know,
You never turn a deaf ear
To my heart's sincere prayer-cries.
My Supreme, my Supreme, my Supreme!

577

My Supreme, my Supreme, my Supreme!
Do come down from wherever You are
To inspect my mind,
To correct my heart
And to perfect my life.
My Supreme, my Supreme, my Supreme!

578

My Supreme, my Supreme, my Supreme!
I shall no more keep You,
My Lord Beloved Supreme,
Waiting.
My Supreme, my Supreme, my Supreme!

579

My Supreme, my Supreme, my Supreme!
Sleeplessly I must think
Only of my Lord's Happiness.
My Supreme, my Supreme, my Supreme!

2 SEPTEMBER 1999

580

My Supreme, my Supreme, my Supreme!
My heart, invoke patience-light.
Behold, Infinity's Peace-Delight
Is fast approaching you.
My Supreme, my Supreme, my Supreme!

581

My Supreme, my Supreme, my Supreme!
In the morning and in the evening
Your Forgiveness and Your Compassion
Ceaselessly talk
To my doubting mind,
And Your Joy and Your Pride
Ceaselessly talk
To my aspiring heart.
My Supreme, my Supreme, my Supreme!

582

My Supreme, my Supreme, my Supreme!
Day and night,
Around the clock,
My Lord Beloved Supreme
Pays blissful Attention
To my unconditional
Surrender-life.
My Supreme, my Supreme, my Supreme!

583

My Supreme, my Supreme, my Supreme!
At every step
On my aspiration-dedication-road,
I clearly see
That my inner fragrance
Is multiplying and multiplying
And multiplying,
And my outer beauty is growing
And growing and growing.
My Supreme, my Supreme, my Supreme!

584

My Supreme, my Supreme, my Supreme!
Alas, You shed bitter Tears
When my mind enjoys
Brooding and spreading doubts.
My Supreme, my Supreme, my Supreme!

585

My Supreme, my Supreme, my Supreme!
Out of Your infinite Bounty,
Every morning
You write something encouraging,
Inspiring, illumining and fulfilling
On the tablet of my aspiration-heart.
My Supreme, my Supreme, my Supreme!

3 SEPTEMBER 1999

586

My Supreme, my Supreme, my Supreme!
My real spirituality
Is my heart-offering
And my life-blossoming,
Not my God-possessing desire.
My Supreme, my Supreme, my Supreme!

587

My Supreme, my Supreme, my Supreme!
My heart goes to Your Heart
With prayer-cries.
Your Heart comes to my heart
With Blessing-Smiles.
My Supreme, my Supreme, my Supreme!

588

My Supreme, my Supreme, my Supreme!
When my heart is on its knees
Before You,
You tell my heart,
"My child,
I am all for you,
I am all for you."
My Supreme, my Supreme, my Supreme!

MY MORNING SOUL-BODY PRAYERS

589

My Supreme, my Supreme, my Supreme!
I am indeed
Your blessingful gift
To Mother Earth.
My Supreme, my Supreme, my Supreme!

4 SEPTEMBER 1999

590

My Supreme, my Supreme, my Supreme!
No desire-dream can forever last.
There comes a time
When it has to burst,
Like a bubble.
My Supreme, my Supreme, my Supreme!

591

My Supreme, my Supreme, my Supreme!
No expectation, no expectation,
No expectation!
Alas, the expectation-boat
Quite often capsizes.
My Supreme, my Supreme, my Supreme!

592

My Supreme, my Supreme, my Supreme!
The pure prayer-heart of a seeker
Is bound to succeed.
My Supreme, my Supreme, my Supreme!

593

My Supreme, my Supreme, my Supreme!
At long last I have come to realise
That ignorance-night
Is terribly and helplessly afraid
Of my prayer-heart.
My Supreme, my Supreme, my Supreme!

594

My Supreme, my Supreme, my Supreme!
My true spirituality
Is the love of Your Breath
In every heart.
My Supreme, my Supreme, my Supreme!

595

My Supreme, my Supreme, my Supreme!
It is indeed an impossible task
To recognise You
In all Your infinite disguises.
My Supreme, my Supreme, my Supreme!

5 SEPTEMBER 1999

596

My Supreme, my Supreme, my Supreme!
Please, please bless me
With a perfection-searching mind,
Perfection-aspiring mind,
Perfection-loving mind
And perfection-living mind.
My Supreme, my Supreme, my Supreme!

597

My Supreme, my Supreme, my Supreme!
May my mind at every moment
Experience peace-light
And peace-delight,
And not anxiety-worry-night.
My Supreme, my Supreme, my Supreme!

598

My Supreme, my Supreme, my Supreme!
You are telling me
That there is only one way
To achieve inner freedom,
And that is through
Constant God-obedience.
My Supreme, my Supreme, my Supreme!

MY MORNING SOUL-BODY PRAYERS

6 SEPTEMBER 1999

599

My Supreme, my Supreme, my Supreme!
Do bless me
With a cheerfully, enthusiastically
And eagerly correctable
Heart, mind, vital and body.
My Supreme, my Supreme, my Supreme!

600

My Supreme, my Supreme, my Supreme!
Do liberate my aspiring heart
And my dedicated life
From this thought-encumbered mind.
My Supreme, my Supreme, my Supreme!

601

My Supreme, my Supreme, my Supreme!
I know, I know,
Peace-achievement
Is not a one-day task.
It is a most serious
Lifelong endeavour.
My Supreme, my Supreme, my Supreme!

602

My Supreme, my Supreme, my Supreme!
Aspiring or desiring—
I unmistakably know
That I belong only
To the golden dust
Of Your Compassion-Forgiveness-Feet.
My Supreme, my Supreme, my Supreme!

603

My Supreme, my Supreme, my Supreme!
You are telling me
Not to enjoy repetition,
But to live in the fulness
Of ever-newness.
My Supreme, my Supreme, my Supreme!

604

My Supreme, my Supreme, my Supreme!
When I am in my mind,
You ask me to be careful.
When I am in my heart,
You ask me to be soulful.
When I am in my soul,
You ask me to be forceful.
When I am in You,
You ask me to remain
Eternally blissful.
My Supreme, my Supreme, my Supreme!

MY MORNING SOUL-BODY PRAYERS

8 SEPTEMBER 1999

605

My Supreme, my Supreme, my Supreme!
Only my heart's aspiration-tears
And my life's dedication-smiles
Can slake my God-thirst.
My Supreme, my Supreme, my Supreme!

606

My Supreme, my Supreme, my Supreme!
I must never, never, never allow
My full God-manifestation-hopes
To dwindle to nothingness.
My Supreme, my Supreme, my Supreme!

607

My Supreme, my Supreme, my Supreme!
You are telling me
That if I want to please You always
In Your own Way,
Then I must triumph over
My self-doubts and my world-criticism.
My Supreme, my Supreme, my Supreme!

9 SEPTEMBER 1999

608

My Supreme, my Supreme, my Supreme!
You want me to live
In the neatness of my body,
In the strictness of my vital,
In the openness of my mind
And in the sweetness of my heart.
My Supreme, my Supreme, my Supreme!

609

My Supreme, my Supreme, my Supreme!
God can easily obliterate
My past blunders
If He sees that the tears of my heart
Are absolutely sincere and pure.
My Supreme, my Supreme, my Supreme!

610

My Supreme, my Supreme, my Supreme!
You want me to be
A seasoned pilgrim
On Eternity's Aspiration-Road.
My Supreme, my Supreme, my Supreme!

611

My Supreme, my Supreme, my Supreme!
Do occupy my mind's desire-house
Exactly the way You have occupied
My heart's aspiration-temple.
My Supreme, my Supreme, my Supreme!

612

My Supreme, my Supreme, my Supreme!
A discouragement-mind—
No, no, no!
An encouragement-heart—
Yes, yes, yes!
An enlightenment-life—
Yes, yes, yes,
A million times!
My Supreme, my Supreme, my Supreme!

10 SEPTEMBER 1999

613

My Supreme, my Supreme, my Supreme!
My life's God-nearness
Entirely depends on
My heart's God-gratitude-progress-tears.
My Supreme, my Supreme, my Supreme!

614

My Supreme, my Supreme, my Supreme!
I shall never, never, never allow
My disbelief-enemy
To enter into
My God-loving, God-searching
And God-crying mind.
My Supreme, my Supreme, my Supreme!

615

My Supreme, my Supreme, my Supreme!
When my ego-monster completely died,
You invited all the cosmic gods,
And most happily and most proudly
Gave them a very special banquet.
My Supreme, my Supreme, my Supreme!

616

My Supreme, my Supreme, my Supreme!
You cheerfully smile
At my simplicity-life.
You proudly shake hands
With my sincerity-mind.
You unreservedly embrace
My purity-heart.
My Supreme, my Supreme, my Supreme!

617

My Supreme, my Supreme, my Supreme!
How I wish You could give me
More, infinitely more,
God-manifestation-responsibilities!
My Supreme, my Supreme, my Supreme!

11 SEPTEMBER 1999

618

My Supreme, my Supreme, my Supreme!
I have come to realise
That when I take pride in thinking
And feeling
That You love me infinitely more
Than anybody else,
That is the time I create
An insurmountable barrier
Between You and me.
My Supreme, my Supreme, my Supreme!

619

My Supreme, my Supreme, my Supreme!
Let me stop talking about
My spirituality –
My aspiration, my dedication,
My love, my devotion, my surrender
And so forth –
Once and for all.
Let me speak only about
Your infinite Compassion
And infinite Forgiveness.
My Supreme, my Supreme, my Supreme!

620

My Supreme, my Supreme, my Supreme!
When my heart is bathed in tears,
I pray to the visible God
For His Compassion and Forgiveness.
When my heart is wreathed in smiles,
I meditate on the invisible God
For His own Satisfaction.
My Supreme, my Supreme, my Supreme!

621

My Supreme, my Supreme, my Supreme!
O my God-disobedience-mind,
Alas, will there come a time
When you will truly be ashamed
Of yourself?
My Supreme, my Supreme, my Supreme!

12 SEPTEMBER 1999

622

My Supreme, my Supreme, my Supreme!
May my life-boat every day ply
Between my heart's hope-shore
And my soul's promise-shore.
My Supreme, my Supreme, my Supreme!

623

My Supreme, my Supreme, my Supreme!
When my mind believes,
My heart receives.
And when my heart receives,
My life achieves.
What does my life achieve?
It achieves Your Compassion,
It achieves Your Satisfaction.
My Supreme, my Supreme, my Supreme!

624

My Supreme, my Supreme, my Supreme!
When I am in my outer existence-life,
I am my body-temple.
When I am in my inner existence-life,
I am my heart-shrine.
When I am in my inmost existence-life,
I am my soul-deity.
My Supreme, my Supreme, my Supreme!

MY MORNING SOUL-BODY PRAYERS

13 SEPTEMBER 1999

625

My Supreme, my Supreme, my Supreme!
My dreamboat-life
Is sailing and sailing and sailing
In my Lord's
Compassion-Heart-Dream-Sea.
My Supreme, my Supreme, my Supreme!

626

My Supreme, my Supreme, my Supreme!
I was born to please You
In Your own Way,
And even when I am dying,
I shall please You in Your own Way.
My Supreme, my Supreme, my Supreme!

627

My Supreme, my Supreme, my Supreme!
Every morning
I renew my unconditional surrender
To Your Will
And immediately I receive
Thunderous applause from Your Heart.
My Supreme, my Supreme, my Supreme!

628

My Supreme, my Supreme, my Supreme!
Today my soul is using
Its adamantine will-power
To compel my mind to touch
The dust of Your Feet
And please You always
In Your own Way.
My Supreme, my Supreme, my Supreme!

629

My Supreme, my Supreme, my Supreme!
Today,
Out of Your infinite Bounty,
You want me to enjoy
The highest flight
On Your Vision-Wings
In Your Infinity's Sky.
My Supreme, my Supreme, my Supreme!

MY MORNING SOUL-BODY PRAYERS

14 SEPTEMBER 1999

630

My Supreme, my Supreme, my Supreme!
Every day, every hour,
Every minute, every second
I must consecrate my earth-existence
To Your Will.
My Supreme, my Supreme, my Supreme!

631

My Supreme, my Supreme, my Supreme!
Every second of my life
I must offer my breath
To absolute God-obedience.
My Supreme, my Supreme, my Supreme!

632

My Supreme, my Supreme, my Supreme!
Sleeplessly
I must keep my heart-eye open
To Your Compassion-flooded Eye.
My Supreme, my Supreme, my Supreme!

633

My Supreme, my Supreme, my Supreme!
I know, I know,
My insecurity gives You
A severe headache;
My jealousy gives You
A real heart attack.

"My child, My child, My child,
To My greatest Joy,
It is your gratitude-heart
That cures My headache;
It is your surrender-life
That cures My heart attack."
My Supreme, my Supreme, my Supreme!

MY MORNING SOUL-BODY PRAYERS

15 SEPTEMBER 1999

634

My Supreme, my Supreme, my Supreme!
I must stop crying
For Your constant Attention.
I must start praying
And meditating
For my mind's purification
And my heart's expansion.
My Supreme, my Supreme, my Supreme!

635

My Supreme, my Supreme, my Supreme!
Every morning,
Out of Your infinite Compassion,
You come to plough
My life's gratitude, obedience
And surrender-fields.
My Supreme, my Supreme, my Supreme!

636

My Supreme, my Supreme, my Supreme!
Your Will has travelled
The entire length and breadth
Of the world.
Alas, only very few aspiring souls
Have responded.
My Supreme, my Supreme, my Supreme!

637

My Supreme, my Supreme, my Supreme!
Those who are living in
The mind-supremacy,
The vital-supremacy
And the body-supremacy
Are destroying the peace-blossom-dream
Of the world.
My Supreme, my Supreme, my Supreme!

638

My Supreme, my Supreme, my Supreme!
Only when I am ready—
When my mind is willing
And my heart is eager—
Do You teach me.
My Supreme, my Supreme, my Supreme!

639

My Supreme, my Supreme, my Supreme!
You gave me the capacity
To surrender unconditionally to You.
Now You have given me the capacity
To reach the zenith-heights
Of spiritual excellence.
My Supreme, my Supreme, my Supreme!

MY MORNING SOUL-BODY PRAYERS

17 SEPTEMBER 1999

640

My Supreme, my Supreme, my Supreme!
My mind's thirst for You,
My heart's hunger for You
And my life's tears and smiles for You
Lovingly, prayerfully, soulfully
And self-givingly
I place at Your Feet.
My Supreme, my Supreme, my Supreme!

641

My Supreme, my Supreme, my Supreme!
May I sleeplessly and breathlessly cry
For the ever-transcending Beyond.
My Supreme, my Supreme, my Supreme!

642

My Supreme, my Supreme, my Supreme!
May my constant self-giving
Be an inspiration
To the citizens of this world
And a joy
To the denizens of the higher worlds.
My Supreme, my Supreme, my Supreme!

643

My Supreme, my Supreme, my Supreme!
The Tears
Of Your Compassion-Eye
And the Smiles
Of Your Forgiveness-Heart
Are the answers
To my life's questions.
My Supreme, my Supreme, my Supreme!

MY MORNING SOUL-BODY PRAYERS

18 SEPTEMBER 1999

644

My Supreme, my Supreme, my Supreme!
My God-devotion
Is the beauty of my heart's tears.
My God-surrender
Is the divinity of my soul's smiles.
My Supreme, my Supreme, my Supreme!

645

My Supreme, my Supreme, my Supreme!
To place myself at Your Forgiveness-Feet
Once again
Is the crying, tearing
And burning hunger
Of my heart.
My Supreme, my Supreme, my Supreme!

646

My Supreme, my Supreme, my Supreme!
O my stupid mind,
My stupid vital, my stupid body,
Come out!
Come out of your spiritual coma.
Our Lord Beloved Supreme
Has so many things
For you to do for Him
Here on earth.
My Supreme, my Supreme, my Supreme!

19 SEPTEMBER 1999

647

My Supreme, my Supreme, my Supreme!
Shake me,
Wake me and shock me,
To make me
A faithful and choice instrument
Of Yours.
My Supreme, my Supreme, my Supreme!

648

My Supreme, my Supreme, my Supreme!
The moment I pray to You
Soulfully and self-givingly
For world peace,
You immediately promise me
An undivided, happy, illumining
And fulfilling oneness-world.
My Supreme, my Supreme, my Supreme!

649

My Supreme, my Supreme, my Supreme!
Like Your dictionary,
My dictionary also will not house
The word "failure".
My Supreme, my Supreme, my Supreme!

MY MORNING SOUL-BODY PRAYERS

650

My Supreme, my Supreme, my Supreme!
To my greatest astonishment
And deepest joy,
When my body speedily runs,
My heart peacefully rests.
My Supreme, my Supreme, my Supreme!

21 SEPTEMBER 1999

651

My Supreme, my Supreme, my Supreme!
Each creation is a very special
Blessing-heart
Of Your transcendental Vision-Eye.
My Supreme, my Supreme, my Supreme!

652

My Supreme, my Supreme, my Supreme!
Each heart carries
A very special Message from God
For the betterment of this world.
My Supreme, my Supreme, my Supreme!

653

My Supreme, my Supreme, my Supreme!
To my heart's greatest joy
And my life's greatest relief,
My doubting mind
Has completely surrendered
To my aspiring heart.
My Supreme, my Supreme, my Supreme!

654

My Supreme, my Supreme, my Supreme!
You bless the seeker
With Your own highest Realisation
Only when he is
A sleeplessly unconditional life
And a breathlessly unconditional heart.
My Supreme, my Supreme, my Supreme!

MY MORNING SOUL-BODY PRAYERS

22 SEPTEMBER 1999

655

My Supreme, my Supreme, my Supreme!
Every morning
May seven new aspiration-flames
Take birth
Inside my heart-temple.
My Supreme, my Supreme, my Supreme!

656

My Supreme, my Supreme, my Supreme!
I must most devotedly kneel down
In the temple of my aspiration-heart
First
And then start praying to You.
My Supreme, my Supreme, my Supreme!

657

My Supreme, my Supreme, my Supreme!
O my God-gratitude-heartbeat,
If you want to remain invisible,
You can,
But I must compel you
To remain audible.
My Supreme, my Supreme, my Supreme!

658

My Supreme, my Supreme, my Supreme!
You are commanding my mind
To take baby steps.
You are commanding my heart
To fly towards You.
You are commanding my life
To sit down and remain
At Your Compassion-Forgiveness-
Protection-Feet.
My Supreme, my Supreme, my Supreme!

MY MORNING SOUL-BODY PRAYERS

23 SEPTEMBER 1999

659

My Supreme, my Supreme, my Supreme!
I love Your beautiful Compassion-Eye.
I love Your blissful Forgiveness-Heart.
I love Your powerful Protection-Feet.
My Supreme, my Supreme, my Supreme!

660

My Supreme, my Supreme, my Supreme!
My mind, why are you so unspiritual?
Why are you such a fool?
Why do you deliberately want to remain
Spiritually unfed or undernourished?
Can you not realise
How much suffering you are creating
For me and my poor heart, my mind?
My Supreme, my Supreme, my Supreme!

661

My Supreme, my Supreme, my Supreme!
May all my prayers and meditations
Every day strengthen
My God-gratitude-heartbeat.
My Supreme, my Supreme, my Supreme!

24 SEPTEMBER 1999

662

My Supreme, my Supreme, my Supreme!
I must liberate my aspiration-heart
And my dedication-life
From my mind's uncertainty-prison.
My Supreme, my Supreme, my Supreme!

663

My Supreme, my Supreme, my Supreme!
With everything that I have
And everything that I am,
May I become
A God-fulfilment-eagerness-dynamo.
My Supreme, my Supreme, my Supreme!

664

My Supreme, my Supreme, my Supreme!
May I be blessed every morning
With a newness-hope-heart
And a fulness-promise-life.
My Supreme, my Supreme, my Supreme!

665

My Supreme, my Supreme, my Supreme!
When I embark
On my heart's pilgrimage
To Your celestial Palace,
I must always carry with me
My heart's devotion-shrine.
My Supreme, my Supreme, my Supreme!

MY MORNING SOUL-BODY PRAYERS

26 SEPTEMBER 1999

666

My Supreme, my Supreme, my Supreme!
If I can have God-closeness,
God-faithfulness and God-devotedness,
Then I have everything that I need.
My Supreme, my Supreme, my Supreme!

667

My Supreme, my Supreme, my Supreme!
Today and every day
I shall pray to You
To see Your smiling Face
Inside each and every
Aspiring heart.
My Supreme, my Supreme, my Supreme!

668

My Supreme, my Supreme, my Supreme!
Your earthly Tears are inside
The broken-hearted.
Your Heavenly Smiles are for
The broken-hearted.
My Supreme, my Supreme, my Supreme!

669

My Supreme, my Supreme, my Supreme!
This morning I looked far beyond
My mind's clouds
And immediately found
My heart's sunshine.
My Supreme, my Supreme, my Supreme!

670

My Supreme, my Supreme, my Supreme!
As the flowers bloom
To receive Your Smile,
Even so, my heart blooms
To love You
And my life blossoms
To serve You.
My Supreme, my Supreme, my Supreme!

671

My Supreme, my Supreme, my Supreme!
On my behalf, my Lord Supreme,
You have chosen
Aspiration-cries for my heart
And dedication-smiles for my life.
My Supreme, my Supreme, my Supreme!

MY MORNING SOUL-BODY PRAYERS

27 SEPTEMBER 1999

672

My Supreme, my Supreme, my Supreme!
In my outer life
You live in the beauty
Of my heart's streaming tears,
And nowhere else.
In my inner life
You live in the fragrance
Of my soul's beaming smiles,
And nowhere else.
My Supreme, my Supreme, my Supreme!

673

My Supreme, my Supreme, my Supreme!
I must increase my faith in You
Immensely.
Otherwise, I shall continue
To stumble and stumble
In my inner running.
My Supreme, my Supreme, my Supreme!

674

My Supreme, my Supreme, my Supreme!
You have taken away
Many uninspiring, unaspiring things
From my life.
Now please take away one more thing:
Frustration, frustration,
Frustration.
My Supreme, my Supreme, my Supreme!

675

My Supreme, my Supreme, my Supreme!
My darkness-mind,
Get out, get out!
My heaviness-heart,
Get out, get out!
My soulfulness-life,
Let us live together
Forever.
My Supreme, my Supreme, my Supreme!

676

My Supreme, my Supreme, my Supreme!
Please inspire my mind,
Please protect my heart,
Please lead my life.
My Supreme, my Supreme, my Supreme!

677

My Supreme, my Supreme, my Supreme!
My today's self-giving dreams
Shall become
My tomorrow's God-satisfying realities.
My Supreme, my Supreme, my Supreme!

678

My Supreme, my Supreme, my Supreme!
I tell God what I can do:
I can pray and meditate for hours
Every day.
God tells me what I must do:
I must sing His Victory-Songs
Sleeplessly.
My Supreme, my Supreme, my Supreme!

679

My Supreme, my Supreme, my Supreme!
My Lord tells me
That in the inner world
There is nothing to discover,
Only to uncover.
My Supreme, my Supreme, my Supreme!

680

My Supreme, my Supreme, my Supreme!
God tells me that my mind-voice
Hurts Him badly
Because it is so sharp.
He also tells me that my heart-voice
Gives Him tremendous joy
Because it is so sweet.
My Supreme, my Supreme, my Supreme!

28 SEPTEMBER 1999

681

My Supreme, my Supreme, my Supreme!
May Your blessingful Presence
And Your cheerful Guidance
Play hide-and-seek
Inside my aspiration-heart-temple.
My Supreme, my Supreme, my Supreme!

682

My Supreme, my Supreme, my Supreme!
I shall never, never try
To understand You.
This is my sole promise to You.
My Supreme, do increase my faith
At every moment
In Your Compassion-Eye,
Forgiveness-Heart
And Protection-Feet.
This is my sole prayer to You.
My Supreme, my Supreme, my Supreme!

683

My Supreme, my Supreme, my Supreme!
Patience, patience,
I need patience
For the complete fulfilment
Of Your Will
In and through me.
My Supreme, my Supreme, my Supreme!

684

My Supreme, my Supreme, my Supreme!
I must realise
That You will come to me
At Your choice Hour—
Neither too soon nor too late!
My Supreme, my Supreme, my Supreme!

685

My Supreme, my Supreme, my Supreme!
O my unconditional surrender
To God's Will,
You are my heart's only joy,
You are my life's only satisfaction.
My Supreme, my Supreme, my Supreme!

686

My Supreme, my Supreme, my Supreme!
I am offering You my prayerful gratitude
For touching my tearful heart.
I am offering You my soulful gratitude
For allowing me to sit
At Your blessingful Feet.
My Supreme, my Supreme, my Supreme!

30 SEPTEMBER 1999

687

My Supreme, my Supreme, my Supreme!
My self-doubt is a ruthless insult
To the fulfilment
Of Your Vision-Eye.
My Supreme, my Supreme, my Supreme!

688

My Supreme, my Supreme, my Supreme!
Self-doubt is indeed
An almost incurable disease.
My Supreme, my Supreme, my Supreme!

689

My Supreme, my Supreme, my Supreme!
My self-doubt takes me away
Farther than the farthest
From Your Compassion-Eye.
Alas, alas!
My Supreme, my Supreme, my Supreme!

690

My Supreme, my Supreme, my Supreme!
O self-doubt,
Get out of my breath,
Get out of my heart,
Get out of my mind,
Get out of my vital,
Get out of my body,
Get out of my earth-existence-life.
Get out, get out immediately,
O self-doubt!
My Supreme, my Supreme, my Supreme!

691

My Supreme, my Supreme, my Supreme!
When I enjoy my self-doubts,
You pitifully cry,
You helplessly shed tears.
Alas, alas,
This is what I do to You,
My Lord Beloved Supreme!
My Supreme, my Supreme, my Supreme!

1 OCTOBER 1999

692

My Supreme, my Supreme, my Supreme!
You want me to grow
Into Your highest Excellence.
But how can I?
"My child,
Certainly you can."
My Supreme, my Supreme, my Supreme!

693

My Supreme, my Supreme, my Supreme!
Love divine
Is Your Compassion-Strength
In my arms.
Peace divine
Is Your Satisfaction-Light
Inside my heart.
My Supreme, my Supreme, my Supreme!

694

My Supreme, my Supreme, my Supreme!
Only the unconditional God-obedience
Knows the surest and shortest way
To God's Heaven-Palace.
My Supreme, my Supreme, my Supreme!

695

My Supreme, my Supreme, my Supreme!
You want me to keep
My heart-eye open
Sleeplessly, soulfully
And self-givingly
To Your all-guiding Will.
My Supreme, my Supreme, my Supreme!

696

My Supreme, my Supreme, my Supreme!
My past is nothing but dust.
I shall satisfy You
Here and now,
Totally, unreservedly
And unconditionally
In Your own Way.
My Supreme, my Supreme, my Supreme!

2 OCTOBER 1999

697

My Supreme, my Supreme, my Supreme!
May my life-boat
Today and every day
Ply between
Your Compassion-Eye-Beauty-Shore
And
Your Forgiveness-Heart-Fragrance-Shore.
My Supreme, my Supreme, my Supreme!

698

My Supreme, my Supreme, my Supreme!
My sleepless heart
Has taken the aspiration-road
To arrive at God's
Transcendental Heights.
My Supreme, my Supreme, my Supreme!

699

My Supreme, my Supreme, my Supreme!
My God-gratitude-heart
Has given me
A God-Beatitude-life.
My Supreme, my Supreme, my Supreme!

700

My Supreme, my Supreme, my Supreme!
When I offer You my aspiration,
You make my road to Your Palace short.
When I offer You my gratitude,
You make it shorter.
When I offer You my surrender,
You make it shortest.
My Supreme, my Supreme, my Supreme!

701

My Supreme, my Supreme, my Supreme!
Your Compassion-Eye,
Your Forgiveness-Heart
And
Your Protection-Feet
Come to me together
Every day
Running at full speed.
My Supreme, my Supreme, my Supreme!

702

My Supreme, my Supreme, my Supreme!
If I do not become a God-dreamer,
God-lover and God-server first,
How can I become a God-pleaser?
My Supreme, my Supreme, my Supreme!

703

My Supreme, my Supreme, my Supreme!
This morning
I had a very, very long
Walk with You.
You simply said to me
Only one thing:
"Shut up! Shut up! Shut up!"
My Supreme, my Supreme, my Supreme!

MY MORNING SOUL-BODY PRAYERS

5 OCTOBER 1999

704

My Supreme, my Supreme, my Supreme!
This morning
You and I had a very long
Private talk.
During our marathon conversation
We shed ceaseless tears
Of mutual affection, love, sweetness
And oneness.
My Supreme, my Supreme, my Supreme!

705

My Supreme, my Supreme, my Supreme!
Cry, cry, cry, my heart,
Cry, cry!
Only then will you be able
To fly
In Infinity's Freedom-Sky.
My Supreme, my Supreme, my Supreme!

706

My Supreme, my Supreme, my Supreme!
May my mind every day
Sing only peace-songs.
May my heart every day
Sing only gratitude-songs.
May my life every day
Sing only surrender-songs.
My Supreme, my Supreme, my Supreme!

707

My Supreme, my Supreme, my Supreme!
To win each and every inner race,
My Supreme,
I need only Your Grace.
My Supreme, my Supreme, my Supreme!

MY MORNING SOUL-BODY PRAYERS

6 OCTOBER 1999

708

My Supreme, my Supreme, my Supreme!
This morning
Unconditionally You have shown me
The measureless depth
Of Your Compassion-Eye.
Do accept the tears
Of my gratitude-heart.
My Supreme, my Supreme, my Supreme!

709

My Supreme, my Supreme, my Supreme!
I am most devotedly seeing
Your Protection-Arms
Around my aspiration-love-
Devotion-surrender-heart.
My Supreme, my Supreme, my Supreme!

710

My Supreme, my Supreme, my Supreme!
I pray to the Feet
Of the unknown God.
I meditate on the Heart
Of the knowable God.
My Supreme, my Supreme, my Supreme!

711

My Supreme, my Supreme, my Supreme!
I have prayerfully and soulfully
Established
My heart, my mind, my vital,
My body and my life
Upon my God-realisation-foundation.
My Supreme, my Supreme, my Supreme!

712

My Supreme, my Supreme, my Supreme!
The mind's freedom-march —
No, no, no!
The heart's devotion-walk —
Yes, yes, yes!
My Supreme, my Supreme, my Supreme!

713

My Supreme, my Supreme, my Supreme!
I have thrown
My body, my vital, my mind
And my heart
Into Your Compassion-Forgiveness-Arms.
My Supreme, my Supreme, my Supreme!

MY MORNING SOUL-BODY PRAYERS

9 OCTOBER 1999

714

My Supreme, my Supreme, my Supreme!
O my inspiration-mind,
O my aspiration-heart,
O my dedication-life,
O my gratitude-breath,
Where are you hiding?
Where?
My Supreme, my Supreme, my Supreme!

715

My Supreme, my Supreme, my Supreme!
My doubting mind is known
As a volcano
In the inner world of my spirituality.
My Supreme, my Supreme, my Supreme!

716

My Supreme, my Supreme, my Supreme!
My suspicious mind is known
As an earthquake
In the inner world of my spirituality.
My Supreme, my Supreme, my Supreme!

717

My Supreme, my Supreme, my Supreme!
My jealous mind is known
As a famine
In the inner world of my spirituality.
My Supreme, my Supreme, my Supreme!

718

My Supreme, my Supreme, my Supreme!
O my doubting mind,
O my suspicious mind,
O my jealous mind,
You immediately need
The blooms and the blossoms
Of a oneness-heart.
My Supreme, my Supreme, my Supreme!

MY MORNING SOUL-BODY PRAYERS

11 OCTOBER 1999

719

My Supreme, my Supreme, my Supreme!
Life is afraid of seeing
The face of death.
Death is afraid of seeing
The immortality of the soul.
My Supreme, my Supreme, my Supreme!

720

My Supreme, my Supreme, my Supreme!
You are commanding me
Only to listen to my aspiring heart
And never to my doubting mind.
I shall prayerfully,
Soulfully and unconditionally
Listen to Your Command.
My Supreme, my Supreme, my Supreme!

721

My Supreme, my Supreme, my Supreme!
Only the unconditional seekers
Are invited by You
To enjoy the ambrosial feast
Of Your Heart.
My Supreme, my Supreme, my Supreme!

722

My Supreme, my Supreme, my Supreme!
Only the tears of my heart
Can carry me and place me
At Your Feet.
My Supreme, my Supreme, my Supreme!

723

My Supreme, my Supreme, my Supreme!
From now on I shall never swerve
Even an inch
From Your Compassion-flooded Will.
This is my prayerful, soulful
And solemn promise to You.
My Supreme, my Supreme, my Supreme!

MY MORNING SOUL-BODY PRAYERS

12 OCTOBER 1999

724

My Supreme, my Supreme, my Supreme!
You teach me only when
I am ready.
Your Compassion teaches me
Even when I am not ready.
Your Forgiveness teaches me
All the time —
Alas, often in vain!
My Supreme, my Supreme, my Supreme!

725

My Supreme, my Supreme, my Supreme!
I am tired, extremely tired.
"My child, I am also extremely tired.
But we must carry on.
The world needs your life's
Service-plants.
The world needs My Heart's
Compassion-Skies."
My Supreme, my Supreme, my Supreme!

726

My Supreme, my Supreme, my Supreme!
My doubting mind,
I am challenging you here and now,
At this very moment,
At this very place.
My Supreme, my Supreme, my Supreme!

727

My Supreme, my Supreme, my Supreme!
Alas, my mind, my vital and I
Are vehemently vetoing
Your World-Vision-Plans.
My Supreme, my Supreme, my Supreme!

MY MORNING SOUL-BODY PRAYERS

13 OCTOBER 1999

728

My Supreme, my Supreme, my Supreme!
Although my body-weightloss-failure-bites
Are very sharp and very painful,
I am sure they are curable.
My Supreme, my Supreme, my Supreme!

729

My Supreme, my Supreme, my Supreme!
I measure my aspiration-heart
With my life's dedication-scale.
My Supreme, my Supreme, my Supreme!

730

My Supreme, my Supreme, my Supreme!
May my faith in You every day
Increase in infinite measure
So that my body, vital, mind and heart
Every day succeed and proceed
And sing the song
Of self-transcendence.
My Supreme, my Supreme, my Supreme!

731

My Supreme, my Supreme, my Supreme!
My sleepless and breathless
God-obedience
Shall carry me to God's
Transcendental Excellence
At His choice Hour.
My Supreme, my Supreme, my Supreme!

732

My Supreme, my Supreme, my Supreme!
God does not know what to do—
Whether to cry or to laugh—
When I say
That mine is the only way
To realise God.
My Supreme, my Supreme, my Supreme!

733

My Supreme, my Supreme, my Supreme!
Only my self-doubt makes me feel
Lonely, weak, useless and miserable.
My Supreme, my Supreme, my Supreme!

MY MORNING SOUL-BODY PRAYERS

14 OCTOBER 1999

734

My Supreme, my Supreme, my Supreme!
I see Your Compassion-Eye,
Your Forgiveness-Heart
And
Your Protection-Feet
Inside my heart's silence-fragrance.
My Supreme, my Supreme, my Supreme!

735

My Supreme, my Supreme, my Supreme!
Even until yesterday
I was a self-enamoured trumpeter.
But from now on I shall only be
Your Compassion-inspired
Victory-trumpeter.
My Supreme, my Supreme, my Supreme!

736

My Supreme, my Supreme, my Supreme!
May my heart and I every day
Please You
With our inner progress-journey.
My Supreme, my Supreme, my Supreme!

737

My Supreme, my Supreme, my Supreme!
May my life's surrender
To God's Will
Be the never-ending song
Of my heart.
My Supreme, my Supreme, my Supreme!

15 OCTOBER 1999

738

My Supreme, my Supreme, my Supreme!
Today
Patience is sour,
But tomorrow
Patience will become sweet,
And the day after tomorrow
Patience will become
Sweetness-perfection.
My Supreme, my Supreme, my Supreme!

739

My Supreme, my Supreme, my Supreme!
Patience is an absolute necessity
In my inner life of aspiration
And
In my outer life of dedication.
My Supreme, my Supreme, my Supreme!

740

My Supreme, my Supreme, my Supreme!
Today I want to offer You
Three very special names:
Patience-Beauty,
Compassion-Fragrance,
Forgiveness-Garden.
My Supreme, my Supreme, my Supreme!

741

My Supreme, my Supreme, my Supreme!
Your Patience-Will
Waits for me.
Your Compassion-Eye
Blesses me.
Your Forgiveness-Heart
Embraces me.
My Supreme, my Supreme, my Supreme!

742

My Supreme, my Supreme, my Supreme!
It is Your infinite Patience
That enables me to achieve
Momentous progress
In my inner life of aspiration
And
Tremendous success
In my outer life of dedication.
My Supreme, my Supreme, my Supreme!

16 OCTOBER 1999

743

My Supreme, my Supreme, my Supreme!
Alas, what am I doing?
Am I not compelling Your Patience
To weep for me?
My Supreme, my Supreme, my Supreme!

744

My Supreme, my Supreme, my Supreme!
All my prayers and meditations
Are under the shelter
Of my Beloved Lord's
Compassion-Umbrella-Eye.
My Supreme, my Supreme, my Supreme!

745

My Supreme, my Supreme, my Supreme!
From now on
I shall not waste
Even a fleeting second
With my self-doubts.
My Supreme, my Supreme, my Supreme!

MY MORNING SOUL-BODY PRAYERS

18 OCTOBER 1999

746

My Supreme, my Supreme, my Supreme!
May every day my aspiration-heart
Feast upon
Your Compassion-flooded Eye.
My Supreme, my Supreme, my Supreme!

747

My Supreme, my Supreme, my Supreme!
The waves
Of Your Heart's Compassion-Sea
Dance
The moment they see my heart's
Tiny aspiration-flames.
My Supreme, my Supreme, my Supreme!

748

My Supreme, my Supreme, my Supreme!
May Your Compassion-Eye
Always keep me
In Your Protection-Arms.
My Supreme, my Supreme, my Supreme!

749

My Supreme, my Supreme, my Supreme!
Today, without fail,
I must put an end
To my self-doubt-life.
My Supreme, my Supreme, my Supreme!

750

My Supreme, my Supreme, my Supreme!
Today my aspiring heart
Is compelling me to compose
God-Victory-songs.
My Supreme, my Supreme, my Supreme!

MY MORNING SOUL-BODY PRAYERS

19 OCTOBER 1999

751

My Supreme, my Supreme, my Supreme!
It is only when the tears of my heart
Place me at God's Feet
That God accepts me unreservedly.
My Supreme, my Supreme, my Supreme!

752

My Supreme, my Supreme, my Supreme!
All the angels of Heaven
Are extremely fond of
And proud of
My God-gratitude-heart-tears.
My Supreme, my Supreme, my Supreme!

753

My Supreme, my Supreme, my Supreme!
Please, please, please bless me
With ever-increasing God-aspiration,
God-dedication and God-manifestation-
Breaths.
My Supreme, my Supreme, my Supreme!

754

My Supreme, my Supreme, my Supreme!
When my soul asks my heart
To love God, serve God and manifest God,
My heart immediately says,
"Yes, I must and I shall."

When my heart asks my mind
To love God, serve God and manifest God,
My mind immediately says,
"Must I? And why should I?"
My Supreme, my Supreme, my Supreme!

755

My Supreme, my Supreme, my Supreme!
God the Mother always worries
About me and my safety.
God the Father always tells me,
"Hurry up, My child, hurry up!
You and I must start walking
Along Eternity's Road."
My Supreme, my Supreme, my Supreme!

MY MORNING SOUL-BODY PRAYERS

20 OCTOBER 1999

756

My Supreme, my Supreme, my Supreme!
My heart's patience-light
Is my life's wisdom-delight
In my God-fulfilment-task.
My Supreme, my Supreme, my Supreme!

757

My Supreme, my Supreme, my Supreme!
Do direct my aspiration-heart
And dedication-life
Towards all Your Necessities
At every moment of my life.
My Supreme, my Supreme, my Supreme!

758

My Supreme, my Supreme, my Supreme!
May my inner life love God-dreams
Sleeplessly.
May my outer life serve God-realities
Unconditionally.
My Supreme, my Supreme, my Supreme!

759

My Supreme, my Supreme, my Supreme!
I must challenge all impossibilities
In my life,
For I am a God-chosen warrior.
My Supreme, my Supreme, my Supreme!

760

My Supreme, my Supreme, my Supreme!
May my life-breath be
The beauty and purity
Of a prayerful and soulful
Rose.
My Supreme, my Supreme, my Supreme!

761

My Supreme, my Supreme, my Supreme!
The unillumined human in me
Is always a problem-seeker.
The illumined divine in me
Is always a problem-shooter.
My Supreme, my Supreme, my Supreme!

MY MORNING SOUL-BODY PRAYERS

22 OCTOBER 1999

762

My Supreme, my Supreme, my Supreme!
If I love You only,
Then I can never be tired
Of loving You.
My Supreme, my Supreme, my Supreme!

763

My Supreme, my Supreme, my Supreme!
Only in my purity-heart-garden
Do Your Satisfaction-Heart-Smiles
Fully blossom.
My Supreme, my Supreme, my Supreme!

764

My Supreme, my Supreme, my Supreme!
You do not want me to be
A cave-dweller-heart.
You do not want me to be
A palace-dweller-mind.
You want me only to be
A temple-dweller-life.
My Supreme, my Supreme, my Supreme!

765

My Supreme, my Supreme, my Supreme!
Gratitude is not an imagination-word
In my mind.
Gratitude is a reality-life
In my heart.
My Supreme, my Supreme, my Supreme!

766

My Supreme, my Supreme, my Supreme!
To me an ingratitude-mind-arrogance
Is the most frightening nightmare.
My Supreme, my Supreme, my Supreme!

MY MORNING SOUL-BODY PRAYERS

25 OCTOBER 1999

767

My Supreme, my Supreme, my Supreme!
My Lord, today You are
Smilingly teaching me
How to write the songs
Of inspiration-buds.
My Supreme, my Supreme, my Supreme!

768

My Supreme, my Supreme, my Supreme!
My Lord, today You are
Compassionately teaching me
How to write the songs
Of aspiration-flames.
My Supreme, my Supreme, my Supreme!

769

My Supreme, my Supreme, my Supreme!
My Lord, today You are
Affectionately teaching me
How to write the songs
Of dedication-drops.
My Supreme, my Supreme, my Supreme!

770

My Supreme, my Supreme, my Supreme!
My Lord, today You are
Proudly teaching me
How to write the songs
Of surrender-smiles.
My Supreme, my Supreme, my Supreme!

771

My Supreme, my Supreme, my Supreme!
My Lord, today You are
Self-givingly teaching me
How to write the songs
Of our hearts' oneness-blossoms.
My Supreme, my Supreme, my Supreme!

772

My Supreme, my Supreme, my Supreme!
My Lord, today You are
Most gloriously teaching me
How to write the songs
Of our souls' ever-transcending
Newness, oneness and fulness-tree.
My Supreme, my Supreme, my Supreme!

MY MORNING SOUL-BODY PRAYERS

26 OCTOBER 1999

773

My Supreme, my Supreme, my Supreme!
I am a soulful worshipper
Of Your Protection-Feet.
You are a blessingful Admirer
Of my dedication-life.
My Supreme, my Supreme, my Supreme!

774

My Supreme, my Supreme, my Supreme!
I am all gratitude to You,
For You have a very special
Secret and sacred Affection-Fondness
For my heart's silence-tears.
My Supreme, my Supreme, my Supreme!

775

My Supreme, my Supreme, my Supreme!
I have many names,
But my most favourite name is
My heart's sleepless
God-satisfaction-cry.
My Supreme, my Supreme, my Supreme!

776

My Supreme, my Supreme, my Supreme!
My heart loves
Your beautiful Eye,
My life loves
Your blessingful Feet
And I love
Your Heart's Forgiveness-Smiles.
My Supreme, my Supreme, my Supreme!

777

My Supreme, my Supreme, my Supreme!
My life's dedication-service
Is my heart's fastest progress-run
Towards You.
My Supreme, my Supreme, my Supreme!

778

My Supreme, my Supreme, my Supreme!
God does not know whether or not
To enjoy a roaring laughter
When my mind says that it is
The only God-knower,
When my heart says that it is
The only God-lover
And when my life says that I am
The only God-fulfiller.
My Supreme, my Supreme, my Supreme!

MY MORNING SOUL-BODY PRAYERS

28 OCTOBER 1999

779

My Supreme, my Supreme, my Supreme!
We must realise
That our confession to God
Is our best lover
And not our worst torturer.
My Supreme, my Supreme, my Supreme!

780

My Supreme, my Supreme, my Supreme!
Finally I have ended
My self-doubt-torture-dance.
My Supreme, my Supreme, my Supreme!

781

My Supreme, my Supreme, my Supreme!
Alas, when will I realise the fact
That my ingratitude-thoughts
Ruthlessly hurt Your Ears?
My Supreme, my Supreme, my Supreme!

782

My Supreme, my Supreme, my Supreme!
Out of Your infinite Compassion,
You are telling me
That my heart's God-gratitude-songs
Make Your Heart dance
With boundless joy.
My Supreme, my Supreme, my Supreme!

783

My Supreme, my Supreme, my Supreme!
My doubting mind
And God's compassionate Eye
Challenge each other.
My God-loving heart
And God's all-illumining Heart
Embrace each other.
My Supreme, my Supreme, my Supreme!

MY MORNING SOUL-BODY PRAYERS

1 NOVEMBER 1999

784

My Supreme, my Supreme, my Supreme!
The body's earthly time
Is passing away.
The soul's Heavenly time
Is blossoming and blossoming
And blossoming
At the Feet of the Lord Beloved Supreme.
My Supreme, my Supreme, my Supreme!

785

My Supreme, my Supreme, my Supreme!
What I desperately need
Is an aspiration-heart
And not a commotion-mind.
My Supreme, my Supreme, my Supreme!

786

My Supreme, my Supreme, my Supreme!
My joy knows no bounds
That my inner life's progress-river
Is running fast, very fast.
My Supreme, my Supreme, my Supreme!

787

My Supreme, my Supreme, my Supreme!
My patience-heart,
You are an unparalleled server
Of my Lord Beloved Supreme.
My Supreme, my Supreme, my Supreme!

788

My Supreme, my Supreme, my Supreme!
Today I am triumphantly enjoying
The ashes of my ego's unmistakable
And permanent death.
My Supreme, my Supreme, my Supreme!

789

My Supreme, my Supreme, my Supreme!
O my gratitude-heart,
Do not delay.
Do establish your soulful friendship
With sleepless Eternity.
My Supreme, my Supreme, my Supreme!

790

My Supreme, my Supreme, my Supreme!
My heart,
Cry and cry and cry!
You and I
Were born to cry for God.
My mind,
Smile and smile and smile!
You and I
Were born to smile at God.
My life,
Surrender and surrender and surrender!
You and I
Were born to surrender to God's Will.
My Supreme, my Supreme, my Supreme!

MY MORNING SOUL-BODY PRAYERS

2 NOVEMBER 1999

791

My Supreme, my Supreme, my Supreme!
I must challenge fear
Fearlessly
And conquer it
Unmistakably.
My Supreme, my Supreme, my Supreme!

792

My Supreme, my Supreme, my Supreme!
May my Lord Beloved Supreme
Smilingly, lovingly, blessingfully
And compassionately
Occupy every space
In my Heaven-climbing aspiration-heart.
My Supreme, my Supreme, my Supreme!

793

My Supreme, my Supreme, my Supreme!
Alas, it seems that my mind's
Self-indulgence
Will never be aware of
My God-effulgence-heart.
My Supreme, my Supreme, my Supreme!

3 NOVEMBER 1999

794

My Supreme, my Supreme, my Supreme!
My spiritual life must entirely depend
Upon my unconditional God-obedience.
My Supreme, my Supreme, my Supreme!

795

My Supreme, my Supreme, my Supreme!
Pride can parade
Only through our division-minds
And never, never, never
Through our oneness-hearts.
My Supreme, my Supreme, my Supreme!

796

My Supreme, my Supreme, my Supreme!
Yours is the Smile
That immediately answers
Every sorrow of my heart.
My Supreme, my Supreme, my Supreme!

797

My Supreme, my Supreme, my Supreme!
To make the fastest progress
In my spiritual life,
I must enliven my aspiration-heart
And dedication-life
With tremendous eagerness, enthusiasm
And energy.
My Supreme, my Supreme, my Supreme!

MY MORNING SOUL-BODY PRAYERS

798

My Supreme, my Supreme, my Supreme!
Each prayer is an indispensable step
Towards humanity's progress-delight.
My Supreme, my Supreme, my Supreme!

SRI CHINMOY

4 NOVEMBER 1999

799

My Supreme, my Supreme, my Supreme!
I serve my Master-Lord, I serve.
Never my heart and I swerve.
My Supreme, my Supreme, my Supreme!

MY MORNING SOUL-BODY PRAYERS

4 NOVEMBER 1999

800

My Supreme, my Supreme, my Supreme!
My Lord Supreme I contact
Long, long before I act.
My Supreme, my Supreme, my Supreme!

801

My Supreme, my Supreme, my Supreme!
What I desperately need
Is a God-surrender-heart
And not
A world-computer-mind.
My Supreme, my Supreme, my Supreme!

802

My Supreme, my Supreme, my Supreme!
Today, to my greatest joy,
I have completely unlocked
My heart-door
To my Master-Lord.
My Supreme, my Supreme, my Supreme!

803

My Supreme, my Supreme, my Supreme!
God's full manifestation-dream
Breathes in every blossom.
My Supreme, my Supreme, my Supreme!

6 NOVEMBER 1999

804

My Supreme, my Supreme, my Supreme!
My freedom without peace
Is impossible.
My peace without my surrender
To God's Will
Is impossible.
My surrender to God's Will
Without God's infinite Compassion
Is impossible.
My Supreme, my Supreme, my Supreme!

805

My Supreme, my Supreme, my Supreme!
For the transformation of human nature
And for the perfection of human life,
This world needs peaceful hearts
And not powerful heads.
My Supreme, my Supreme, my Supreme!

806

My Supreme, my Supreme, my Supreme!
God's Compassion-Eye
And
God's Forgiveness-Heart
Envelop the entire earth.
My Supreme, my Supreme, my Supreme!

807

My Supreme, my Supreme, my Supreme!
With my heart's love, devotion
And surrender-flower
I shall today prayerfully
And soulfully encircle
The Lotus-Feet
Of my Lord Beloved Supreme.
My Supreme, my Supreme, my Supreme!

808

My Supreme, my Supreme, my Supreme!
God's Eye plays with our smiles,
God's Heart plays with our tears
And
God plays with our satisfaction-hearts,
Satisfaction-minds, satisfaction-vitals
And satisfaction-bodies
Only when they live
In their divine consciousness.
My Supreme, my Supreme, my Supreme!

8 NOVEMBER 1999

809

My Supreme, my Supreme, my Supreme!
My life has to be rooted and grounded
In my sleepless love of God.
My Supreme, my Supreme, my Supreme!

810

My Supreme, my Supreme, my Supreme!
I must first have sleepless
And breathless love for You.
Only then can I have
Abiding faith in You.
My Supreme, my Supreme, my Supreme!

811

My Supreme, my Supreme, my Supreme!
Out of Your infinite Bounty,
Every day You allow me
To have a lovely and lively
Conversation with You
At least for an hour.
My Supreme, my Supreme, my Supreme!

812

My Supreme, my Supreme, my Supreme!
May my heart's new hopes
And my soul's new promises
Replace my mind's old doubts
And old fears.
My Supreme, my Supreme, my Supreme!

813

My Supreme, my Supreme, my Supreme!
At every moment each seeker has to be
Extremely alert.
At any moment his spiritual life
Can descend into steep decline.
My Supreme, my Supreme, my Supreme!

814

My Supreme, my Supreme, my Supreme!
In my spiritual life,
I shall have to be
A dauntless runner
With determined and measured strides
To arrive at my Destination.
My Supreme, my Supreme, my Supreme!

14 NOVEMBER 1999

815

My Supreme, my Supreme, my Supreme!
God does not want me to be
A God-preacher.
He wants me to be
A God-dreamer.
My Supreme, my Supreme, my Supreme!

816

My Supreme, my Supreme, my Supreme!
God does not want me to be
A God-scholar.
He wants me to be
A God-lover.
My Supreme, my Supreme, my Supreme!

817

My Supreme, my Supreme, my Supreme!
God does not want me to be
A God-author.
He wants me to be
A God-learner.
My Supreme, my Supreme, my Supreme!

818

My Supreme, my Supreme, my Supreme!
God does not want me to be
A God-drummer.
He wants me to be
A God-flutist.
My Supreme, my Supreme, my Supreme!

819

My Supreme, my Supreme, my Supreme!
God does not want me to be
A world-renouncer.
He wants me to be
A God-server.
My Supreme, my Supreme, my Supreme!

820

My Supreme, my Supreme, my Supreme!
God does not want me to be
A world-mind-computer.
He wants me to be
A world-heart-commuter.
My Supreme, my Supreme, my Supreme!

15 NOVEMBER 1999

821

My Supreme, my Supreme, my Supreme!
O ignorance-night-sleep,
Not a temporary
But a permanent break
I am taking from you.
My Supreme, my Supreme, my Supreme!

822

My Supreme, my Supreme, my Supreme!
My heart's unconditional surrender
To God's Will
Is the full blossom of my life.
My Supreme, my Supreme, my Supreme!

823

My Supreme, my Supreme, my Supreme!
You are telling me
That I have chatted enough
With You.
Now I must start chanting
Your Name.
My Supreme, my Supreme, my Supreme!

824

My Supreme, my Supreme, my Supreme!
Long before I sought,
My Beloved's Lotus-Feet
Had caught my heart.
My Supreme, my Supreme, my Supreme!

MY MORNING SOUL-BODY PRAYERS

825

My Supreme, my Supreme, my Supreme!
You are asking my mind's readiness,
My life's willingness
And my heart's eagerness
To hurry up,
And You are also asking
My doubting and suspecting mind
To slow down and stop forever.
My Supreme, my Supreme, my Supreme!

26 NOVEMBER 1999

826

My Supreme, my Supreme, my Supreme!
The life-expectancy
Of a God-lover
Is unlimited.
My Supreme, my Supreme, my Supreme!

827

My Supreme, my Supreme, my Supreme!
My Beloved Lord Supreme,
You are spoiling me
With Your Indulgence-Abundance.
"My child,
I cannot help it."
My Supreme, my Supreme, my Supreme!

828

My Supreme, my Supreme, my Supreme!
My eagerness-heart
Shall never retire
From God-service.
My Supreme, my Supreme, my Supreme!

829

My Supreme, my Supreme, my Supreme!
Is there anybody on earth
Who does not suffer from
Insecurity-cancer?
My Supreme, my Supreme, my Supreme!

MY MORNING SOUL-BODY PRAYERS

830

My Supreme, my Supreme, my Supreme!
My soul is begging my wild mind
To give God
At least a temporary pass.
My Supreme, my Supreme, my Supreme!

831

My Supreme, my Supreme, my Supreme!
My 700 pounds, I salute you,
I love you and I need you
To manifest the Will
Of my Lord Beloved Supreme.
My Supreme, my Supreme, my Supreme!

30 NOVEMBER 1999

832

My Supreme, my Supreme, my Supreme!
My sleepless faithfulness
And
My breathless devotedness
Have brought Your blessingful Presence
To me
Faster than the fastest.
My Supreme, my Supreme, my Supreme!

833

My Supreme, my Supreme, my Supreme!
Do give me the capacity
Not only to love and serve
But also to become inseparably one with
The troubled world.
My Supreme, my Supreme, my Supreme!

834

My Supreme, my Supreme, my Supreme!
You are Your Compassion-Eye,
You are Your Forgiveness-Heart.
I am my surrender-life,
I am my gratitude-breath.
My Supreme, my Supreme, my Supreme!

835

My Supreme, my Supreme, my Supreme!
The only wisdom-light I need
Is this:
My sleepless love
For Your Compassion-flooded Feet.
My Supreme, my Supreme, my Supreme!

836

My Supreme, my Supreme, my Supreme!
Mine is a life
That is sleeplessly eager
For God's full Examination.
Mine is a heart
That is breathlessly eager
For God's full Satisfaction.
My Supreme, my Supreme, my Supreme!

5 DECEMBER 1999

837

My Supreme, my Supreme, my Supreme!
My devotion-heart
And my surrender-life
Lovingly, happily and proudly
Live together.
My Supreme, my Supreme, my Supreme!

838

My Supreme, my Supreme, my Supreme!
I practise and treasure patience,
For patience
Is an invaluable gift of God
To humanity.
My Supreme, my Supreme, my Supreme!

839

My Supreme, my Supreme, my Supreme!
At every moment
We must declare war
On uncomely and undivine thoughts,
For they are extremely, extremely
Destructive.
My Supreme, my Supreme, my Supreme!

MY MORNING SOUL-BODY PRAYERS

6 DECEMBER 1999

840

My Supreme, my Supreme, my Supreme!
The mind-walker hesitantly walks
Towards the Destination,
But, alas, the Destination remains
A far cry.
The heart-runner runs fast, very fast,
Towards the Destination
And reaches the Destination
To please God in His own Way.
My Supreme, my Supreme, my Supreme!

841

My Supreme, my Supreme, my Supreme!
At the end of every day
May my life become
A God-fulfilled promise.
My Supreme, my Supreme, my Supreme!

842

My Supreme, my Supreme, my Supreme!
May my mind be freed
From constant
Thought-interruption-torture.
My Supreme, my Supreme, my Supreme!

8 DECEMBER 1999

843

My Supreme, my Supreme, my Supreme!
How beautiful, how peaceful
And how blissful
Is the silence of my heart's
Meditation-room.
My Supreme, my Supreme, my Supreme!

844

My Supreme, my Supreme, my Supreme!
Our mind's frustration-sighs
Are
Our life's God-denials.
My Supreme, my Supreme, my Supreme!

845

My Supreme, my Supreme, my Supreme!
I must think of God's
Frustration-Heart first.
Then I should look at God's
Compassion-Eye.
My Supreme, my Supreme, my Supreme!

MY MORNING SOUL-BODY PRAYERS

9 DECEMBER 1999

846

My Supreme, my Supreme, my Supreme!
May every heart be cradled
By boundless faith.
My Supreme, my Supreme, my Supreme!

847

My Supreme, my Supreme, my Supreme!
I talk sleeplessly.
You talk so little.
Why? Why? Why?
My Supreme, my Supreme, my Supreme!

848

My Supreme, my Supreme, my Supreme!
I am telling the truth
That my heart is as beautiful
As Your Eye.
My Supreme, my Supreme, my Supreme!

13 DECEMBER 1999

849

My Supreme, my Supreme, my Supreme!
The problem of problems
For my poor Lord Beloved Supreme
Is my mind's unwillingness.
My Supreme, my Supreme, my Supreme!

850

My Supreme, my Supreme, my Supreme!
You are telling me
That we all must develop
Inner muscles of iron.
My Supreme, my Supreme, my Supreme!

851

My Supreme, my Supreme, my Supreme!
I shall not allow You
To overstrain
Your Compassion-Eye for me.
My Supreme, my Supreme, my Supreme!

852

My Supreme, my Supreme, my Supreme!
My Lord Beloved Supreme,
I shall no more
Permit Your Heart
To bleed
For my abominable misdeeds.
My Supreme, my Supreme, my Supreme!

MY MORNING SOUL-BODY PRAYERS

14 DECEMBER 1999

853

My Supreme, my Supreme, my Supreme!
Invariably
Every heart-plus needs
A mind-minus first.
My Supreme, my Supreme, my Supreme!

854

My Supreme, my Supreme, my Supreme!
I desperately need help
From You.
I really want to escape
From my mind-prison.
My Supreme, my Supreme, my Supreme!

855

My Supreme, my Supreme, my Supreme!
Do You really love me?
Do You really care for me?
If so, do scold me most powerfully
Every day.
My Supreme, my Supreme, my Supreme!

15 DECEMBER 1999

856

My Supreme, my Supreme, my Supreme!
A God-disobedience-life
Is
A happiness-heart-killer.
My Supreme, my Supreme, my Supreme!

857

My Supreme, my Supreme, my Supreme!
For years and years and years
I shall have to climb
To reach my transcendental heights.
Please do not allow me to miss
Even a second.
My Supreme, my Supreme, my Supreme!

858

My Supreme, my Supreme, my Supreme!
You are telling
All the God-seekers and God-lovers
That, for them, there is no such thing
As a passing infatuation
With worldliness.
My Supreme, my Supreme, my Supreme!

MY MORNING SOUL-BODY PRAYERS

16 DECEMBER 1999

859

My Supreme, my Supreme, my Supreme!
I must love God the Creator
And serve God the creation
Simultaneously
If I want to please God completely
In His own Way.
My Supreme, my Supreme, my Supreme!

860

My Supreme, my Supreme, my Supreme!
My soul-enlightenment-Maker
Is
My heart-attachment-breaker.
My Supreme, my Supreme, my Supreme!

861

My Supreme, my Supreme, my Supreme!
You are telling me
That in our spiritual life
All our heart-ultramarathons
Are sponsored by God Himself.
My Supreme, my Supreme, my Supreme!

17 DECEMBER 1999

862

My Supreme, my Supreme, my Supreme!
Each day is a golden opportunity
For the blossoming of my self-offering
To God's Will.
My Supreme, my Supreme, my Supreme!

863

My Supreme, my Supreme, my Supreme!
My aspiring heart radiates
Abundant peace and bliss
Only when my mind
Is completely desireless.
My Supreme, my Supreme, my Supreme!

864

My Supreme, my Supreme, my Supreme!
May each day the tears and smiles
Of my heart
Develop a deeper, stronger and greater
God-hunger.
My Supreme, my Supreme, my Supreme!

865

My Supreme, my Supreme, my Supreme!
Every day
My mind concentrates to succeed,
My heart meditates to proceed
And
My soul contemplates to feed.
Whom? God.
My Supreme, my Supreme, my Supreme!

MY MORNING SOUL-BODY PRAYERS

20 DECEMBER 1999

866

My Supreme, my Supreme, my Supreme!
My God-surrender-life
Accepts
No desire-invitations.
My Supreme, my Supreme, my Supreme!

867

My Supreme, my Supreme, my Supreme!
When I do not do well spiritually,
Your Compassion-Eye cries and cries
And
Your Tolerance-Heart sighs and sighs.
My Supreme, my Supreme, my Supreme!

868

My Supreme, my Supreme, my Supreme!
My aspiration-heart-sky
Is the place
Of my rainbow-sunrise.
My Supreme, my Supreme, my Supreme!

21 DECEMBER 1999

869

My Supreme, my Supreme, my Supreme!
My heart is cheerfully, faithfully,
Devotedly and self-givingly
Following
Your moonlit Ecstasy-Steps.
My Supreme, my Supreme, my Supreme!

870

My Supreme, my Supreme, my Supreme!
In all our God-fulfilment-promise-races,
We must take proper and perfect starts.
If not,
We shall be disqualified.
What is a proper and perfect start?
Our heart's intensity-cry for God.
My Supreme, my Supreme, my Supreme!

871

My Supreme, my Supreme, my Supreme!
May my heart, mind, vital,
Body and life
Never wane in enthusiasm,
Even for a fleeting second.
My Supreme, my Supreme, my Supreme!

MY MORNING SOUL-BODY PRAYERS

22 DECEMBER 1999

872

My Supreme, my Supreme, my Supreme!
You are telling me
That God-realisation
Is not monkey-banana-eating.
God-realisation
Is a self-giving God-lover's
Seventy million times
Himaloy-climbing.
My Supreme, my Supreme, my Supreme!

873

My Supreme, my Supreme, my Supreme!
A true God-lover does not have to prove
To the world
That he is a God-lover.
God's boundless Pride-Heart
Is his witness.
My Supreme, my Supreme, my Supreme!

23 DECEMBER 1999

874

My Supreme, my Supreme, my Supreme!
My mind says to me:
"Accept a disciple –
Face untold responsibilities."
My heart says to me:
"Accept a disciple –
Embrace a new impossibility."
My Supreme, my Supreme, my Supreme!

875

My Supreme, my Supreme, my Supreme!
My mind says to me:
"Accept a disciple –
A new frustration-attack."
My heart says to me:
"Accept a disciple –
Feast on a new God-Dream."
My Supreme, my Supreme, my Supreme!

876

My Supreme, my Supreme, my Supreme!
My mind says to me:
"Accept a disciple –
Your life is chained
To a huge bondage-rock."
My heart says to me:
"Accept a disciple –
Your life has added
A new God-blossom-tree."
My Supreme, my Supreme, my Supreme!

877

My Supreme, my Supreme, my Supreme!
My mind says to me:
"Accept a disciple –
Two colossal failures appear
From nowhere."
My heart says to me:
"Accept a disciple –
Your life will receive
A choice satisfaction-award
From God Himself."
My Supreme, my Supreme, my Supreme!

25 DECEMBER 1999

878

My Supreme, my Supreme, my Supreme!
Two giant question marks
Stand before me:
Do I love God only?
Will I be able to realise God
In this incarnation?
My Supreme, my Supreme, my Supreme!

879

My Supreme, my Supreme, my Supreme!
Your Compassion-Eye fondly
And sleeplessly cradles
My unconditional surrender-life.
My Supreme, my Supreme, my Supreme!

880

My Supreme, my Supreme, my Supreme!
Only a fully awakened heart
And
A fully surrendered life
Can make the God-climbing progress.
My Supreme, my Supreme, my Supreme!

881

My Supreme, my Supreme, my Supreme!
My highest Heaven
Is where
My God-devotion cries.
My Supreme, my Supreme, my Supreme!

MY MORNING SOUL-BODY PRAYERS

27 DECEMBER 1999

882

My Supreme, my Supreme, my Supreme!
My Lord Beloved Supreme,
You have taken me into
Your Confidence-Seraglio.
I must prove myself to be worthy.
My Supreme, my Supreme, my Supreme!

883

My Supreme, my Supreme, my Supreme!
My life has many goals,
But my life's penultimate goal
Is Your transcendental Vision-Eye,
And my life's ultimate goal
Is Your ever-blossoming
And ever-transcending Smile.
My Supreme, my Supreme, my Supreme!

884

My Supreme, my Supreme, my Supreme!
I am not yet ready
Even to look at Your Feet,
But
You are already so eager
To embrace my heart.
My Supreme, my Supreme, my Supreme!

885

My Supreme, my Supreme, my Supreme!
Seated on my heart-tree's
Highest, longest and largest branch,
You are singing and smiling,
You are smiling and singing.
My Supreme, my Supreme, my Supreme!

MY MORNING SOUL-BODY PRAYERS

28 DECEMBER 1999

886

My Supreme, my Supreme, my Supreme!
Your Concern-Eye drives me
From behind,
And Your Bliss-Heart beckons me
From afar.
My Supreme, my Supreme, my Supreme!

887

My Supreme, my Supreme, my Supreme!
My possession-hunger
Is a big minus-life.
My renunciation-meal
Is an infinitely bigger
Plus-life.
My Supreme, my Supreme, my Supreme!

888

My Supreme, my Supreme, my Supreme!
My mind's cheerfulness-blessing
Is an invaluable gift for You.
My Supreme, my Supreme, my Supreme!

889

My Supreme, my Supreme, my Supreme!
My restive mind and my aggressive vital
Ceaselessly beat war drums.
My blissful soul and my peaceful heart
Sleeplessly hear God's Songs
Sung by God Himself.
My Supreme, my Supreme, my Supreme!

31 DECEMBER 1999

890

My Supreme, my Supreme, my Supreme!
I know, I know, I know,
There is no proper cure
For Your absence in my heart.
My Supreme, my Supreme, my Supreme!

891

My Supreme, my Supreme, my Supreme!
Every morning may I find myself
Fully awake
With a new God-manifestation-promise
On earth.
My Supreme, my Supreme, my Supreme!

892

My Supreme, my Supreme, my Supreme!
In my life,
God walks only upon
My heart's humility-carpet
And nowhere else.
My Supreme, my Supreme, my Supreme!

MY MORNING SOUL-BODY PRAYERS

1 JANUARY 2000

893

My Supreme, my Supreme, my Supreme!
Every day, for everything,
My heart loves to quote God
Because He is the only reliable,
Irrefutable and inevitable Source.
My Supreme, my Supreme, my Supreme!

894

My Supreme, my Supreme, my Supreme!
God gladly accepts
My sleep-necessity,
But
He vehemently rejects
My sleep-luxury.
My Supreme, my Supreme, my Supreme!

895

My Supreme, my Supreme, my Supreme!
Like my soul,
May my heart, my mind, my vital
And my body
Be inexorably drawn towards God.
My Supreme, my Supreme, my Supreme!

896

My Supreme, my Supreme, my Supreme!
My cheerful surrender-life
Has a free access
To God's Heart-Kingdom.
My Supreme, my Supreme, my Supreme!

897

My Supreme, my Supreme, my Supreme!
When will You feed me
With Your Nectar-Delight?
"My child, I shall feed you
With My Nectar-Delight
Only when I see
That you have freed yourself
From all earth-bound desires."
My Supreme, my Supreme, my Supreme!

898

My Supreme, my Supreme, my Supreme!
I dream and dream
Of a fully God-blossomed
And God-manifested world.
My Supreme, my Supreme, my Supreme!

899

My Supreme, my Supreme, my Supreme!
We have many divine virtues.
Our God-obedience-virtue
Is, indeed, unparalleled.
My Supreme, my Supreme, my Supreme!

MY MORNING SOUL-BODY PRAYERS

3 JANUARY 2000

900

My Supreme, my Supreme, my Supreme!
Each human being is rich
Not only in God-realisation-possibilities
But also
In God-realisation-inevitabilities.
My Supreme, my Supreme, my Supreme!

901

My Supreme, my Supreme, my Supreme!
I have turned my desire-life
Towards Your
Blessingful and blissful Feet.
My Supreme, my Supreme, my Supreme!

902

My Supreme, my Supreme, my Supreme!
God does not answer
Some of our prayers
Precisely because
His infinite Love for us
Is absolutely genuine.
My Supreme, my Supreme, my Supreme!

5 JANUARY 2000

903

My Supreme, my Supreme, my Supreme!
When I am in the company
Of my heart's tears,
I fly and fly with them
Until I have reached God's Feet
And have taken shelter.
My Supreme, my Supreme, my Supreme!

904

My Supreme, my Supreme, my Supreme!
I must develop
An irresistible attraction
For everything that You love —
Such as compassion, forgiveness, harmony,
Peace and bliss.
My Supreme, my Supreme, my Supreme!

905

My Supreme, my Supreme, my Supreme!
An unconditional surrender-life-route
Is chosen for me
By You
And nobody else.
My Supreme, my Supreme, my Supreme!

906

My Supreme, my Supreme, my Supreme!
Every morning God inspires me,
Encourages me and helps me
To reach a higher height
In my meditation.
My Supreme, my Supreme, my Supreme!

907

My Supreme, my Supreme, my Supreme!
Like the phoenix,
I must rise from the ashes
Of my destruction-desire-life
To the light
Of my transcendental heights.
My Supreme, my Supreme, my Supreme!

908

My Supreme, my Supreme, my Supreme!
Please bless me
With abundant capacities
So that my spiritual children
Do not make daily complaints to You
Against me.
They are telling You that
They are unsought, unasked, unassisted,
Unappreciated, unadmired, unloved
And even unnoticed by me.
I wish to put an end
To this slogan of theirs.
My Supreme, my Supreme, my Supreme!

MY MORNING SOUL-BODY PRAYERS

8 JANUARY 2000

909

My Supreme, my Supreme, my Supreme!
The dreamer in me
Is God's Newness-Eye.
The dream-fulfiller
Is God's Sweetness-Heart.
My Supreme, my Supreme, my Supreme!

910

My Supreme, my Supreme, my Supreme!
Out of Your infinite Bounty,
You are replacing
My disappointment-tears
With Your Enlightenment-Smiles.
My Supreme, my Supreme, my Supreme!

911

My Supreme, my Supreme, my Supreme!
An eagerness-stride of my heart
Is
A progress-mile of my life.
My Supreme, my Supreme, my Supreme!

9 JANUARY 2000

912

My Supreme, my Supreme, my Supreme!
God wants the tears of my heart
To accompany His Heart.
God wants the smiles of my soul
To accompany His Eye.
My Supreme, my Supreme, my Supreme!

913

My Supreme, my Supreme, my Supreme!
A fearlessness-life
Lives only
In a vastness and oneness-heart.
My Supreme, my Supreme, my Supreme!

914

My Supreme, my Supreme, my Supreme!
Many are God-dreamers,
A few are God-seekers and servers,
But very, very few are true God-lovers.
My Supreme, my Supreme, my Supreme!

915

My Supreme, my Supreme, my Supreme!
A tragic end
Is another name
For God-disobedience.
My Supreme, my Supreme, my Supreme!

MY MORNING SOUL-BODY PRAYERS

11 JANUARY 2000

916

My Supreme, my Supreme, my Supreme!
Enthusiasm is second to none.
Enthusiasm means all done.
My Supreme, my Supreme, my Supreme!

917

My Supreme, my Supreme, my Supreme!
Enthusiasm, enthusiasm, enthusiasm!
You have freed my life
From my mind-chasm.
My Supreme, my Supreme, my Supreme!

918

My Supreme, my Supreme, my Supreme!
Enthusiasm is
My soul's mightiest roar.
Enthusiasm is
My life's brightest shore.
My Supreme, my Supreme, my Supreme!

13 JANUARY 2000

919

My Supreme, my Supreme, my Supreme!
Forgiveness-delight can never be
Totally exhausted.
My Supreme, my Supreme, my Supreme!

920

My Supreme, my Supreme, my Supreme!
Your Compassion-Eye starts;
Your Forgiveness-Heart completes.
My Supreme, my Supreme, my Supreme!

921

My Supreme, my Supreme, my Supreme!
My forgiveness most surprisingly
Increases
My God-wisdom-depth.
My Supreme, my Supreme, my Supreme!

MY MORNING SOUL-BODY PRAYERS

14 JANUARY 2000

922

My Supreme, my Supreme, my Supreme!
Alas, quite often our mind-inventions
Are founded upon
Our evil intentions.
My Supreme, my Supreme, my Supreme!

923

My Supreme, my Supreme, my Supreme!
Every morning You command me
To walk with You for an hour
With my heart's beauty
And my soul's fragrance.
My Supreme, my Supreme, my Supreme!

924

My Supreme, my Supreme, my Supreme!
May my heart be as beautiful,
Charming, illumining
And perfect
As a smile born in Heaven.
My Supreme, my Supreme, my Supreme!

925

My Supreme, my Supreme, my Supreme!
I cried for You,
But nothing happened.
I smiled at You,
But nothing happened.
When I cried *with* You,
When I smiled *with* You,
Everything happened —
Inspiring, aspiring, illumining
And fulfilling.
My Supreme, my Supreme, my Supreme!

MY MORNING SOUL-BODY PRAYERS

15 JANUARY 2000

926

My Supreme, my Supreme, my Supreme!
You are calling me.
Alas, my ears do not want to listen
To You.
They do not want me to hear
Your Blessing-Message.
My Supreme, my Supreme, my Supreme!

927

My Supreme, my Supreme, my Supreme!
How fortunate I am!
Every morning You cradle my heart
With a Smile of Your Heart's Beauty.
My Supreme, my Supreme, my Supreme!

18 JANUARY 2000

928

My Supreme, my Supreme, my Supreme!
Spirituality blind:
A computerised mind.
My Supreme, my Supreme, my Supreme!

929

My Supreme, my Supreme, my Supreme!
A computerised mind
Alas, nowhere can find
Supreme Lord's Beauty-Eye —
A total failure-sigh.
My Supreme, my Supreme, my Supreme!

930

My Supreme, my Supreme, my Supreme!
A computerised mind
Remains farthest behind.
It values not God-quest
And God hides His Heart-Nest.
My Supreme, my Supreme, my Supreme!

931

My Supreme, my Supreme, my Supreme!
A computerised mind
Can never be as kind
As a God-surrender-soul.
God-Joy his only goal.
My Supreme, my Supreme, my Supreme!

MY MORNING SOUL-BODY PRAYERS

20 JANUARY 2000

932

My Supreme, my Supreme, my Supreme!
God-slaves are more reliable,
More dependable, more sociable,
More serviceable and more capable
Than anybody else.
My Supreme, my Supreme, my Supreme!

933

My Supreme, my Supreme, my Supreme!
The slave says:
"Master, throughout Eternity,
I shall be with you, in you, for you."
The Master says:
"My slave, you are my heart's
Most treasured wealth here on earth,
There in Heaven."
My Supreme, my Supreme, my Supreme!

934

My Supreme, my Supreme, my Supreme!
Today's faithful slave
Is
Tomorrow's blissful Master.
My Supreme, my Supreme, my Supreme!

935

My Supreme, my Supreme, my Supreme!
A self-giving slave
Eventually becomes
A God-flowering Master.
My Supreme, my Supreme, my Supreme!

MY MORNING SOUL-BODY PRAYERS

21 JANUARY 2000

936

My Supreme, my Supreme, my Supreme!
I deeply appreciate, admire and adore
And I simply love
Your firm grip on my life.
My Supreme, my Supreme, my Supreme!

937

My Supreme, my Supreme, my Supreme!
O New Millennium,
You have brought
The beauty of newness
To my mind.
You have brought
The fragrance of newness
To my heart.
You have brought
The perfection of newness
To my life.
My Supreme, my Supreme, my Supreme!

23 JANUARY 2000

938

My Supreme, my Supreme, my Supreme!
I must not surprise You any more
With my life's new ignorance-night.
My Supreme, my Supreme, my Supreme!

939

My Supreme, my Supreme, my Supreme!
Tomorrow God wants me to be present
Inside my heart
When He comes to visit me.
This is, indeed, His express Command.
My Supreme, my Supreme, my Supreme!

MY MORNING SOUL-BODY PRAYERS

26 JANUARY 2000

940

My Supreme, my Supreme, my Supreme!
This morning I embarked
On a new journey
To fulfil all my impossible dreams.
My Supreme, my Supreme, my Supreme!

941

My Supreme, my Supreme, my Supreme!
I am such a fool!
I expect Infinity's Nectar-Delight
From my desire-mind.
My Supreme, my Supreme, my Supreme!

942

My Supreme, my Supreme, my Supreme!
Every morning I love to do
My inner intensity-training.
My Supreme, my Supreme, my Supreme!

27 JANUARY 2000

943

My Supreme, my Supreme, my Supreme!
He who gives is loved;
He who becomes is claimed;
He who surrenders becomes
A supremely chosen member
Of God's inner circle.
My Supreme, my Supreme, my Supreme!

944

My Supreme, my Supreme, my Supreme!
A God-realised soul comes into the world
To make spirituality,
Which is God's inner life,
Crystal clear for the God-dreamers,
God-seekers, God-lovers
And God-servers.
My Supreme, my Supreme, my Supreme!

945

My Supreme, my Supreme, my Supreme!
The day a seeker can prayerfully,
Soulfully, sleeplessly,
Breathlessly and self-givingly
Cry for God
Is, indeed, a triumph-day for him.
My Supreme, my Supreme, my Supreme!

946

My Supreme, my Supreme, my Supreme!
God says to my mind,
"Please do Me a big favour:
Shorten your complaint list."
My Supreme, my Supreme, my Supreme!

28 JANUARY 2000

947

My Supreme, my Supreme, my Supreme!
A sleepless and breathless
God-surrender
Is an inexhaustible God-Love-fund.
My Supreme, my Supreme, my Supreme!

948

My Supreme, my Supreme, my Supreme!
Time is too short,
But my love of God is not only long,
Very long,
But also eternal.
My Supreme, my Supreme, my Supreme!

MY MORNING SOUL-BODY PRAYERS

3 FEBRUARY 2000

949

My Supreme, my Supreme, my Supreme!
There are certain things
That hurt me so deeply.
How is it that I do not want
To renounce them immediately?
My Supreme, my Supreme, my Supreme!

950

My Supreme, my Supreme, my Supreme!
As unconsciously I cherish my problems,
Even so, consciously I want
To place them at Your Feet.
My Supreme, my Supreme, my Supreme!

951

My Supreme, my Supreme, my Supreme!
God has no time for those
Who deliberately do not listen
To Him.
My Supreme, my Supreme, my Supreme!

5 FEBRUARY 2000

952

My Supreme, my Supreme, my Supreme!
Long before I say something,
Long before I do something,
I must eagerly take
Your cheerful Approval.
My Supreme, my Supreme, my Supreme!

953

My Supreme, my Supreme, my Supreme!
God gives supreme importance
To the Master-disciple
Oneness-heart-tears
And
Oneness-soul-smiles.
My Supreme, my Supreme, my Supreme!

954

My Supreme, my Supreme, my Supreme!
God's Compassion-Eye
Does not criticise any human being.
God's Forgiveness-Heart
Does not accuse any human being.
My Supreme, my Supreme, my Supreme!

MY MORNING SOUL-BODY PRAYERS

7 FEBRUARY 2000

955

My Supreme, my Supreme, my Supreme!
A God-gratitude-heart
Is
A fulness-life-joy.
My Supreme, my Supreme, my Supreme!

956

My Supreme, my Supreme, my Supreme!
For years I have been trying so hard
To be a member of God's
Delight-association.
Finally, today I am successful.
My Supreme, my Supreme, my Supreme!

957

My Supreme, my Supreme, my Supreme!
My self-giving life
Is the most powerful weapon
In my heart-armoury.
My Supreme, my Supreme, my Supreme!

8 FEBRUARY 2000

958

My Supreme, my Supreme, my Supreme!
Today my Absolute Lord
Commands my negativity-mind
To disappear
Once and for all.
My Supreme, my Supreme, my Supreme!

959

My Supreme, my Supreme, my Supreme!
Your unconditional Grace
Is the only way for me to make
Any progress in any field.
My Supreme, my Supreme, my Supreme!

960

My Supreme, my Supreme, my Supreme!
Because of Your unconditional Grace,
I hope, I promise and I fulfil.
My Supreme, my Supreme, my Supreme!

MY MORNING SOUL-BODY PRAYERS

10 FEBRUARY 2000

961

My Supreme, my Supreme, my Supreme!
A gratitude-heart is the unparalleled
Wonder of the world.
My Supreme, my Supreme, my Supreme!

962

My Supreme, my Supreme, my Supreme!
Do You really read my troubled heart
Every day?
"Yes, My child, I do.
In fact,
I pay first and foremost attention
To your troubled heart every day."
My Supreme, my Supreme, my Supreme!

963

My Supreme, my Supreme, my Supreme!
The moment I demolished
My ego-mansion,
You blessed me with
Your supreme Pride-Reward.
My Supreme, my Supreme, my Supreme!

12 FEBRUARY 2000

964

My Supreme, my Supreme, my Supreme!
My Lord,
Your Compassion-Delight-Voice
Is my heart's secret and sacred choice.
My Supreme, my Supreme, my Supreme!

965

My Supreme, my Supreme, my Supreme!
Every morning
God, in His Heart of Delight,
Invites me to sing with Him,
To run with Him
And
To play with Him.
My Supreme, my Supreme, my Supreme!

966

My Supreme, my Supreme, my Supreme!
The delight in self-giving says:
Eternity I have.
The delight in God-becoming says:
Infinity I am.
My Supreme, my Supreme, my Supreme!

MY MORNING SOUL-BODY PRAYERS

14 FEBRUARY 2000

967

My Supreme, my Supreme, my Supreme!
O impersonal God,
I like You, I appreciate You, I admire You.
O personal God,
I love You, I adore You, I need You.
My Supreme, my Supreme, my Supreme!

968

My Supreme, my Supreme, my Supreme!
O impersonal God,
You inspire me profusely.
O personal God,
You aspire in and through me regularly.
My Supreme, my Supreme, my Supreme!

969

My Supreme, my Supreme, my Supreme!
O impersonal God,
You are my rainbow-dream-reality.
O personal God,
You are my realisation-sun-revelation.
My Supreme, my Supreme, my Supreme!

16 FEBRUARY 2000

970

My Supreme, my Supreme, my Supreme!
What is Your Grace?
Your Grace is Your Omnipresence-Love.
My Supreme, my Supreme, my Supreme!

971

My Supreme, my Supreme, my Supreme!
What is Your Grace?
Your Grace is Your Omniscience-Joy.
My Supreme, my Supreme, my Supreme!

972

My Supreme, my Supreme, my Supreme!
What is Your Grace?
Your Grace
Is Your Omnipotence-Embrace.
My Supreme, my Supreme, my Supreme!

MY MORNING SOUL-BODY PRAYERS

18 FEBRUARY 2000

973

My Supreme, my Supreme, my Supreme!
May each day be a God-Victory-day
For all God-lovers and God-servers.
My Supreme, my Supreme, my Supreme!

974

My Supreme, my Supreme, my Supreme!
May my mind's readiness,
My life's willingness
And
My heart's eagerness
Sleeplessly respond to the Will
Of my Lord Beloved Supreme.
My Supreme, my Supreme, my Supreme!

975

My Supreme, my Supreme, my Supreme!
Finally You are accepting me
As Your own, very own.
Today my lifelong dream
Has come true.
My Supreme, my Supreme, my Supreme!

19 FEBRUARY 2000

976

My Supreme, my Supreme, my Supreme!
Today it will be a symbolic lift.
My Supreme, my Supreme, my Supreme!
Today I am embarking on
A very, very, very long journey.
While I am taking each step forward,
I am going to offer You
My heart's gratitude-tears.
I do hope that one day,
Out of Your infinite Bounty,
You will take me to my destination.
My Supreme, my Supreme, my Supreme!

977

My Supreme, my Supreme, my Supreme!
Indeed, a mystic journey
In the weightlifting world.
My Supreme, my Supreme, my Supreme!

MY MORNING SOUL-BODY PRAYERS

21 FEBRUARY 2000

978

My Supreme, my Supreme, my Supreme!
Please, please never allow me
To run out of
Aspiration-energy-cry-supplies.
Please, please never allow me
To run out of
Dedication-energy-smile-supplies.
My Supreme, my Supreme, my Supreme!

23 FEBRUARY 2000

979

My Supreme, my Supreme, my Supreme!
I must love You more,
Infinitely more.
Only then all the obstacles
With their hostilities
Will surrender to me.
My Supreme, my Supreme, my Supreme!

980

My Supreme, my Supreme, my Supreme!
Do give me the capacity
To ring Your Victory-Ecstasy-Bell
Every morning and every evening
In my heart of aspiration
And
In my life of dedication.
My Supreme, my Supreme, my Supreme!

MY MORNING SOUL-BODY PRAYERS

24 FEBRUARY 2000

981

My Supreme, my Supreme, my Supreme!
May my mind every day
Run for God's Eye.
May my heart every day
Sprint for God's Heart.
May my life every day
Kiss the dust of my Lord's Feet.
My Supreme, my Supreme, my Supreme!

982

My Supreme, my Supreme, my Supreme!
May my God-love, God-devotion
And God-surrender
Increase every day
At least by an inch.
My Supreme, my Supreme, my Supreme!

983

My Supreme, my Supreme, my Supreme!
Your infinite Grace is telling me
That my heart-hermitage
Is Your celestial Palace.
My Supreme, my Supreme, my Supreme!

25 FEBRUARY 2000

984

My Supreme, my Supreme, my Supreme!
I am absolutely convinced
That my God-manifestation
Here on earth
Is not an eyeless, hopeless
And useless hunger-quest.
My Supreme, my Supreme, my Supreme!

985

My Supreme, my Supreme, my Supreme!
May my life be an untiring
Self-offering
To humanity's God-aspiring heart.
My Supreme, my Supreme, my Supreme!

986

My Supreme, my Supreme, my Supreme!
I am my ceaseless gratitude-heart;
God is His Compassion-flooded,
Ceaseless, sunlit Smile.
My Supreme, my Supreme, my Supreme!

MY MORNING SOUL-BODY PRAYERS

26 FEBRUARY 2000

987

My Supreme, my Supreme, my Supreme!
No more clamouring mind-confusion,
No more!
God-satisfaction more, infinitely more,
Eternally more.
My Supreme, my Supreme, my Supreme!

988

My Supreme, my Supreme, my Supreme!
I am my gratitude-heart
And
You are Your Compassion-Eye.
Your Compassion-Eye is telling me
That my summit-meditation
Is Your Heart-treasure.
My Supreme, my Supreme, my Supreme!

989

My Supreme, my Supreme, my Supreme!
The god of sincerity
And
The goddess of purity
Always live inside my heart-temple.
They never, never live inside
My unlit mind-room.
My Supreme, my Supreme, my Supreme!

28 FEBRUARY 2000

990

My Supreme, my Supreme, my Supreme!
No matter what befalls me,
My heart and I shall sleeplessly sing
Your Victory-Songs.
My Supreme, my Supreme, my Supreme!

991

My Supreme, my Supreme, my Supreme!
May my life become an endless river
Of God-gratitude-tears
And smiles.
My Supreme, my Supreme, my Supreme!

992

My Supreme, my Supreme, my Supreme!
Where do I live?
I live in my Lord's
Compassion-Heart-Sky.
How?
By constantly flying and flying
And flying.
My Supreme, my Supreme, my Supreme!

MY MORNING SOUL-BODY PRAYERS

I MARCH 2000

993

My Supreme, my Supreme, my Supreme!
My mind whispers to me:
"God is always busy.
I am sure He is not going to come
And visit you."
My heart whispers to me:
"God loves you so much.
Look, He is coming to visit you!"
My Supreme, my Supreme, my Supreme!

994

My Supreme, my Supreme, my Supreme!
My world has two very special names:
My aspiration-heart-beauty
And
My dedication-life-fragrance.
My Supreme, my Supreme, my Supreme!

995

My Supreme, my Supreme, my Supreme!
Alas, God-gratitude-tears
Are never to be found in my mind.
My Supreme, my Supreme, my Supreme!

2 MARCH 2000

996

My Supreme, my Supreme, my Supreme!
God wants me to carry
My love-devotion-surrender-identification
With me wherever I go.
My Supreme, my Supreme, my Supreme!

997

My Supreme, my Supreme, my Supreme!
There are many, many charming,
Inspiring, encouraging
And illumining stations
Along the road to Infinity's Bliss.
My Supreme, my Supreme, my Supreme!

998

My Supreme, my Supreme, my Supreme!
When I say, "I do not,"
My Lord cries and cries and cries.
When I say, "I cannot,"
My Lord laughs and laughs and laughs.
When I say, "I can,"
My Lord smiles and smiles and smiles.
When I say, "I have done,"
My Lord immediately says,
"My child, I am making you
Another God, a future God."
My Supreme, my Supreme, my Supreme!

999

My Supreme, my Supreme, my Supreme!
God does not want me to carry
A credit card.
He wants me to carry always with me
The mighty dollar
To remind me that I am, indeed,
A child of the Almighty.
My Lord, will people not laugh
At my cleverness?
"My child, cleverness is far better
Than foolishness.
When you use your cash, your inner pride
And the cashier's inner joy
Sing, play and dance together."
Finally, God becomes serious.
He tells me, "My child,
Money-power conquers only the inferiors.
Heart-power conquers everybody —
The superiors, the inferiors
And the equals,
Plus Me and My All."
My Supreme, my Supreme, my Supreme!

3 MARCH 2000

1000

My Supreme, my Supreme, my Supreme!
My enthusiasm-life
Has a great and equal partner:
My eagerness-heart.
My Supreme, my Supreme, my Supreme!

1001

My Supreme, my Supreme, my Supreme!
Eventually desire-life fades
And aspiration-heart
Succeeds and flourishes.
My Supreme, my Supreme, my Supreme!

1002

My Supreme, my Supreme, my Supreme!
I must pass well,
Sleeplessly and breathlessly,
All my God-surrender-examinations.
My Supreme, my Supreme, my Supreme!

MY MORNING SOUL-BODY PRAYERS

5 MARCH 2000

1003

My Supreme, my Supreme, my Supreme!
Alas, my mind has blindfolded
My heart's vision-eye.
My Supreme, my Supreme, my Supreme!

1004

My Supreme, my Supreme, my Supreme!
I must never allow
My sleepless God-attention
And
My breathless God-devotion
To waver.
My Supreme, my Supreme, my Supreme!

1005

My Supreme, my Supreme, my Supreme!
God experienced –
God-Love, God-Joy, God-Peace
And God-Bliss
Expressed, revealed and manifested.
My Supreme, my Supreme, my Supreme!

6 MARCH 2000

1006

My Supreme, my Supreme, my Supreme!
My God expresses
His extreme bewilderment
When I tell Him
That I am not inspired any more
To do His God-manifestation-work.
My Supreme, my Supreme, my Supreme!

1007

My Supreme, my Supreme, my Supreme!
God's Compassion-Eye
Has introduced me
To God's Pinnacle-Height.
My Supreme, my Supreme, my Supreme!

1008

My Supreme, my Supreme, my Supreme!
My God-obedience is the shortest
And the safest road
To my God-Destination.
My Supreme, my Supreme, my Supreme!

MY MORNING SOUL-BODY PRAYERS

7 MARCH 2000

1009

My Supreme, my Supreme, my Supreme!
I must give a heart-smile to have
A true life-friend.
A true life-friend is, indeed,
A rare achievement.
My Supreme, my Supreme, my Supreme!

1010

My Supreme, my Supreme, my Supreme!
My old mind says
That there is nothing new
And there will not be anything new.
My new heart says
That everything is not only new,
But inspiring, encouraging, energising,
Illumining and fulfilling.
My Supreme, my Supreme, my Supreme!

1011

My Supreme, my Supreme, my Supreme!
Every morning do bless me
With indomitable waves
Of enthusiasm-energy.
My Supreme, my Supreme, my Supreme!

9 MARCH 2000

1012

My Supreme, my Supreme, my Supreme!
An unconditional self-giver
Is the winner
Of God's Peace Award.
My Supreme, my Supreme, my Supreme!

1013

My Supreme, my Supreme, my Supreme!
My sleepless and breathless
God-gratitude-heart
Is the shortest and safest stairway
To arrive at
God's Transcendental Height.
My Supreme, my Supreme, my Supreme!

1014

My Supreme, my Supreme, my Supreme!
I shall never allow
My aspiration-heart, my dedication-life
And my God-manifestation-accounts
To ever be empty.
My Supreme, my Supreme, my Supreme!

MY MORNING SOUL-BODY PRAYERS

11 MARCH 2000

1015

My Supreme, my Supreme, my Supreme!
My mind says to me,
"Stop! Stop! Danger ahead."
My heart says to me,
"Go on! Go on! Look,
Your Destination is beckoning you."
My Supreme, my Supreme, my Supreme!

1016

My Supreme, my Supreme, my Supreme!
I know how to maximise and amplify
My prayers.
God knows how to glorify
My prayers
And intensify His Grace.
My Supreme, my Supreme, my Supreme!

1017

My Supreme, my Supreme, my Supreme!
My prayers lengthen My God-service-life.
My meditations strengthen
My God-oneness-heart.
My Supreme, my Supreme, my Supreme!

1018

My Supreme, my Supreme, my Supreme!
My mind knows only
How to assail the world constantly.
My heart knows not only
How to sail my life-boat
But God's Life-Boat, too.
My Supreme, my Supreme, my Supreme!

1019

My Supreme, my Supreme, my Supreme!
I love God the man to be happy.
I serve man the God to be perfect.
My Supreme, my Supreme, my Supreme!

1020

My Supreme, my Supreme, my Supreme!
When I look at my Lord's Eye,
He gives me a most beautiful flower
From His Heart-Garden.
When I smile at His Heart,
He gives me His All.
My Supreme, my Supreme, my Supreme!

MY MORNING SOUL-BODY PRAYERS

16 MARCH 2000

1021

My Supreme, my Supreme, my Supreme!
Please help me fly far beyond
The skies of fears, worries
And anxieties.
My Supreme, my Supreme, my Supreme!

1022

My Supreme, my Supreme, my Supreme!
This morning God gave me
A surprise call.
He said to me, "My son,
You must keep your promise.
You must fight for Me
Against ignorance—
Sleeplessly, breathlessly, eternally."
My Supreme, my Supreme, my Supreme!
I am at Your Feet throughout Eternity.
I shall be at Your Feet to please You
And to fulfil You in Your own Way.
My Supreme, my Supreme, my Supreme!

1023

My Supreme, my Supreme, my Supreme!
If I do not improve myself,
Then how can You wait for me
Indefinitely?
What right do I have
To beg You to wait for me?
My Supreme, my Supreme, my Supreme!

SRI CHINMOY

18 MARCH 2000

1024

My Supreme, my Supreme, my Supreme!
From this moment on,
I shall see everything
In Your own Way,
I shall feel everything
In Your own Way
And
I shall do everything
In Your own Way
Without having a thought
For my own self.
My Supreme, my Supreme, my Supreme!

MY MORNING SOUL-BODY PRAYERS

20 MARCH 2000

1025

My Supreme, my Supreme, my Supreme!
The Hour of God is waiting for me
Today.
The Hour of God will watch me
Tomorrow.
The Hour of God will examine me
The day after.
My Supreme, my Supreme, my Supreme!

1026

My Supreme, my Supreme, my Supreme!
Finally, today I have discarded
My mind's complaint-list.
My Supreme, my Supreme, my Supreme!

1027

My Supreme, my Supreme, my Supreme!
My mind still enjoys
Avid discussions.
To my great joy, my heart enjoys
Only sweet God-conversations.
My Supreme, my Supreme, my Supreme!

21 MARCH 2000

1028

My Supreme, my Supreme, my Supreme!
Each Smile I receive from You
Is, indeed,
A very special Blessing-Gift
From Your Heart.
My Supreme, my Supreme, my Supreme!

1029

My Supreme, my Supreme, my Supreme!
May my heart's aspiration-flames
And
My life's dedication-flowers
Please Your Eye, please Your Heart
And please Your Feet
Simultaneously.
My Supreme, my Supreme, my Supreme!

1030

My Supreme, my Supreme, my Supreme!
Each obstacle I face
Along the road of my spirituality
Is an opportunity for me to express
My love for You infinitely more.
My Supreme, my Supreme, my Supreme!

MY MORNING SOUL-BODY PRAYERS

23 MARCH 2000

1031

My Supreme, my Supreme, my Supreme!
What a fool I am!
I am delaying and delaying and delaying
Looking at my Lord's Compassion-Eye.
My Supreme, my Supreme, my Supreme!

1032

My Supreme, my Supreme, my Supreme!
Can there be a greater fool than I am?
I am delaying and delaying and delaying
Placing myself at the Feet
Of my Lord Supreme
For His Forgiveness-Blessings.
My Supreme, my Supreme, my Supreme!

1033

My Supreme, my Supreme, my Supreme!
What a fool I am!
I have received Forgiveness-Delight
From my Lord Beloved Supreme,
Yet I am not praying every day
In the small hours of the morning
For His Supreme Victory on earth.
My Supreme, my Supreme, my Supreme!

25 MARCH 2000

1034

My Supreme, my Supreme, my Supreme!
Please, please bind my heart,
Please, please bind my mind,
Please, please bind my vital,
Please, please bind my body,
So that they can be only Yours
In their inner existence
And
In their outer existence.
My Supreme, my Supreme, my Supreme!

1035

My Supreme, my Supreme, my Supreme!
My undivine mind grabs
And throws away
My heart's "Do Not Disturb" sign.
My Supreme, my Supreme, my Supreme!

1036

My Supreme, my Supreme, my Supreme!
I know, I know,
Your powerful Warning
Is another name
For Your Protection-Blessing.
My Supreme, my Supreme, my Supreme!

MY MORNING SOUL-BODY PRAYERS

27 MARCH 2000

1037

My Supreme, my Supreme, my Supreme!
No more impurity-mind,
Insecurity-heart
And inferiority-life
Can darken my meditation-room.
My Supreme, my Supreme, my Supreme!

29 MARCH 2000

1038

My Supreme, my Supreme, my Supreme!
Only unconditionally surrendered
Seekers
Have God's private and unlisted
Number.
My Supreme, my Supreme, my Supreme!

1039

My Supreme, my Supreme, my Supreme!
May I develop
Desperate desperation-hunger
For Your full manifestation
Here on earth.
My Supreme, my Supreme, my Supreme!

1040

My Supreme, my Supreme, my Supreme!
I beg and pray
For my life's complete
Transformation-day.
My Supreme, my Supreme, my Supreme!

1041

My Supreme, my Supreme, my Supreme!
Miracle-performances are
Problem-makers.
God-preferences are
Problem-strangers.
My Supreme, my Supreme, my Supreme!

MY MORNING SOUL-BODY PRAYERS

31 MARCH 2000

1042

My Supreme, my Supreme, my Supreme!
I must purify my mind,
I must intensify my heart,
I must simplify my life
To be of real service to You.
My Supreme, my Supreme, my Supreme!

1043

My Supreme, my Supreme, my Supreme!
I must not stop dreaming
If I want to become
A God-fulfilling reality.
My Supreme, my Supreme, my Supreme!

1044

My Supreme, my Supreme, my Supreme!
Every day You want me to sing
With the soaring horizons
Of my God-representative-soul.
My Supreme, my Supreme, my Supreme!

SRI CHINMOY

2 APRIL 2000

1045

My Supreme, my Supreme, my Supreme!
No aspiration-heart,
No surrender-courage,
No God-Satisfaction!
My Supreme, my Supreme, my Supreme!

MY MORNING SOUL-BODY PRAYERS

3 APRIL 2000

1046

My Supreme, my Supreme, my Supreme!
May my soul, my heart, my mind,
My vital and my body
Always remain
In Your Protection-Cradle.
My Supreme, my Supreme, my Supreme!

1047

My Supreme, my Supreme, my Supreme!
Every morning You bless me
With Your Heart's Rainbow-Smile
The moment I wake up.
My Supreme, my Supreme, my Supreme!

4 APRIL 2000

1048

My Supreme, my Supreme, my Supreme!
May my ceaseless heart-cries
Hasten my Lord's full manifestation
Here on earth.
My Supreme, my Supreme, my Supreme!

1049

My Supreme, my Supreme, my Supreme!
My mind-road takes me nowhere.
My heart-road leads me everywhere,
Plus, at the end,
I see my Lord smiling at me.
My Supreme, my Supreme, my Supreme!

1050

My Supreme, my Supreme, my Supreme!
Each time I sing a heart-song,
I take a step forward
Towards my Destination.
My Supreme, my Supreme, my Supreme!

MY MORNING SOUL-BODY PRAYERS

6 APRIL 2000

1051

My Supreme, my Supreme, my Supreme!
Not even for one breath
Do I belong to ignorance-hunger
And ignorance-pride.
I belong only to You and Your Feet.
My Supreme, my Supreme, my Supreme!

1052

My Supreme, my Supreme, my Supreme!
I must cross over
All my temptation-hurdles
In order to reach my life's
Liberation-Destination.
My Supreme, my Supreme, my Supreme!

1053

My Supreme, my Supreme, my Supreme!
Today I have replaced
My fault-finding mind
With my world-oneness-loving heart.
My Supreme, my Supreme, my Supreme!

10 APRIL 2000

1054

My Supreme, my Supreme, my Supreme!
Out of Your infinite Bounty,
You value my heart-smiles.
Again, out of Your infinite Bounty,
You value my life-tears
Infinitely more.
My Supreme, my Supreme, my Supreme!

1055

My Supreme, my Supreme, my Supreme!
I do not allow my mind to have
Even an inch
Of negativity-space.
My Supreme, my Supreme, my Supreme!

1056

My Supreme, my Supreme, my Supreme!
In my life there is only one
Supreme Blessing
And that Supreme Blessing
Is to kiss the dust of Your Feet
At every moment.
My Supreme, my Supreme, my Supreme!

MY MORNING SOUL-BODY PRAYERS

12 APRIL 2000

1057

My Supreme, my Supreme, my Supreme!
My final Destination
Is my Lord's full manifestation
Here on earth.
My Supreme, my Supreme, my Supreme!

1058

My Supreme, my Supreme, my Supreme!
God has not sanctioned
Even one single holiday
For a God-realised person
In the inner world.
My Supreme, my Supreme, my Supreme!

1059

My Supreme, my Supreme, my Supreme!
I equally love and value
My heart's aspiration-flames
And
My life's dedication-blossoms.
My Supreme, my Supreme, my Supreme!

SRI CHINMOY

14 APRIL 2000

1060

My Supreme, my Supreme, my Supreme!
The human life is nothing but
The morning joy
And the evening sorrow.
My Supreme, my Supreme, my Supreme!

1061

My Supreme, my Supreme, my Supreme!
Each soul has a unique way
To manifest God here on earth.
My Supreme, my Supreme, my Supreme!

MY MORNING SOUL-BODY PRAYERS

20 APRIL 2000

1062

My Supreme, my Supreme, my Supreme!
My God-aspiration shows me the way.
My God-dedication takes me
To my Destination.
My God-manifestation is my Lord's
Complete Satisfaction.
My Supreme, my Supreme, my Supreme!

1063

My Supreme, my Supreme, my Supreme!
My mind's God-imagination
Is a real friend
Of my heart's aspiration.
My Supreme, my Supreme, my Supreme!

1064

My Supreme, my Supreme, my Supreme!
My heart, dream, dream.
Dreaming is realising.
Realising is becoming
The Highest Absolute.
Therefore, my heart, stop not dreaming.
My Supreme, my Supreme, my Supreme!

22 April 2000

1065

My Supreme, my Supreme, my Supreme!
A God-willingness-seeker
Is always the winner
In the inner race.
My Supreme, my Supreme, my Supreme!

1066

My Supreme, my Supreme, my Supreme!
For me to choose is to lose
In my God-oneness-game.
My Supreme, my Supreme, my Supreme!

1067

My Supreme, my Supreme, my Supreme!
No matter where I roam,
Your Compassion-Eye
And Forgiveness-Heart
Follow me unconditionally.
My Supreme, my Supreme, my Supreme!

MY MORNING SOUL-BODY PRAYERS

28 APRIL 2000

1068

My Supreme, my Supreme, my Supreme!
The union of life
Is deep within.
The separation of death
Is all around.
My Supreme, my Supreme, my Supreme!

1069

My Supreme, my Supreme, my Supreme!
My heart wishes to be touched
By Your Compassion-Eye.
My life wishes to be caught
By Your Forgiveness-Feet.
My Supreme, my Supreme, my Supreme!

1070

My Supreme, my Supreme, my Supreme!
Ignorance-night wants to trick us
And kick us.
Wisdom-light wants to love us
And bless us.
My Supreme, my Supreme, my Supreme!

1 MAY 2000

1071

My Supreme, my Supreme, my Supreme!
I have only one prayer:
Do give me the capacity
To utter Your Name prayerfully,
Soulfully and self-givingly
With every heartbeat of mine.
My Supreme, my Supreme, my Supreme!

1072

My Supreme, my Supreme, my Supreme!
In sacred secrecy supreme
You are telling me
That You want from my life
The fastest progress
Both in the inner world
And in the outer world.
My Supreme, my Supreme, my Supreme!

1073

My Supreme, my Supreme, my Supreme!
In my spiritual life
My only real death
Is my God-forgetfulness.
My Supreme, my Supreme, my Supreme!

MY MORNING SOUL-BODY PRAYERS

3 MAY 2000

1074

My Supreme, my Supreme, my Supreme!
Forgiveness, forgiveness, forgiveness —
This is my morning prayer.
Love and transform —
This is my evening prayer.
My Supreme, my Supreme, my Supreme!

1075

My Supreme, my Supreme, my Supreme!
Injustice-night, injustice-night,
Injustice-night — everywhere.
Justice-light, justice-light,
Justice-light — nowhere.
But, my Lord, do give my life
The capacity to grow into
Your universal Justice-Light.
My Supreme, my Supreme, my Supreme!

4 MAY 2000

1076

My Supreme, my Supreme, my Supreme!
Every day God sends
A special peace-message
To my mind,
But my mind summarily rejects it.
My Supreme, my Supreme, my Supreme!

1077

My Supreme, my Supreme, my Supreme!
Do give me the capacity
To feed only Your Need
And nothing else,
Nothing else.
My Supreme, my Supreme, my Supreme!

1078

My Supreme, my Supreme, my Supreme!
Any time, any place
Is perfect to please God
In His own Way.
My Supreme, my Supreme, my Supreme!

1079

My Supreme, my Supreme, my Supreme!
God is never interested
In my mind-explanation.
He is always interested
In my heart-illumination.
My Supreme, my Supreme, my Supreme!

MY MORNING SOUL-BODY PRAYERS

9 MAY 2000

1080

My Supreme, my Supreme, my Supreme!
A desire-life is, indeed,
A long run of expectation,
Frustration and destruction.
My Supreme, my Supreme, my Supreme!

11 MAY 2000

1081

My Supreme, my Supreme, my Supreme!
Today I must plant my roots
Inside Your Heart-Garden.
My Supreme, my Supreme, my Supreme!

1082

My Supreme, my Supreme, my Supreme!
I must not picture my future.
I must live in my promise-fulfilment
Of the Eternal Now.
My Supreme, my Supreme, my Supreme!

MY MORNING SOUL-BODY PRAYERS

13 MAY 2000

1083

My Supreme, my Supreme, my Supreme!
My crying heart triumphantly smiles
When it can sit at the Feet
Of my Lord Beloved Supreme.
My Supreme, my Supreme, my Supreme!

1084

My Supreme, my Supreme, my Supreme!
My heart's hope-flames
Are bound to grow
Into my life's promise-sun.
My Supreme, my Supreme, my Supreme!

1085

My Supreme, my Supreme, my Supreme!
No God-surrender, no life-progress.
No life-progress, no God-Smile.
My Supreme, my Supreme, my Supreme!

15 MAY 2000

1086

My Supreme, my Supreme, my Supreme!
The mind is a doubt-mountain.
The heart is a faith-fountain.
My Supreme, my Supreme, my Supreme!

1087

My Supreme, my Supreme, my Supreme!
Your Compassion-Train
Has liberated my life
From its bondage-chain.
My Supreme, my Supreme, my Supreme!

MY MORNING SOUL-BODY PRAYERS

18 MAY 2000

1088

My Supreme, my Supreme, my Supreme!
The world-doubting mind
Is a torturer.
The soul-doubting mind
Is a sufferer.
My Supreme, my Supreme, my Supreme!

1089

My Supreme, my Supreme, my Supreme!
God's Will is not familiar with
A trifle-disobedience.
My Supreme, my Supreme, my Supreme!

1090

My Supreme, my Supreme, my Supreme!
I must never lose sight of
Your Forgiveness-Footsteps.
My Supreme, my Supreme, my Supreme!

1091

My Supreme, my Supreme, my Supreme!
An unconditional Forgiveness
Is only God's forte.
My Supreme, my Supreme, my Supreme!

20 MAY 2000

1092

My Supreme, my Supreme, my Supreme!
Only Your Will-fulfilment
From the beginning of my journey
To the end of my journey.
My Supreme, my Supreme, my Supreme!

1093

My Supreme, my Supreme, my Supreme!
I shall no more waste
My precious time
In expectation-snare.
My Supreme, my Supreme, my Supreme!

1094

My Supreme, my Supreme, my Supreme!
May my heart all the time
Dream of the Beauty and Delight
Of the highest Heavens.
My Supreme, my Supreme, my Supreme!

MY MORNING SOUL-BODY PRAYERS

22 MAY 2000

1095

My Supreme, my Supreme, my Supreme!
Happiness I create
By silencing my mind.
Happiness I create
By bringing my heart to the fore.
My Supreme, my Supreme, my Supreme!

1096

My Supreme, my Supreme, my Supreme!
Every day may my heart
Soulfully become
God-service-happiness.
My Supreme, my Supreme, my Supreme!

23 MAY 2000

1097

My Supreme, my Supreme, my Supreme!
God will love me infinitely more
If I can laugh at my outer failures.
My Supreme, my Supreme, my Supreme!

1098

My Supreme, my Supreme, my Supreme!
An unaspiring heart
Adds loneliness
To the life.
My Supreme, my Supreme, my Supreme!

1099

My Supreme, my Supreme, my Supreme!
My heart-sorrows
Are my life-treasures.
My Supreme, my Supreme, my Supreme!

MY MORNING SOUL-BODY PRAYERS

24 MAY 2000

1100

My Supreme, my Supreme, my Supreme!
May my soulful actions speak
And not my boastful words.
My Supreme, my Supreme, my Supreme!

1101

My Supreme, my Supreme, my Supreme!
Your timetable never fails.
You are always prompt
In answering my prayers.
It is I who fail again and again
In obeying You promptly.
My Supreme, my Supreme, my Supreme!

SRI CHINMOY

25 MAY 2000

1102

My Supreme, my Supreme, my Supreme!
My soul-bird sleeplessly sings
Peace-songs
Inside my heart.
My Supreme, my Supreme, my Supreme!

1103

My Supreme, my Supreme, my Supreme!
My intuition-speed
Is the whisper-message
Of my all-seeing soul.
My Supreme, my Supreme, my Supreme!

MY MORNING SOUL-BODY PRAYERS

26 MAY 2000

1104

My Supreme, my Supreme, my Supreme!
Everything that I have
And everything that I am
I am prayerfully and devotedly
Placing at the Feet
Of my Lord Beloved Supreme.
My Supreme, my Supreme, my Supreme!

1105

My Supreme, my Supreme, my Supreme!
Every day my high experiences
Plough my soul's fertile soil.
My Supreme, my Supreme, my Supreme!

1106

My Supreme, my Supreme, my Supreme!
To reach my ultimate Goal,
Only one thing I need:
Your Compassion-flooded Eye.
My Supreme, my Supreme, my Supreme!

SRI CHINMOY

30 MAY 2000

1107

My Supreme, my Supreme, my Supreme!
My today's patience-life
Will tomorrow grow into
My peace-heart.
My Supreme, my Supreme, my Supreme!

1108

My Supreme, my Supreme, my Supreme!
I take sincere pride in my heart.
Therefore, You take enormous pride
In me.
My Supreme, my Supreme, my Supreme!

MY MORNING SOUL-BODY PRAYERS

1 JUNE 2000

1109

My Supreme, my Supreme, my Supreme!
Man is man's overdue
Gratitude-heart to God.
My Supreme, my Supreme, my Supreme!

1110

My Supreme, my Supreme, my Supreme!
For me, today is the day
Of my unconditional surrender
To Your express Will.
My Supreme, my Supreme, my Supreme!

4 JUNE 2000

1111

My Supreme, my Supreme, my Supreme!
The heart cannot live
Without loving God,
But the mind can.
My Supreme, my Supreme, my Supreme!

1112

My Supreme, my Supreme, my Supreme!
At last I have found my identification.
My identification is my love
For a oneness-world.
My Supreme, my Supreme, my Supreme!

MY MORNING SOUL-BODY PRAYERS

5 JUNE 2000

1113

My Supreme, my Supreme, my Supreme!
The mind conceives;
The heart achieves.
My Supreme, my Supreme, my Supreme!

SRI CHINMOY

13 JUNE 2000

1114

My Supreme, my Supreme, my Supreme!
My life-complacency
Is my self-destruction.
My heart-confidence
Is my God-preparation.
My Supreme, my Supreme, my Supreme!

MY MORNING SOUL-BODY PRAYERS

18 JUNE 2000

1115

My Supreme, my Supreme, my Supreme!
This morning, out of His infinite Bounty,
God has struck my name
From ignorance-night-list.
My Supreme, my Supreme, my Supreme!

1116

My Supreme, my Supreme, my Supreme!
I am my God-oneness-hope.
God is His God-Fulness-Promise.
My Supreme, my Supreme, my Supreme!

1117

My Supreme, my Supreme, my Supreme!
Do bless me with one million hearts
To love You.
Do bless me with two million hands
To serve You.
My Supreme, my Supreme, my Supreme!

19 JUNE 2000

1118

My Supreme, my Supreme, my Supreme!
Those who are now peace-dreamers
And God-lovers
Were definitely born with
God-aspiration-flames deep within.
My Supreme, my Supreme, my Supreme!

1119

My Supreme, my Supreme, my Supreme!
I am my heart's gratitude-song.
You are Your Heart's Sweetness-Flute.
My Supreme, my Supreme, my Supreme!

MY MORNING SOUL-BODY PRAYERS

20 JUNE 2000

1120

My Supreme, my Supreme, my Supreme!
Today my heart's
God-manifestation-bird
Is flying high, very high,
And far, very far.
My Supreme, my Supreme, my Supreme!

1121

My Supreme, my Supreme, my Supreme!
My inspiration says, "I *can*."
My aspiration says, "I *have*."
My realisation says, "I *am*."
My Supreme, my Supreme, my Supreme!

1122

My Supreme, my Supreme, my Supreme!
Who am I?
I am an insignificant God-lover
In my inner life of aspiration.
I am an insignificant God-server
In my outer life of dedication.
My Supreme, my Supreme, my Supreme!

1123

My Supreme, my Supreme, my Supreme!
Mountains appear only to disappear
The moment God's Grace descends.
My Supreme, my Supreme, my Supreme!

SRI CHINMOY

21 JUNE 2000

1124

My Supreme, my Supreme, my Supreme!
Your Forgiveness ends
My helpless days.
Your Compassion begins
My hopeful days.
My Supreme, my Supreme, my Supreme!

1125

My Supreme, my Supreme, my Supreme!
At long last I have unmistakably won
My life's self-discipline-battle.
My Supreme, my Supreme, my Supreme!

MY MORNING SOUL-BODY PRAYERS

22 JUNE 2000

1126

My Supreme, my Supreme, my Supreme!
In the inner world
Our deliberate blindness
Disappoints Your Mind
And
Disheartens Your Heart.
My Supreme, my Supreme, my Supreme!

1127

My Supreme, my Supreme, my Supreme!
What is my confidence,
If not my Lord's
Unconditional Compassion?
My Supreme, my Supreme, my Supreme!

23 JUNE 2000

1128

My Supreme, my Supreme, my Supreme!
Every morning I must quicken
My aspiration-heart
And stretch out
My aspiration-hands.
My Supreme, my Supreme, my Supreme!

1129

My Supreme, my Supreme, my Supreme!
I must never allow
My God-manifestation-readiness,
My God-manifestation-willingness
And
My God-manifestation-eagerness
To slow down.
My Supreme, my Supreme, my Supreme!

MY MORNING SOUL-BODY PRAYERS

24 JUNE 2000

1130

My Supreme, my Supreme, my Supreme!
Not an early death
But an immediate death of my ego
I need.
My Supreme, my Supreme, my Supreme!

1131

My Supreme, my Supreme, my Supreme!
No hesitation-mind,
But a determination-mind.
Not my capacity,
But God's unconditional Bounty.
My Supreme, my Supreme, my Supreme!

1132

My Supreme, my Supreme, my Supreme!
Out of Your infinite Bounty,
You have taught me many, many,
Many things.
Please teach me one more thing:
How I can be prayerfully, soulfully,
Sleeplessly and breathlessly
Grateful to You.
My Supreme, my Supreme, my Supreme!

SRI CHINMOY

26 JUNE 2000

1133

My Supreme, my Supreme, my Supreme!
I shall never allow
My unconditional God-obedience-book
To be out of print.
My Supreme, my Supreme, my Supreme!

1134

My Supreme, my Supreme, my Supreme!
Humanity's aspiration-hearts
Are moving the world inward,
Driving the world forward
And
Raising the world upward.
My Supreme, my Supreme, my Supreme!

1135

My Supreme, my Supreme, my Supreme!
How fortunate I am to have You
As my heart's inner Instructor
And my life's outer Instructor.
My Supreme, my Supreme, my Supreme!

1136

My Supreme, my Supreme, my Supreme!
I shall not allow
Your expectation-fulfilment of my life
To remain a far cry.
My Supreme, my Supreme, my Supreme!

MY MORNING SOUL-BODY PRAYERS

1137

My Supreme, my Supreme, my Supreme!
My Lord Supreme,
As my life has taken shelter
At Your Protection-Feet,
Even so, I am placing my Goal
At Your Satisfaction-Feet.
My Supreme, my Supreme, my Supreme!

27 JUNE 2000

1138

My Supreme, my Supreme, my Supreme!
May my heart be made of
God-gratitude-smiles.
My Supreme, my Supreme, my Supreme!

1139

My Supreme, my Supreme, my Supreme!
When I please You in Your own Way,
I clearly see the celestials
Dancing Your Victory-Dance
In my heart-sky.
My Supreme, my Supreme, my Supreme!

1140

My Supreme, my Supreme, my Supreme!
May my God-love, God-devotion
And God-surrender
Be as sincere, as serious
And as pure as possible.
My Supreme, my Supreme, my Supreme!

1141

My Supreme, my Supreme, my Supreme!
When I please You in Your own Way,
You ask me to carry Your Heart-Smiles
Wherever I go,
And You will carry my heart-tears
Wherever You go.
My Supreme, my Supreme, my Supreme!

MY MORNING SOUL-BODY PRAYERS

28 JUNE 2000

1142

My Supreme, my Supreme, my Supreme!
Your ceaseless Compassion-Rain
Has totally destroyed
My mind's limitation-bondage-chain.
My Supreme, my Supreme, my Supreme!

1143

My Supreme, my Supreme, my Supreme!
Every day, every hour,
Every minute, every second
You try to keep me happy,
Yet I do not have a gratitude-heart.
Alas! Alas!
My Supreme, my Supreme, my Supreme!

1144

My Supreme, my Supreme, my Supreme!
What I need is patience, patience,
Patience.
You have Your own Hour to please me
In Your own Way.
My Supreme, my Supreme, my Supreme!

1145

My Supreme, my Supreme, my Supreme!
My constant and cheerful surrender
To Your Will
Is the most powerful joy in my life.
My Supreme, my Supreme, my Supreme!

1146

My Supreme, my Supreme, my Supreme!
May my gratitude-heart-flower
Always remain divinely fresh
And supremely pure.
My Supreme, my Supreme, my Supreme!

1147

My Supreme, my Supreme, my Supreme!
God's Grace is the only Power
That silences the pride
Of impossibility.
My Supreme, my Supreme, my Supreme!

MY MORNING SOUL-BODY PRAYERS

30 JUNE 2000

1148

My Supreme, my Supreme, my Supreme!
Time and again I have broken
My God-fulfilment-promises,
Yet my Lord's Compassion,
Love and Affection
In infinite measure
Remain the same for me.
My Supreme, my Supreme, my Supreme!

SRI CHINMOY

3 JULY 2000

1149

My Supreme, my Supreme, my Supreme!
Insecurity disappears
The moment the heart-singer
Starts singing only God-songs.
My Supreme, my Supreme, my Supreme!

MY MORNING SOUL-BODY PRAYERS

5 JULY 2000

1150

My Supreme, my Supreme, my Supreme!
When the mind unjustly prospers,
The poor heart terribly suffers.
My Supreme, my Supreme, my Supreme!

6 JULY 2000

1151

My Supreme, my Supreme, my Supreme!
My concentration
Is my world-success-winner.
My meditation
Is my God-Smile-lover.
My Supreme, my Supreme, my Supreme!

MY MORNING SOUL-BODY PRAYERS

7 JULY 2000

1152

My Supreme, my Supreme, my Supreme!
I am absolutely sure
That my heart's God-search-pilgrimage
Shall be crowned with success.
My Supreme, my Supreme, my Supreme!

SRI CHINMOY

8 JULY 2000

1153

My Supreme, my Supreme, my Supreme!
My fastest progress
Is in my constant
God-surrender-breath.
My Supreme, my Supreme, my Supreme!

MY MORNING SOUL-BODY PRAYERS

9 JULY 2000

1154

My Supreme, my Supreme, my Supreme!
My God-fulfilment-obedience-eagerness
Gives me the strength
Of a million elephants.
My Supreme, my Supreme, my Supreme!

1155

My Supreme, my Supreme, my Supreme!
My heart's eagerness-fire
Has burnt and destroyed
All my mind's unwillingness-walls.
My Supreme, my Supreme, my Supreme!

10 JULY 2000

1156

My Supreme, my Supreme, my Supreme!
My desire-mind ran forth
For world-possession.
My aspiration-life is now racing
For God-satisfaction.
My Supreme, my Supreme, my Supreme!

1157

My Supreme, my Supreme, my Supreme!
The moment my heart sings,
My mind rises immediately
And proudly.
My Supreme, my Supreme, my Supreme!

1158

My Supreme, my Supreme, my Supreme!
Every morning I pray to You
To bless me with only two things:
God-reliance and patience –
And every day You fulfil my desire.
My Supreme, my Supreme, my Supreme!

MY MORNING SOUL-BODY PRAYERS

11 JULY 2000

1159

My Supreme, my Supreme, my Supreme!
God's unconditional Compassion-Eye
Is the only Source of my strength.
My Supreme, my Supreme, my Supreme!

SRI CHINMOY

13 JULY 2000

1160

My Supreme, my Supreme, my Supreme!
Today my heart is bursting
With my Lord's Compassion-Smiles.
My Supreme, my Supreme, my Supreme!

MY MORNING SOUL-BODY PRAYERS

14 JULY 2000

1161

My Supreme, my Supreme, my Supreme!
Every day my aspiration-heart
Travels to an ever-new horizon.
My Supreme, my Supreme, my Supreme!

1162

My Supreme, my Supreme, my Supreme!
My Lord's Compassion-Smiles
And my heart's gratitude-tears
Are always found together.
My Supreme, my Supreme, my Supreme!

16 JULY 2000

1163

My Supreme, my Supreme, my Supreme!
Only when I love You only
Do You show me how
We belong to each other eternally.
My Supreme, my Supreme, my Supreme!

1164

My Supreme, my Supreme, my Supreme!
The attachment-chain
Is extremely difficult to break,
But the aspiration-fire
Can burn it completely
And turn it to ashes.
My Supreme, my Supreme, my Supreme!

MY MORNING SOUL-BODY PRAYERS

17 JULY 2000

1165

My Supreme, my Supreme, my Supreme!
Please give me a little more time.
"My child, what have you been doing?
It is already so late!"
My Supreme, my Supreme, my Supreme!

1166

My Supreme, my Supreme, my Supreme!
My heart, you are my true friend.
Why?
Because you are the only one
Who is eagerly longing to please God
In His own Way.
My Supreme, my Supreme, my Supreme!

1167

My Supreme, my Supreme, my Supreme!
I really love all the games
That You play with me,
Except one game: indifference.
My Supreme, my Supreme, my Supreme!

SRI CHINMOY

18 JULY 2000

1168

My Supreme, my Supreme, my Supreme!
Finally, my mind's ignorance-night
Has completely surrendered
To my heart's wisdom-light.
My Supreme, my Supreme, my Supreme!

1169

My Supreme, my Supreme, my Supreme!
To a purity-heart,
Everything is the Beauty
Of God's Eye
And the Fragrance
Of God's Heart.
My Supreme, my Supreme, my Supreme!

MY MORNING SOUL-BODY PRAYERS

19 JULY 2000

1170

My Supreme, my Supreme, my Supreme!
A sleeplessly self-giving life
To God's Will
Takes the least possible time
To discover God.
My Supreme, my Supreme, my Supreme!

1171

My Supreme, my Supreme, my Supreme!
God cannot convince the human mind
Of anything.
Yet God loves the human mind.
My Supreme, my Supreme, my Supreme!

1172

My Supreme, my Supreme, my Supreme!
The mind does not believe
In the existence-reality
Of the peace-horizon.
My Supreme, my Supreme, my Supreme!

1173

My Supreme, my Supreme, my Supreme!
A new record means a new joy.
I am prayerfully offering
My heart's new joy to the world
To increase its inspiration
And aspiration
For the betterment of the world.
My Supreme, my Supreme, my Supreme!

21 JULY 2000

1174

My Supreme, my Supreme, my Supreme!
Today is my 800-pound bench press
Journey's start.
I am my gratitude-heart
And
I am my surrender-life.
My Supreme, my Supreme, my Supreme!

1175

My Supreme, my Supreme, my Supreme!
A desire-life can never be liberated
From the stumbling blocks
Of misfortune.
My Supreme, my Supreme, my Supreme!

1176

My Supreme, my Supreme, my Supreme!
I practise, I practise, I practise
Only to make myself perfect
And to make You proud of me.
My Supreme, my Supreme, my Supreme!

1177

My Supreme, my Supreme, my Supreme!
A life without heart-tears for God
Is no life.
My Supreme, my Supreme, my Supreme!

MY MORNING SOUL-BODY PRAYERS

22 JULY 2000

1178

My Supreme, my Supreme, my Supreme!
I do not strain every nerve
To please You.
I just surrender myself to You
Unconditionally all the time,
And You are fully satisfied with me
And mightily proud of me.
My Supreme, my Supreme, my Supreme!

1179

My Supreme, my Supreme, my Supreme!
My mind says to me,
"Can you not see that God has left you
For good?"
My heart says to me,
"Look, look! God is returning."
It also says to me
That it will keep God permanently
With its devotion-strength
And surrender-length.
My Supreme, my Supreme, my Supreme!

23 JULY 2000

1180

My Supreme, my Supreme, my Supreme!
I know, I know,
No matter how undivine
The human mind is,
It is not beyond the reach
Of Your Compassion-Eye
And Forgiveness-Heart.
My Supreme, my Supreme, my Supreme!

1181

My Supreme, my Supreme, my Supreme!
My conscious God-disobedience
Is my life's unpardonable crime.
My Supreme, my Supreme, my Supreme!

MY MORNING SOUL-BODY PRAYERS

24 JULY 2000

1182

My Supreme, my Supreme, my Supreme!
Sooner or later,
The mind's outer darkness surrenders
To the heart's inner dawn.
My Supreme, my Supreme, my Supreme!

1183

My Supreme, my Supreme, my Supreme!
May my aspiration-heart
And dedication-life please You
Every inch of the way
To Your celestial Palace.
My Supreme, my Supreme, my Supreme!

1184

My Supreme, my Supreme, my Supreme!
Every day I prayerfully and soulfully
Celebrate God's Will
With my gratitude-heart-tears
And smiles.
My Supreme, my Supreme, my Supreme!

25 JULY 2000

1185

My Supreme, my Supreme, my Supreme!
Every day
God happily and unconditionally
Gives me good advice.
To my great sorrow,
My mind does not allow me
To accept it.
My Supreme, my Supreme, my Supreme!

1186

My Supreme, my Supreme, my Supreme!
My Lord tells me,
If I really want to please Him
In His own Way,
Then I must do it as quickly as possible.
Otherwise, it will be of no avail.
My Supreme, my Supreme, my Supreme!

MY MORNING SOUL-BODY PRAYERS

26 JULY 2000

1187

My Supreme, my Supreme, my Supreme!
Every heart is Your precious
Treasure-home.
My Supreme, my Supreme, my Supreme!

1188

My Supreme, my Supreme, my Supreme!
To please God on the largest scale,
My ceaselessly surrendered life
Is of paramount importance.
My Supreme, my Supreme, my Supreme!

1189

My Supreme, my Supreme, my Supreme!
My heart implores and imports
God's free and unconditional
Blessing-Light
From the highest Heaven.
My Supreme, my Supreme, my Supreme!

27 JULY 2000

1190

My Supreme, my Supreme, my Supreme!
Even Eternity's life is too short
To manifest Your infinite Light
Here on earth.
My Supreme, my Supreme, my Supreme!

1191

My Supreme, my Supreme, my Supreme!
God loves my love
Only when it is not tainted
By the selfishness
Of my impure mind.
My Supreme, my Supreme, my Supreme!

MY MORNING SOUL-BODY PRAYERS

28 JULY 2000

1192

My Supreme, my Supreme, my Supreme!
May my heart-speed every day increase
To reach the Feet
Of my Lord Beloved Supreme.
My Supreme, my Supreme, my Supreme!

SRI CHINMOY

28 JULY 2000

1193

My Supreme, my Supreme, my Supreme!
God proudly comes to visit
My heart-garden
Only when it is full
Of sweet fragrance.
My Supreme, my Supreme, my Supreme!

1194

My Supreme, my Supreme, my Supreme!
O humanity,
Revive your lost faith!
God wants you to be
His dearest and choicest instrument
To manifest Him fully
Here on earth.
My Supreme, my Supreme, my Supreme!

MY MORNING SOUL-BODY PRAYERS

31 JULY 2000

1195

My Supreme, my Supreme, my Supreme!
My deliberate confinement
To my mind-jungle
Is shocking and disgraceful
To say the least!
My Supreme, my Supreme, my Supreme!

1196

My Supreme, my Supreme, my Supreme!
May I proclaim Your supreme Victory
In my soul, heart, mind, vital and body
Every day, every hour, every minute
And every second.
My Supreme, my Supreme, my Supreme!

1197

My Supreme, my Supreme, my Supreme!
Never, never, never shall I break
My God-manifestation-vow
Here on earth.
My Supreme, my Supreme, my Supreme!

5 AUGUST 2000

1198

My Supreme, my Supreme, my Supreme!
May my heart be a soaring
God-fulfilment-dream-reality.
My Supreme, my Supreme, my Supreme!

1199

My Supreme, my Supreme, my Supreme!
May the waves
Of my God-devotion-tears
Break open my heart-doors.
My Supreme, my Supreme, my Supreme!

MY MORNING SOUL-BODY PRAYERS

6 AUGUST 2000

1200

My Supreme, my Supreme, my Supreme!
Impossibility is in man's dictionary.
Grace is in God's Dictionary.
Impossibility must surrender
To God's Grace unconditional.
My Supreme, my Supreme, my Supreme!

7 AUGUST 2000

1201

My Supreme, my Supreme, my Supreme!
My life's most valuable possession
Is my God-gratitude-heart.
My Supreme, my Supreme, my Supreme!

1202

My Supreme, my Supreme, my Supreme!
Your infinite Compassion has enabled
My aspiration-heart and dedication-life
To be in excellent condition.
My Supreme, my Supreme, my Supreme!

MY MORNING SOUL-BODY PRAYERS

8 AUGUST 2000

1203

My Supreme, my Supreme, my Supreme!
Today my aspiration-breath
Has returned.
The moment I saw You
Blessingfully smiling at me,
My long-lost aspiration-heart-breath
Came back to me.
My Supreme, my Supreme, my Supreme!

1204

My Supreme, my Supreme, my Supreme!
You are always eager to play
In my child-heart-garden.
My Supreme, my Supreme, my Supreme!

SRI CHINMOY

9 AUGUST 2000

1205

My Supreme, my Supreme, my Supreme!
True, I am not in close touch
With God's Omniscience
And God's Omnipresence,
But I am definitely in close touch
With God's Forgiveness-Heart
And God's Compassion-Eye.
Therefore, I am mightily happy.
My Supreme, my Supreme, my Supreme!

1206

My Supreme, my Supreme, my Supreme!
Pleasing God requires no austerity.
Pleasing God requires only simplicity,
Sincerity, purity and integrity.
My Supreme, my Supreme, my Supreme!

1207

My Supreme, my Supreme, my Supreme!
O my mind, do not wait
Until it is too late
For you to accept God's Will
As your own.
My Supreme, my Supreme, my Supreme!

MY MORNING SOUL-BODY PRAYERS

10 AUGUST 2000

1208

My Supreme, my Supreme, my Supreme!
Every day I must avail myself
Of all God-manifestation-opportunities.
My Supreme, my Supreme, my Supreme!

1209

My Supreme, my Supreme, my Supreme!
Every morning,
Out of His infinite Bounty,
God's Compassion-Eye from Heaven
Imports my gratitude-heart-tears.
My Supreme, my Supreme, my Supreme!

1210

My Supreme, my Supreme, my Supreme!
With all my heart-tears
I am praying to You
Never to relax
Your Forgiveness, Compassion
And Concern-Grips on my life.
My Supreme, my Supreme, my Supreme!

12 AUGUST 2000

1211

My Supreme, my Supreme, my Supreme!
May my life-tree grow
In the faith-garden
Of my heart.
My Supreme, my Supreme, my Supreme!

1212

My Supreme, my Supreme, my Supreme!
Alas, my life's time-river
Is flowing by,
And I have accomplished nothing special
To please God
In His full manifestation on earth.
My Supreme, my Supreme, my Supreme!

1213

My Supreme, my Supreme, my Supreme!
Infinite is my joy
When I happily and self-givingly
Row my God-obedience-boat.
My Supreme, my Supreme, my Supreme!

MY MORNING SOUL-BODY PRAYERS

13 AUGUST 2000

1214

My Supreme, my Supreme, my Supreme!
God is the Supreme Doer.
He wants me to be
Mankind's aspiration-collector.
My Supreme, my Supreme, my Supreme!

SRI CHINMOY

14 AUGUST 2000

1215

My Supreme, my Supreme, my Supreme!
May my heart-garden be the smile
Of all oneness-peace-nations.
My Supreme, my Supreme, my Supreme!

1216

My Supreme, my Supreme, my Supreme!
When I am in my heart-garden,
You smile and smile and smile.
When I am in my mind-jungle,
You sigh and sigh and sigh.
My Supreme, my Supreme, my Supreme!

MY MORNING SOUL-BODY PRAYERS

15 AUGUST 2000

1217

My Supreme, my Supreme, my Supreme!
May my heart be a sleepless
And breathless
God-manifestation-rain
On earth.
My Supreme, my Supreme, my Supreme!

1218

My Supreme, my Supreme, my Supreme!
Please, please bless me
With the capacity to place
Every day
My devotion-heart-blossoms
At Your Feet.
My Supreme, my Supreme, my Supreme!

16 AUGUST 2000

1219

My Supreme, my Supreme, my Supreme!
I admire the head of science,
But I love the heart of spirituality
And I want to be inseparably one
With the heart of spirituality
Before long.
My Supreme, my Supreme, my Supreme!

1220

My Supreme, my Supreme, my Supreme!
God speaks,
And then He smilingly, lovingly,
Compassionately and self-givingly
Touches humanity's heart.
But humanity is not convinced
And does not want to be convinced.
My Supreme, my Supreme, my Supreme!

MY MORNING SOUL-BODY PRAYERS

17 AUGUST 2000

1221

My Supreme, my Supreme, my Supreme!
Alas, for untold ages
God has been waiting
For humanity to respond
To His Compassion-flooded Eye.
My Supreme, my Supreme, my Supreme!

1222

My Supreme, my Supreme, my Supreme!
Out of Your infinite Bounty,
You are telling me
That although Your Heights
Are unimaginably high,
They are quite accessible.
My Supreme, my Supreme, my Supreme!

SRI CHINMOY

19 AUGUST 2000

1223

My Supreme, my Supreme, my Supreme!
I must fulfil You in every way
As quickly and as perfectly
As You hope.
My Supreme, my Supreme, my Supreme!

1224

My Supreme, my Supreme, my Supreme!
On the nineteenth of February
I started practising 1,300 pounds.
Today I complete five long months.
Alas, satisfaction is still a far cry.
My Supreme,
My heart is all gratitude to You
For You have inundated me
With Your Compassion-Patience-Light.
My Supreme, my Supreme, my Supreme!

MY MORNING SOUL-BODY PRAYERS

21 AUGUST 2000

1225

My Supreme, my Supreme, my Supreme!
My God-gratitude-flames
Grow beautifully, soulfully
And powerfully
Only in my peace-heart-garden.
My Supreme, my Supreme, my Supreme!

1226

My Supreme, my Supreme, my Supreme!
I really love my soul's requests,
But I love my soul's commands
Infinitely more.
My Supreme, my Supreme, my Supreme!

22 AUGUST 2000

1227

My Supreme, my Supreme, my Supreme!
Our God-manifestation-fulfilment-
Opportunities
Are very, very vast in number.
My Supreme, my Supreme, my Supreme!

1228

My Supreme, my Supreme, my Supreme!
When God is extremely tired,
He rests on my unconditional life's
Surrender-pillow.
My Supreme, my Supreme, my Supreme!

1229

My Supreme, my Supreme, my Supreme!
It is only my gratitude-heart
That enables me to clasp Your Feet
And embrace Your Heart.
My Supreme, my Supreme, my Supreme!

MY MORNING SOUL-BODY PRAYERS

23 AUGUST 2000

1230

My Supreme, my Supreme, my Supreme!
May my heart-garden be always full
Of God-gratitude-rose-blossoms.
My Supreme, my Supreme, my Supreme!

1231

My Supreme, my Supreme, my Supreme!
O seekers, have more faith in God
And in yourselves.
When your consciousness is low,
He will definitely lift you up,
Wipe your tears
And give you strength
To smile once again.
My Supreme, my Supreme, my Supreme!

SRI CHINMOY

24 AUGUST 2000

1232

My Supreme, my Supreme, my Supreme!
God is God's Compassion-Eye
And
I am my gratitude-heart.
My Supreme, my Supreme, my Supreme!

1233

My Supreme, my Supreme, my Supreme!
My life is Your Compassion.
My heart is Your Compassion.
My breath is Your Compassion.
I lived, I live and I shall forever live
On Your Compassion-Love,
Compassion-Concern,
Compassion-Forgiveness
And Compassion-Fulfilment.
My Supreme, my Supreme, my Supreme!

MY MORNING SOUL-BODY PRAYERS

25 AUGUST 2000

1234

My Supreme, my Supreme, my Supreme!
O mind, discard immediately
All your God-disobeying
And God-displeasing thoughts.
My Supreme, my Supreme, my Supreme!

1235

My Supreme, my Supreme, my Supreme!
O mind, are you not ashamed
Of your absurd God-existence-doubts?
My Supreme, my Supreme, my Supreme!

1236

My Supreme, my Supreme, my Supreme!
O mind, you deliberately indulge
In doubts, suspicions, jealousies,
Supremacies and insecurities.
To me, you are worse than useless!
My Supreme, my Supreme, my Supreme!

31 AUGUST 2000

1237

My Supreme, my Supreme, my Supreme!
May my heart-garden be always full
Of God-surrender-blossoms.
My Supreme, my Supreme, my Supreme!

1238

My Supreme, my Supreme, my Supreme!
God's Clarion Call is only
For a sleepless God-gratitude-heart.
My Supreme, my Supreme, my Supreme!

1239

My Supreme, my Supreme, my Supreme!
I do not want an exciting mind.
I want an aspiring heart
And a serving life.
My Supreme, my Supreme, my Supreme!

MY MORNING SOUL-BODY PRAYERS

1 SEPTEMBER 2000

1240

My Supreme, my Supreme, my Supreme!
May I be a heart-cry in my inner life
For You
And may I be a life-smile in my outer life
For You.
My Supreme, my Supreme, my Supreme!

3 SEPTEMBER 2000

1241

My Supreme, my Supreme, my Supreme!
A real God-seeker's life
Is
A God-manifestation-fulfilment-promise.
My Supreme, my Supreme, my Supreme!

1242

My Supreme, my Supreme, my Supreme!
Only inside a self-giving heart
Is the home of peace.
My Supreme, my Supreme, my Supreme!

1243

My Supreme, my Supreme, my Supreme!
Only when I sincerely
Love and serve the world
Do You allow my life to blossom
In Your own Heart-Garden.
My Supreme, my Supreme, my Supreme!

MY MORNING SOUL-BODY PRAYERS

4 SEPTEMBER 2000

1244

My Supreme, my Supreme, my Supreme!
May my life, my heart
And my breath
Be made of my God-gratitude-tears.
My Supreme, my Supreme, my Supreme!

5 SEPTEMBER 2000

1245

My Supreme, my Supreme, my Supreme!
When my mind prays to You
And when my mind thinks of You
Most sincerely,
It sees ignorance-darkness-night-abyss
Nowhere.
My Supreme, my Supreme, my Supreme!

1246

My Supreme, my Supreme, my Supreme!
I am so fortunate that every day
Your Compassion-Eye-Flame-Waves
Feed my heart unconditionally.
My Supreme, my Supreme, my Supreme!

1247

My Supreme, my Supreme, my Supreme!
My cheerfulness pleases You.
My soulfulness pleases You
Abundantly more.
My selflessness pleases You
Infinitely more.
My Supreme, my Supreme, my Supreme!

MY MORNING SOUL-BODY PRAYERS

8 SEPTEMBER 2000

1248

My Supreme, my Supreme, my Supreme!
Every day God enjoys watching
His Compassion-Eye
And my aspiration-heart
Playing together.
My Supreme, my Supreme, my Supreme!

1249

My Supreme, my Supreme, my Supreme!
My prayer-life teaches me
How to realise God.
My meditation-heart teaches me
How to manifest God
On earth.
My Supreme, my Supreme, my Supreme!

1250

My weightlifting is my prayer-life
To inspire my sisters and brothers
Of the entire world.

1251

My Supreme, my Supreme, my Supreme!
When I soulfully pray,
I see myself seated
Inside God's Dream-Boat
And God Himself is piloting the Boat.
When I sleeplessly meditate,
I see myself singing and smiling
At God's Reality-Shore.
My Supreme, my Supreme, my Supreme!

1252

My Supreme, my Supreme, my Supreme!
May my heart always live
In the rainbow-beauty
Of glowing hopes.
My Supreme, my Supreme, my Supreme!

1253

My Supreme, my Supreme, my Supreme!
May my life always live
In the mountain-height
Of lightning-promises.
My Supreme, my Supreme, my Supreme!

MY MORNING SOUL-BODY PRAYERS

9 SEPTEMBER 2000

1254

My Supreme, my Supreme, my Supreme!
O seeker,
Your God-Compassion-doubt
Is
Your spirituality's immediate death.
My Supreme, my Supreme, my Supreme!

1255

My Supreme, my Supreme, my Supreme!
The Smiles of Your Compassion-Eye
Have liberated me from my mind's
Bondage-ignorance-night-abyss.
My Supreme, my Supreme, my Supreme!

1256

My Supreme, my Supreme, my Supreme!
I must conquer my mind's frustrations.
I must conquer my heart's depressions.
I must conquer my life's failures.
My Supreme, my Supreme, my Supreme!

10 SEPTEMBER 2000

1257

My Supreme, my Supreme, my Supreme!
I do not want You to be on my side.
I want my very existence on earth
To be always on Your side.
My Supreme, my Supreme, my Supreme!

1258

My Supreme, my Supreme, my Supreme!
May each morning be for me
A golden God-yearning, God-loving,
God-serving and God-manifesting
Opportunity.
My Supreme, my Supreme, my Supreme!

1259

My Supreme, my Supreme, my Supreme!
How far my mind is away from God,
God alone knows.
But how far my heart is away from God,
Not only God knows but I also know.
The distance is most astonishingly
Negligible.
My Supreme, my Supreme, my Supreme!

MY MORNING SOUL-BODY PRAYERS

12 SEPTEMBER 2000

1260

My Supreme, my Supreme, my Supreme!
When the human in me ascends,
You smile and smile and smile.
When the divine in me descends,
You cry and cry and cry.
My Supreme, my Supreme, my Supreme!

1261

My Supreme, my Supreme, my Supreme!
Will it ever happen
That I shall think of You
Before You think of me?
Will it ever happen
That I shall love You
Before You love me?

"My child, I shall help you.
When you succeed,
I shall be infinitely happier
Than you can ever imagine."
My Supreme, my Supreme, my Supreme!

13 SEPTEMBER 2000

1262

My Supreme, my Supreme, my Supreme!
My sleepless and breathless
God-gratitude-tears
Are infinitely sweeter and purer
Than anything else.
My Supreme, my Supreme, my Supreme!

1263

My Supreme, my Supreme, my Supreme!
My mind, there is only one way
To have happiness,
And that way is to surrender
To God's Will
All the time.
My Supreme, my Supreme, my Supreme!

MY MORNING SOUL-BODY PRAYERS

14 SEPTEMBER 2000

1264

My Supreme, my Supreme, my Supreme!
God will never allow a true seeker
To escape His Will.
My Supreme, my Supreme, my Supreme!

1265

My Supreme, my Supreme, my Supreme!
My mind,
Not thick attachment-fog,
But blue detachment-sky!
My Supreme, my Supreme, my Supreme!

1266

My Supreme, my Supreme, my Supreme!
The divine beauty of life
Depends on the purity of the mind.
My Supreme, my Supreme, my Supreme!

SRI CHINMOY

15 SEPTEMBER 2000

1267

My Supreme, my Supreme, my Supreme!
May my mind be silenced
By my soul's ecstasy-breath.
My Supreme, my Supreme, my Supreme!

1268

My Supreme, my Supreme, my Supreme!
May my life be liberated
By my soul's ecstasy-embrace.
My Supreme, my Supreme, my Supreme!

MY MORNING SOUL-BODY PRAYERS

16 SEPTEMBER 2000

1269

My Supreme, my Supreme, my Supreme!
I must aspire first,
Before I love God.
I must love God first,
Before I serve God.
I must serve God first,
Before I manifest God.
This is the only way
I can please God in His own Way.
My Supreme, my Supreme, my Supreme!

1270

My Supreme, my Supreme, my Supreme!
God's Compassion-Eye
Thrills my heart.
God's Forgiveness-Feet
Thrill my heart abundantly more.
The Nectar-dust of God's Feet
Thrills my heart infinitely more.
My Supreme, my Supreme, my Supreme!

20 SEPTEMBER 2000

1271

My Supreme, my Supreme, my Supreme!
Whenever I do anything unconditionally
For You,
I take You by surprise.
My Supreme, my Supreme, my Supreme!

1272

My Supreme, my Supreme, my Supreme!
God tells me never to underestimate
The power of surrender.
My Supreme, my Supreme, my Supreme!

1273

My Supreme, my Supreme, my Supreme!
God's Silence-Smile
Is always eager to teach me.
My Supreme, my Supreme, my Supreme!

MY MORNING SOUL-BODY PRAYERS

21 SEPTEMBER 2000

1274

My Supreme, my Supreme, my Supreme!
When I help the soul,
I reach a new goal.
My Supreme, my Supreme, my Supreme!

1275

My Supreme, my Supreme, my Supreme!
A confusion-mind destroys
A golden dream of humankind.
My Supreme, my Supreme, my Supreme!

SRI CHINMOY

22 SEPTEMBER 2000

1276

My Supreme, my Supreme, my Supreme!
Your Compassion-Eye awakens me.
Your Forgiveness-Heart feeds me.
Your Protection-Feet illumine me
And my all.
My Supreme, my Supreme, my Supreme!

1277

My Supreme, my Supreme, my Supreme!
My God-aspiration has no finish line.
My God-realisation has no finish line.
My God-revelation has no finish line.
My God-manifestation has no finish line.
My Supreme,
You have given me the Message
Of sleepless and breathless
Self-transcendence.
My Supreme, my Supreme, my Supreme!

MY MORNING SOUL-BODY PRAYERS

25 SEPTEMBER 2000

1278

My Supreme, my Supreme, my Supreme!
Every day I need an indomitable will
To succeed in my outer life
And to proceed in my inner life.
My Supreme, my Supreme, my Supreme!

1279

My Supreme, my Supreme, my Supreme!
May my heart and my life,
Like my soul-bird,
Fly in Infinity's Sky,
Singing the Victory-Songs
Of my Lord Absolute Beloved Supreme.
My Supreme, my Supreme, my Supreme!

SRI CHINMOY

26 SEPTEMBER 2000

1280

My Supreme, my Supreme, my Supreme!
May my life be a constant
Inspiration-service to humanity.
My Supreme, my Supreme, my Supreme!

MY MORNING SOUL-BODY PRAYERS

28 SEPTEMBER 2000

1281

My Supreme, my Supreme, my Supreme!
May I have a new name: Grace,
And this name will be all Yours.
My Supreme, my Supreme, my Supreme!

1282

My Supreme, my Supreme, my Supreme!
Your Grace, Your Grace, Your Grace!
An iota of Your Grace
Can make my heart beautiful
And my life fruitful.
My Supreme, my Supreme, my Supreme!

1283

My Supreme, my Supreme, my Supreme!
Your unconditional Grace
Is my heart's only hope for goodness
And my life's only promise for greatness.
My Supreme, my Supreme, my Supreme!

29 SEPTEMBER 2000

1284

My Supreme, my Supreme, my Supreme!
In the worlds of God-realisation
And God-manifestation,
Time never runs out.
My Supreme, my Supreme, my Supreme!

1285

My Supreme, my Supreme, my Supreme!
It is an extremely difficult task
For the mind to learn even one
God-surrender-song.
My Supreme, my Supreme, my Supreme!

MY MORNING SOUL-BODY PRAYERS

30 SEPTEMBER 2000

1286

My Supreme, my Supreme, my Supreme!
Your Compassion is boundless.
Your Forgiveness is boundless.
Alas, yet I fail to love You
Wholeheartedly.
My Supreme, my Supreme, my Supreme!

1287

My Supreme, my Supreme, my Supreme!
Your Compassion-Eye
Awakens my heart.
Your Forgiveness-Heart
Fulfils my life.
My Supreme, my Supreme, my Supreme!

1 OCTOBER 2000

1288

My Supreme, my Supreme, my Supreme!
Since everything has an end,
I am sure my desire-life
Also will come to an end.
My Supreme, my Supreme, my Supreme!

1289

My Supreme, my Supreme, my Supreme!
My mind says: punishment.
My heart says: enlightenment.
My Supreme, my Supreme, my Supreme!

MY MORNING SOUL-BODY PRAYERS

2 OCTOBER 2000

1290

My Supreme, my Supreme, my Supreme!
My mind says to me:
God is only for Sunday worship.
My heart says to me:
God is not only for everyday worship,
But also for every hour, every minute
And every second worship.
My Supreme, my Supreme, my Supreme!

1291

My Supreme, my Supreme, my Supreme!
God wants my heart
To be His own Beauty's angel.
My Supreme, my Supreme, my Supreme!

SRI CHINMOY

3 OCTOBER 2000

1292

My Supreme, my Supreme, my Supreme!
May my Lord Beloved Absolute Supreme
Always find me willing, eager
And self-giving.
My Supreme, my Supreme, my Supreme!

MY MORNING SOUL-BODY PRAYERS

3 OCTOBER 2000

1293

My Supreme, my Supreme, my Supreme!
Your Compassion and Concern
Have travelled far and long
To meet with an unconditionally
Surrendered seeker.
My Supreme, my Supreme, my Supreme!

4 OCTOBER 2000

1294

My Supreme, my Supreme, my Supreme!
My desire-mind leads me
To greatness-might.
My aspiration-heart leads me
To goodness-delight.
My Supreme, my Supreme, my Supreme!

1295

My Supreme, my Supreme, my Supreme!
Two things I really love:
My heart's aspiration-height
And
My life's dedication-delight.
My Supreme, my Supreme, my Supreme!

MY MORNING SOUL-BODY PRAYERS

5 OCTOBER 2000

1296

My Supreme, my Supreme, my Supreme!
You are telling me that
My prayers to You
Shall save my life
And my meditations on You
Shall fulfil my heart.
My Supreme, my Supreme, my Supreme!

1297

My Supreme, my Supreme, my Supreme!
The human in me enjoys
Resting and sleeping.
The divine in me enjoys
Serving and manifesting.
My Supreme, my Supreme, my Supreme!

1298

My Supreme, my Supreme, my Supreme!
Alas, my ego-mind cannot appreciate
My Lord's Compassion-flooded Presence.
My Supreme, my Supreme, my Supreme!

7 OCTOBER 2000

1299

My Supreme, my Supreme, my Supreme!
You are telling me
That the devotion-tears
Of my gratitude-heart
Are extremely precious to You.
My Supreme, my Supreme, my Supreme!

1300

My Supreme, my Supreme, my Supreme!
The beauty of my life
Lies in the God-worshipping tears
Of my heart.
My Supreme, my Supreme, my Supreme!

MY MORNING SOUL-BODY PRAYERS

9 OCTOBER 2000

1301

My Supreme, my Supreme, my Supreme!
With God-loving tears
I came into the world.
With God-serving smiles
I shall depart.
My Supreme, my Supreme, my Supreme!

1302

My Supreme, my Supreme, my Supreme!
A selfless action is immediately followed
By a sweet satisfaction.
My Supreme, my Supreme, my Supreme!

1303

My Supreme, my Supreme, my Supreme!
A heart of depth
Is a life of height, light
And delight.
My Supreme, my Supreme, my Supreme!

14 OCTOBER 2000

1304

My Supreme, my Supreme, my Supreme!
Alas, I have two serious problems:
My mind is dry;
My heart cannot cry.
My Supreme, my Supreme, my Supreme!

1305. MP1305

My Supreme, my Supreme, my Supreme!
Faith, more faith.
That means
Joy, more joy.
My Supreme, my Supreme, my Supreme!

1306

My physical weightlifting-journey ends,
But my spiritual God-crying-journey
Shall never end.

MY MORNING SOUL-BODY PRAYERS

12 DECEMBER 2004

1307

My Supreme, my Supreme!
The God of Silence
Is blooming now
Inside my heart.
My Supreme, my Supreme!

1308

My Supreme, my Supreme!
The God of Silence
Has fully blossomed now
Inside my heart.
My Supreme, my Supreme!

13 DECEMBER 2004

1309

My Supreme, my Supreme!
What do I need?
I need a sleeplessly
God-crying heart.
My Supreme, my Supreme!

1310

My Supreme, my Supreme!
In the small hours of the morning
I take the surrender-express train
To arrive at my Destination.
My Supreme, my Supreme!

MY MORNING SOUL-BODY PRAYERS

15 DECEMBER 2004

1311

My Supreme, my Supreme!
I have locked my aspiration-eyes
On Your Compassion-Eyes.
My Supreme, my Supreme!

1312

My Supreme, my Supreme!
You have already accepted my heart.
Please, please now accept me
And my all.
My Supreme, my Supreme!

16 DECEMBER 2004

1313

My Supreme, my Supreme!
You are telling me
That my unconditional, sleepless
And breathless love for You
Is the beauty of my heart.
My Supreme, my Supreme!

1314

My Supreme, my Supreme!
You are telling me
That my unconditional, sleepless
And breathless surrender
To Your Will
Is the fragrance of my soul.
My Supreme, my Supreme!

MY MORNING SOUL-BODY PRAYERS

16 DECEMBER 2004

1315

My Supreme, my Supreme!
I need only one thing from You:
Your Compassion-Breath
At every moment of my life.
My Supreme, my Supreme!

1316

My Supreme, my Supreme!
You are telling me,
"My child, how is it that
My Friendship is not enough for you?
Why do you need human friendship?"
My Supreme, my Supreme!

18 DECEMBER 2004

1317

My Supreme, my Supreme!
To approach You with devotion
Is to swim in Your Ecstasy-Sea.
My Supreme, my Supreme!

1318

My Supreme, my Supreme!
You are telling me that
You brought me into the world
Only to act for You –
Inwardly, outwardly,
Consciously and self-givingly.
My Supreme, my Supreme!

MY MORNING SOUL-BODY PRAYERS

20 DECEMBER 2004

1319

My Supreme, my Supreme!
O seeker, the sunlit path
Is right in front of you.
Delay not, delay not!
My Supreme, my Supreme!

1320

My Supreme, my Supreme!
Silence, silence, silence!
Silence is God's most sacred Name.
Silence, silence, silence!
My Supreme, my Supreme!

22 DECEMBER 2004

1321

My Supreme, my Supreme!
Each seeker receives
A special dream from You:
How to realise You.
My Supreme, my Supreme!

1322

My Supreme, my Supreme!
The outer strength attacks the enemy.
The inner strength,
Which is infinitely stronger
Than the outer strength, suffers.
The inner strength has no enemy.
The inner strength is all love –
Love for God the Father,
Love for God the Mother,
Love for God the Creator,
Love for God the creation.
My Supreme, my Supreme!

MY MORNING SOUL-BODY PRAYERS

23 DECEMBER 2004

1323

My Supreme, my Supreme!
I pray to You to keep me
As a Compassion-beggar of Yours
Forever and forever.
My Supreme, You are telling me,
"My child, if you are not going to be
My Victory-fighter,
My Victory-proclaimer
And My Mission-on-earth-fulfiller,
Then who will be,
Who will be, My child?"
My Supreme, my Supreme!

1324

My Supreme, my Supreme!
My Supreme,
I have a most sincere question.
I shall be so grateful to You
If You answer my question.
"What is your question, My child?"
My Supreme, how long do I have to stay
In this weightlifting world?
"My child, I answer only
Your sensible questions!"
My Supreme, my Supreme!

25 DECEMBER 2004

1325

My Supreme, my Supreme!
You have given my soul the capacity
To thrive on inner challenges.
You have given my eyes the capacity
To thrive on outer challenges.
My Supreme, my Supreme!

1326

My Supreme, my Supreme!
You want me to catch,
You want me to hold
And You want me to keep
The bird of silence.
My Supreme, my Supreme!

MY MORNING SOUL-BODY PRAYERS

26 DECEMBER 2004

1327

My Supreme, my Supreme!
I pray to the God
Known and knowable.
I meditate on the God
Unknown and unknowable.
My Supreme, my Supreme!

1328

My Supreme, my Supreme!
My occult power says:
"I can and I do."
My spiritual power says:
"You only have and you only are."
My Supreme, my Supreme!

27 DECEMBER 2004

1329

My Supreme, my Supreme!
O my mind, rest assured,
You will never die of overwork!
My Supreme, my Supreme!

1330

My Supreme, my Supreme!
You do not count
How many years I have in my life,
But You do count
How many lives I have in my years.
My Supreme, my Supreme!

MY MORNING SOUL-BODY PRAYERS

28 DECEMBER 2004

1331

My Supreme, my Supreme!
I love God-newness.
My heart loves God-oneness.
My life loves God-fulness.
My Supreme, my Supreme!

1332

My Supreme, my Supreme!
Self-giving is absolutely necessary
To establish a close and personal
Connection with God.
My Supreme, my Supreme!

29 DECEMBER 2004

1333

My Supreme, my Supreme!
Please give me the capacity
To fix my prayerful eyes
On Your Golden Feet
All the time.
My Supreme, my Supreme!

1334

My Supreme, my Supreme!
You are telling me that
The depth of Your Forgiveness
And the height of my happiness
Are inseparable.
My Supreme, my Supreme!

MY MORNING SOUL-BODY PRAYERS

31 DECEMBER 2004

1335

My Supreme, my Supreme!
A oneness-heart
Is
A rainbow God-manifested dream.
My Supreme, my Supreme!

1336

My Supreme, my Supreme!
I am determined to emigrate
To the heart-gratitude-country
And settle there.
My Supreme, my Supreme!

SRI CHINMOY

1 JANUARY 2005

1337

My Supreme, my Supreme!
The New Year
Is the year of the
Mind-Astonishment,
Heart-Government
And
Life-Fulfilment.
My Supreme, my Supreme!

1338

My Supreme, my Supreme!
The message of self-transcendence
My soul receives from You every day,
My heart receives from my soul every day
And I receive from my heart every day.
My Supreme, my Supreme!

MY MORNING SOUL-BODY PRAYERS

2 JANUARY 2005

1339

My Supreme, my Supreme!
No length of time,
No strength of time,
Will ever dare to separate
My heart from Your Heart.
My Supreme, my Supreme!

1340

My Supreme, my Supreme!
My hope is my Lord's
Heaven-climber.
My promise is my Lord's
Earth-supporter.
My Supreme, my Supreme!

3 JANUARY 2005

1341

My Supreme, my Supreme!
I have travelled far and wide
And yet I have not seen
A seeker of soul-beauty.
My Supreme, my Supreme!

1342

My Supreme, my Supreme!
Angels from Heaven come down
To see my God-gratitude-heart-tears.
My Supreme, my Supreme!

MY MORNING SOUL-BODY PRAYERS

4 JANUARY 2005

1343

My Supreme, my Supreme!
You want my aspiration-heart
To be the richness
Of Your inner Life.
My Supreme, my Supreme!

1344

My Supreme, my Supreme!
My eagerness-heart
Knows only one thing:
The full manifestation
Of Your Light here on earth.
My Supreme, my Supreme!

6 JANUARY 2005

1345

My Supreme, my Supreme!
My hope ascends to Heaven
To enjoy Your Beauty.
My Supreme, my Supreme!

1346

My Supreme, my Supreme!
My promise descends to earth
To perform
My God-manifestation-duty.
My Supreme, my Supreme!

MY MORNING SOUL-BODY PRAYERS

7 JANUARY 2005

1347

My Supreme, my Supreme!
Every morning
A new divinity-sun rises
In my aspiration-heart-sky.
My Supreme, my Supreme!

1348

My Supreme, my Supreme!
My soul and my heart
Have already become members
Of Your Inner Circle.
Like them, I, too, wish to become
A member of Your Inner Circle.
My Supreme, my Supreme!

SRI CHINMOY

8 JANUARY 2005

1349

My Supreme, my Supreme!
A self-giving life
Is a very fast approach
To God.
My Supreme, my Supreme!

1350

My Supreme, my Supreme!
My God-obedience
And my God-ecstasy
Are next-door neighbours.
My Supreme, my Supreme!

MY MORNING SOUL-BODY PRAYERS

9 JANUARY 2005

1351

My Supreme, my Supreme!
The outer success dies in the dust,
But not the inner progress.
The inner progress is immortal.
My Supreme, my Supreme!

1352

My Supreme, my Supreme!
I walk and jog and run
Only on Your inner track.
My Supreme, my Supreme!

10 JANUARY 2005

1353

My Supreme, my Supreme!
Wherever I look, I see only
Your ever-blossoming Compassion-Eye.
My Supreme, my Supreme!

1354

My Supreme, my Supreme!
Loneliness cannot attack
A true God-lover.
My Supreme, my Supreme!

MY MORNING SOUL-BODY PRAYERS

14 JANUARY 2005

1355

My Supreme, my Supreme!
Our indulgence-imperfections
Prevent us from arriving
At Your Heart-Door.
My Supreme, my Supreme!

1356

My Supreme, my Supreme!
The power of silence
Conquers all —
No exception, no exception!
My Supreme, my Supreme!

15 JANUARY 2005

1357

My Supreme, my Supreme!
My aspiration-heart
Is
Your ever-blossoming Victory-Song.
My Supreme, my Supreme!

1358

My Supreme, my Supreme!
I know, I know
That ignorance-night
Is bound to betray us,
Sooner or later.
My Supreme, my Supreme!

MY MORNING SOUL-BODY PRAYERS

16 JANUARY 2005

1359

My Supreme, my Supreme!
No self-doubt-extinction,
No real God-realisation.
My Supreme, my Supreme!

1360

My Supreme, my Supreme!
A sweetness-fragrance –
This is what precisely
A God-seeker's heart is.
My Supreme, my Supreme!

SRI CHINMOY

17 JANUARY 2005

1361

My Supreme, my Supreme!
Your visible Nearness-Presence
I love and I love,
My Supreme, my Supreme.
Your invisible Nearness-Presence
I worship and I worship.
My Supreme, my Supreme!

1362

My Supreme, my Supreme!
Silence,
You are the only friend
That I need and treasure.
My Supreme, my Supreme!

MY MORNING SOUL-BODY PRAYERS

19 JANUARY 2005

1363

My Supreme, my Supreme!
Today my heart is extremely happy
Because my mind has finally surrendered
All its freedom
To our Beloved Lord Supreme.
My Supreme, my Supreme!

1364

My Supreme, my Supreme!
Today my soul, my heart, my mind,
My vital and my body
Are exceedingly happy
Precisely because our prayer has won
The highest flying race
And our meditation has won
The deepest diving race.
My Supreme, my Supreme!

SRI CHINMOY

25 JANUARY 2005

1365

My Supreme, my Supreme!
You want me to be
A most reliable representative
Of both Heaven and earth.
My Supreme, my Supreme!

1366

My Supreme, my Supreme!
Every morning God sounds
My receptivity-depths.
My Supreme, my Supreme!

MY MORNING SOUL-BODY PRAYERS

26 JANUARY 2005

1367

My Supreme, my Supreme!
You are telling me that
My world-indifference-desire
Is the height of my stupidity.
My Supreme, my Supreme!

1368

My Supreme, my Supreme!
My soul is a member
Of the Heaven-fragrance-society.
My heart is a member
Of the earth-beauty-society.
And I am a member
Of God's Will-fulfilment-society.
My Supreme, my Supreme!

28 JANUARY 2005

1369

My Supreme, my Supreme!
The joy of my aspiration-heart
Is unimaginable.
My Supreme, my Supreme!

1370

My Supreme, my Supreme!
I must try to inspire
The whole world
With the silence
Of my meditation.
My Supreme, my Supreme!

MY MORNING SOUL-BODY PRAYERS

31 JANUARY 2005

1371

My Supreme, my Supreme!
You are telling me
That the receptivity-seekers
Are Your most favourite children.
My Supreme, my Supreme!

1372

My Supreme, my Supreme!
I am inspired only by God-News
And by no other news.
My Supreme, my Supreme!

7 FEBRUARY 2005

1373

My Supreme, my Supreme!
Your philosophy does not
Believe in tomorrow.
Your philosophy is
Here and Now.
My Supreme, my Supreme!

1374

My Supreme, my Supreme!
You wonder why it is not possible
For us to think of You,
Pray to You and meditate on You
At least four hours a day
Out of twenty-four hours.
My Supreme, my Supreme!

MY MORNING SOUL-BODY PRAYERS

8 FEBRUARY 2005

1375

My Supreme, my Supreme!
You are so kind to me.
You have blessed me
With endless ways to please You
In Your own Way.
My Supreme, my Supreme!

1376

My Supreme, my Supreme!
Today my heart's aspiration-boat
Is sailing extremely fast.
My Supreme, my Supreme!

SRI CHINMOY

9 FEBRUARY 2005

1377

My Supreme, my Supreme!
I do excellent meditations
Only when I meditate
In my God-heart-temple.
My Supreme, my Supreme!

1378

My Supreme, my Supreme!
Every day I play
On the blue violin of my heart
To invoke the blessingful presence
Of my Goddess-Mother Saraswati.
My Supreme, my Supreme!

MY MORNING SOUL-BODY PRAYERS

10 FEBRUARY 2005

1379

My Supreme, my Supreme!
I love and adore
The tranquil voice
Of my meditation-heart.
My Supreme, my Supreme!

1380

My Supreme, my Supreme!
I have come to realise
That the happiness of my mind
Has a shockingly short breath.
My Supreme, my Supreme!

SRI CHINMOY

13 FEBRUARY 2005

1381

My Supreme, my Supreme!
Please, please
Do not allow my mind
To have ambition-fire.
My Supreme, my Supreme,
Please give my heart
Aspiration-flames
To illumine my entire life.
My Supreme, my Supreme!

1382

My Supreme, my Supreme!
Every morning
We exchange our possessions:
I give You
The sorrows of my heart;
You give me
The Smiles of Your Eye.
My Supreme, my Supreme!

MY MORNING SOUL-BODY PRAYERS

15 FEBRUARY 2005

1383

My Supreme, my Supreme!
The God-fulfilling,
God-pleasing inner journey
Never ends, never, never!
My Supreme, my Supreme!

1384

My Supreme, my Supreme!
I have only one desire:
I wish to claim You
At every moment
As my own, very own.
My Supreme, my Supreme!

(AFTER PERFORMING THE SONGS)

This is the end of our journey.

26 NOVEMBER 2005

1385

My Supreme, my Supreme, my Supreme!
I am enamoured only of Your Feet.
Why? Because Your Feet forgive me
Sooner than the soonest,
Whereas Your Eye and Your Heart
Take time.
My Supreme, my Supreme, my Supreme!

MY MORNING SOUL-BODY PRAYERS

27 NOVEMBER 2005

1386

My Supreme, my Supreme, my Supreme!
You are telling me that
My soul's morning rose-smiles
And
My heart's morning Heaven-climbing tears
Are Your fondest children.
My Supreme, my Supreme, my Supreme!

SRI CHINMOY

28 NOVEMBER 2005

1387

My Supreme, my Supreme, my Supreme!
You are beautiful
In the lives of human beings.
You are infinitely more beautiful
In the heart of Nature.
My Supreme, my Supreme, my Supreme!

MY MORNING SOUL-BODY PRAYERS

29 NOVEMBER 2005

1388

My Supreme, my Supreme, my Supreme!
My Lord, I begin my day
With Your descending
Blue Compassion-Blessings.
"My child, I begin My day
With your ascending
Green gratitude-songs."
My Supreme, my Supreme, my Supreme!

30 NOVEMBER 2005

1389

My Supreme, my Supreme, my Supreme!
You are now blessing me
With a rainbow-joy-dawn-hope,
And I am offering You
My sleepless and selfless
Determination-promise
For the manifestation
Of Your infinite Light
In the heart of humanity.
My Supreme, my Supreme, my Supreme!

MY MORNING SOUL-BODY PRAYERS

1 DECEMBER 2005

1390

My Supreme, my Supreme, my Supreme!
I pray to God the Singular,
I meditate on God the Singular,
But I serve God the Plural,
I manifest God the Plural.
My Supreme, my Supreme, my Supreme!

2 DECEMBER 2005

1391

My Supreme, my Supreme, my Supreme!
This morning I find myself
In Your Golden Boat.
I am right beside You.
You are carrying me
To the Golden Shore.
My Supreme, my Supreme, my Supreme!

MY MORNING SOUL-BODY PRAYERS

3 DECEMBER 2005

1392

My Supreme, my Supreme, my Supreme!
You are happily congratulating me
And blessingfully honouring me
Because I have done very well
In my obedience and gratitude-examinations.
My Supreme, my Supreme, my Supreme!

SRI CHINMOY

4 DECEMBER 2005

1393

My Supreme, my Supreme, my Supreme!
I give You nothing!
Even my readiness, my willingness
And my eagerness
Are Your invaluable Blessing-Presents.
My Supreme, my Supreme, my Supreme!

MY MORNING SOUL-BODY PRAYERS

5 DECEMBER 2005

1394

My Supreme, my Supreme, my Supreme!
Out of Your infinite Bounty,
You and Your Will follow me
Wherever I go
And whatever I do.
When I go out climbing,
You and Your Will go out with me climbing.
When I go out swimming,
You and Your Will go out with me swimming.
When I go out running,
You and Your Will go out with me running.
And even when I go out shopping,
You and Your Will go out with me shopping.
What a strange experience You are giving me,
My Lord Supreme!
Instead of my following You,
You and Your Will are following me.
My Supreme, my Supreme, my Supreme!

6 DECEMBER 2005

1395

My Supreme, my Supreme, my Supreme!
Each wee earth-seed
Is a Heaven-climbing prayer
And a world-awakening realisation.
My Supreme, my Supreme, my Supreme!

MY MORNING SOUL-BODY PRAYERS

7 DECEMBER 2005

1396

My Supreme, my Supreme, my Supreme!
My heart is all tearful gratitude to You
Because You have given me
An aspiration-heart
That never fails You and never falls.
My Supreme, my Supreme, my Supreme!

SRI CHINMOY

8 DECEMBER 2005

1397

My Supreme, my Supreme, my Supreme!
You are Your Kindness infinite.
Every morning
I receive a handwritten
Compassion-Inspiration-Letter
From You.
Every evening
I receive a handwritten
Satisfaction-Pride-Letter
From You.
My Supreme, my Supreme, my Supreme!

MY MORNING SOUL-BODY PRAYERS

9 DECEMBER 2005

1398

My Supreme, my Supreme, my Supreme!
Each time I look at Your Eye
And each time I touch Your Feet,
I feel as fresh as a breath
Of beauty-purity's dawn.
My Supreme, my Supreme, my Supreme!

SRI CHINMOY

13 DECEMBER 2005

1399

My Supreme, my Supreme, my Supreme!
You are telling me that a self-winner
Is by far the best
God-dreamer and God-lover in Heaven
And God-server on earth.
My Supreme, my Supreme, my Supreme!

MY MORNING SOUL-BODY PRAYERS

14 DECEMBER 2005

1400

My Supreme, my Supreme, my Supreme!
At the journey's start,
Life may make serious mistakes,
But at the journey's close,
The same life will become
Perfect perfection.
My Supreme, my Supreme, my Supreme!

SRI CHINMOY

15 DECEMBER 2005

1401

My Supreme, my Supreme, my Supreme!
The earth-mind-connection-thought
Fails.
The Heaven-heart-connection-will
Sails.
My Supreme, my Supreme, my Supreme!

MY MORNING SOUL-BODY PRAYERS

16 DECEMBER 2005

1402

My Supreme, my Supreme, my Supreme!
Every day my soul's smiles
And my heart's tears
Take the earth-Heaven shuttle
To work with You
And to work for You.
My Supreme, my Supreme, my Supreme!

SRI CHINMOY

17 DECEMBER 2005

1403

My Supreme, my Supreme, my Supreme!
Every morning
God blesses my soul
With a new God-climbing dream.
My Supreme, my Supreme, my Supreme!

MY MORNING SOUL-BODY PRAYERS

18 DECEMBER 2005

1404

My Supreme, my Supreme, my Supreme!
When I think of You,
You smile at me.
When I pray to You like a child,
You happily and proudly clap.
When I meditate on You,
You immediately embrace me.
When I give You
All that I have and all that I am,
You command me
To take a very special part
In Your Cosmic Play.
My Supreme, my Supreme, my Supreme!

SRI CHINMOY

19 DECEMBER 2005

1405

My Supreme, my Supreme, my Supreme!
I love You
Because You are all mine.
You love me
Because You want to make me
Your ever-blossoming child divine.
My Supreme, my Supreme, my Supreme!

MY MORNING SOUL-BODY PRAYERS

20 DECEMBER 2005

1406

My Supreme, my Supreme, my Supreme!
Every morning
You carry my blooming heart
And my blossoming soul
In Your Golden Boat
To a newly discovered Shore.
My Supreme, my Supreme, my Supreme!

21 DECEMBER 2005

1407

My Supreme, my Supreme, my Supreme!
Slowly, steadily and unerringly,
My gratitude-heart-train is moving
Towards God's Heart-Embrace-Station.
My Supreme, my Supreme, my Supreme!

MY MORNING SOUL-BODY PRAYERS

22 DECEMBER 2005

1408

My Supreme, my Supreme, my Supreme!
I love You,
I need You,
I am all for You.
You have given me
A new name:
"Transformation".
My Supreme, my Supreme, my Supreme!

SRI CHINMOY

23 DECEMBER 2005

1409

My Supreme, my Supreme, my Supreme!
My aspiring life's blooms and blossoms
Are the revelations and manifestations
Of my gratitude-heart-song.
My Supreme, my Supreme, my Supreme!

MY MORNING SOUL-BODY PRAYERS

24 DECEMBER 2005

1410

My Supreme, my Supreme, my Supreme!
When I pray,
I wish to be
As sweet and beautiful
As a child.
When I meditate,
I wish to be
As powerful and peaceful
As a Yogi.
My Supreme, my Supreme, my Supreme!

25 DECEMBER 2005

1411

My Supreme, my Supreme, my Supreme!
No escape!
Life has to face
Earth's justice-hours.
True, absolutely true —
God embraces life
At God's choice Hour.
My Supreme, my Supreme, my Supreme!

MY MORNING SOUL-BODY PRAYERS

26 DECEMBER 2005

1412

My Supreme, my Supreme, my Supreme!
I am praying to You
Only for one thing:
Patience, patience, patience,
Patience infinite.
My Supreme, my Supreme, my Supreme!

27 DECEMBER 2005

1413

My Supreme, my Supreme, my Supreme!
Please, please, please bless me
With a voice that will sing
Only Your Victory-Songs
Through every aspiring heart.
My Supreme, my Supreme, my Supreme!

MY MORNING SOUL-BODY PRAYERS

28 DECEMBER 2005

1414

My Supreme, my Supreme, my Supreme!
Heaven and earth
Are equally precious.
Heaven's Smiles and earth's tears
Are equally precious.
God the Dreamer in Heaven
And God the Doer on earth
Are equally precious.
My Supreme, my Supreme, my Supreme!

29 DECEMBER 2005

1415

My Supreme, my Supreme, my Supreme!
Every morning God accepts,
Readily and gladly,
A non-stop gratitude-flooded invitation
From my heart-nest.
My Supreme, my Supreme, my Supreme!

MY MORNING SOUL-BODY PRAYERS

30 DECEMBER 2005

1416

My Supreme, my Supreme, my Supreme!
The tears of my heart
And the smiles of my soul
Enjoy their sweetness, fondness
And oneness
In Your Infinity's Sky.
My Supreme, my Supreme, my Supreme!

SRI CHINMOY

31 DECEMBER 2005

1417

My Supreme, my Supreme, my Supreme!
I have come to realise
That each life
Is a very, very special prayer
To Heaven.
My Supreme, my Supreme, my Supreme!

MY MORNING SOUL-BODY PRAYERS

1 JANUARY 2006

1418

My Supreme, my Supreme, my Supreme!
Happy New Year!
Happy New Year!
Happy New Year!
From today on,
Every day You expect from
Your supremely chosen children
A divinely dignified spiritual life.
My Supreme, my Supreme, my Supreme!

SRI CHINMOY

2 JANUARY 2006

1419

My Supreme, my Supreme, my Supreme!
My Mother Earth is beauty.
My Father Heaven is light.
And I am their Eternity's
Reality-existence.
My Supreme, my Supreme, my Supreme!

MY MORNING SOUL-BODY PRAYERS

3 JANUARY 2006

1420

My Supreme, my Supreme, my Supreme!
You are Your Compassion-Eye
And I am my aspiration-heart.
Together we live and fulfil each other.
My Supreme, my Supreme, my Supreme!

SRI CHINMOY

4 JANUARY 2006

1421

My Supreme, my Supreme, my Supreme!
Every day
Do give me the capacity
To sow a new aspiration-seed
In my heart-garden.
My Supreme, my Supreme, my Supreme!

MY MORNING SOUL-BODY PRAYERS

5 JANUARY 2006

1422

My Supreme, my Supreme, my Supreme!
Every morning
My aspiration-heart runs and runs
To touch the peace-sea-shore.
Every evening
The peace-sea-shore comes and blesses
My aspiration-heart.
My Supreme, my Supreme, my Supreme!

SRI CHINMOY

6 JANUARY 2006

1423

My Supreme, my Supreme, my Supreme!
My morning prayers and meditations
Give me the joy of the higher worlds.
My evening prayers and meditations
Give me the joy of the inner worlds.
My Supreme, my Supreme, my Supreme!

MY MORNING SOUL-BODY PRAYERS

7 JANUARY 2006

1424

My Supreme, my Supreme, my Supreme!
May the singing and dancing
Of divine melodies
Awaken my heart
Every morning.
My Supreme, my Supreme, my Supreme!

8 JANUARY 2006

1425

My Supreme, my Supreme, my Supreme!
My heart-bird sings and sings
Your Victory-Songs
Even when my body, my vital,
My mind and I
Are fast asleep.
My Supreme, my Supreme, my Supreme!

MY MORNING SOUL-BODY PRAYERS

9 JANUARY 2006

1426

My Supreme, my Supreme, my Supreme!
All are caught by Time.
Nobody – nobody! – can hide
From Time.
My Supreme, my Supreme, my Supreme!

SRI CHINMOY

10 JANUARY 2006

1427

My Supreme, my Supreme, my Supreme!
I am sailing and sailing and sailing
My life-boat
Towards the shore
Of the Unknowable.
My Supreme, my Supreme, my Supreme!

MY MORNING SOUL-BODY PRAYERS

11 JANUARY 2006

1428

My Supreme, my Supreme, my Supreme!
Now that I live
In aspiration-sunshine-days,
I must not think of
My desire-ignorance-nights.
My Supreme, my Supreme, my Supreme!

12 JANUARY 2006

1429

My Supreme, my Supreme, my Supreme!
My God-worship
Is my heart's intimacy
And not my life's secrecy.
My Supreme, my Supreme, my Supreme!

MY MORNING SOUL-BODY PRAYERS

13 JANUARY 2006

1430

My Supreme, my Supreme, my Supreme!
May my heart be
An ever-steady and ever-climbing
Aspiration-flame.
My Supreme, my Supreme, my Supreme!

SRI CHINMOY

14 JANUARY 2006

1431

My Supreme, my Supreme, my Supreme!
My sleeplessly climbing aspiration-heart
Is the richest, fondest treasure
Of my soul.
My Supreme, my Supreme, my Supreme!

MY MORNING SOUL-BODY PRAYERS

15 JANUARY 2006

1432

My Supreme, my Supreme, my Supreme!
My morning sincerity-heart
Is speaking:
"I am for God;
I am all for God;
I am only for God."
My Supreme, my Supreme, my Supreme!

16 JANUARY 2006

1433

My Supreme, my Supreme, my Supreme!
The closer a seeker is to God,
The more strict God becomes –
A fact undeniable!
But once the seeker realises God,
Nothing remains impossible.
My Supreme, my Supreme, my Supreme!

MY MORNING SOUL-BODY PRAYERS

17 JANUARY 2006

1434

My Supreme, my Supreme, my Supreme!
I have written many, many, many books.
My God-Forgiveness-book
Is by far the best.
My Supreme, my Supreme, my Supreme!

SRI CHINMOY

18 JANUARY 2006

1435

My Supreme, my Supreme, my Supreme!
When I pray to You,
You give me a beautiful Smile.
When I pray for You,
You give me one hundred
Most powerful Smiles
In a row.
My Supreme, my Supreme, my Supreme!

MY MORNING SOUL-BODY PRAYERS

19 JANUARY 2006

1436

My Supreme, my Supreme, my Supreme!
Please bless me
With a very deep God-thirst
And a very strong God-hunger.
My Supreme, my Supreme, my Supreme!

SRI CHINMOY

20 JANUARY 2006

1437

My Supreme, my Supreme, my Supreme!
My morning prayer
And my evening meditation
Have transformed my heart
Into beauty's rose garden.
My Supreme, my Supreme, my Supreme!

MY MORNING SOUL-BODY PRAYERS

21 JANUARY 2006

1438

My Supreme, my Supreme, my Supreme!
This morning my heart-bird-wings
Are flying and flying,
Singing Your Victory-Songs
In Infinity's Sky.
My Supreme, my Supreme, my Supreme!

23 JANUARY 2006

1439

My Supreme, my Supreme, my Supreme!
Silence is the newness of my heart.
Silence is the fulness of my life.
My Supreme, my Supreme, my Supreme!

1440

My Supreme, my Supreme, my Supreme!
My life I surrender to God's Eye.
My heart I surrender to God's Feet.
My Supreme, my Supreme, my Supreme!

MY MORNING SOUL-BODY PRAYERS

24 JANUARY 2006

1441

My Supreme, my Supreme, my Supreme!
The more I love You,
The more I need You.

"My child, I am adding something:
The more you love Me,
The more you need Me,
The more I am proud of you."
My Supreme, my Supreme, my Supreme!

26 JANUARY 2006

1442

My Supreme, my Supreme, my Supreme!
God and vacation do not rhyme.
Chinmoy and vacation also do not rhyme.
My Supreme, my Supreme, my Supreme!

MY MORNING SOUL-BODY PRAYERS

28 JANUARY 2006

1443

My Supreme, my Supreme, my Supreme!
Where is true happiness?

"My child, happiness is
Far beyond the domain
Of the doubting and binding mind."
My Supreme, my Supreme, my Supreme!

SRI CHINMOY

29 JANUARY 2006

1444

My Supreme, my Supreme, my Supreme!
God Himself has taught me
Seventy-four of His Heartbeat-Songs
Most compassionately
And most affectionately.
My Supreme, my Supreme, my Supreme!

MY MORNING SOUL-BODY PRAYERS

30 JANUARY 2006

1445

My Supreme, my Supreme, my Supreme!
Who am I?
I am a full
God-manifestation-hero-warrior-promise
Here on earth.
My Supreme, my Supreme, my Supreme!

SRI CHINMOY

31 JANUARY 2006

1446

My Supreme, my Supreme, my Supreme!
May my God-gratitude-heart
Blossom most beautifully
Every day.
My Supreme, my Supreme, my Supreme!

MY MORNING SOUL-BODY PRAYERS

1 FEBRUARY 2006

1447

My Supreme, my Supreme, my Supreme!
What can I do?
"My child,
Sit down at My Feet
And keep quiet."
My Supreme, my Supreme, my Supreme!

SRI CHINMOY

2 FEBRUARY 2006

1448

My Supreme, my Supreme, my Supreme!
Today I am on a new wave
Of determination-promise
To please You
At every moment of my life
In Your own Way.
My Supreme, my Supreme, my Supreme!

MY MORNING SOUL-BODY PRAYERS

3 FEBRUARY 2006

1449

My Supreme, my Supreme, my Supreme!
Delight is our source.
Delight is our course.
In delight we end our journey.
My Supreme, my Supreme, my Supreme!

SRI CHINMOY

5 FEBRUARY 2006

1450

My Supreme, my Supreme, my Supreme!
My heart's first morning smile
Thrills my Lord Beloved Supreme.
My Supreme, my Supreme, my Supreme!

MY MORNING SOUL-BODY PRAYERS

6 FEBRUARY 2006

1451

My Supreme, my Supreme, my Supreme!
I am a sleepless lover
Of Infinity's peace-hunger.
My Supreme, my Supreme, my Supreme!

SRI CHINMOY

7 FEBRUARY 2006

1452

My Supreme, my Supreme, my Supreme!
I do not want to live any more
In the expectation-world.
The expectation-world is
Very, very painful.
My Supreme, my Supreme, my Supreme!

MY MORNING SOUL-BODY PRAYERS

8 FEBRUARY 2006

1453

My Supreme, my Supreme, my Supreme!
I see Your Face
Inside my heart
And not before my eyes.
Why?
"My child,
Heart is the right place."
My Supreme, my Supreme, my Supreme!

9 FEBRUARY 2006

1454

My Supreme, my Supreme, my Supreme!
Individuals may fail,
But not mankind's promise to God
For the fulfilment of His Will.
My Supreme, my Supreme, my Supreme!

1455

My Supreme, my Supreme, my Supreme!
Today I am extremely happy
Because I have pleased my Lord Supreme
In His own Way.
My Supreme, my Supreme, my Supreme!

MY MORNING SOUL-BODY PRAYERS

10 FEBRUARY 2006

1456

My Supreme, my Supreme, my Supreme!
My Lord,
How can I please You
All the time?
"My child, easy!
Just think of Me all the time
And do not think of yourself."
My Supreme, my Supreme, my Supreme!

12 FEBRUARY 2006

1457

My Supreme, my Supreme, my Supreme!
God-realisation, God-revelation
And God-manifestation
Take place only here
In the heart of Mother Earth.
My Supreme, my Supreme, my Supreme!

1458

My Supreme, my Supreme, my Supreme!
I love God's Name
More than I love God.
My heart loves God
More than it loves God's Name.
What is the difference
Between God's Name and God?
"Greatness is the Name of God's Name.
Goodness is the Name of God.
God's Greatness and God's Goodness
Can never be separated.
They always live together."
My Supreme, my Supreme, my Supreme!

MY MORNING SOUL-BODY PRAYERS

13 FEBRUARY 2006

1459

My Supreme, my Supreme, my Supreme!
Every day we think of You,
We pray to You, we meditate on You,
We see You, we even talk to You.
But, alas, we just do not recognise You.
My Supreme, my Supreme, my Supreme!

14 FEBRUARY 2006

1460

My Supreme, my Supreme, my Supreme!
The desire-life
Is to possess the world.
The aspiration-life
Is to surrender to God's Will.
The realisation-life
Is to be possessed by God Himself.
My Supreme, my Supreme, my Supreme!

1461

My Supreme, my Supreme, my Supreme!
God tells me
That every morning
If I pray to Him
To give me a pure heart,
A sincere mind
And a simple life,
Then I will be
His most favourite child.
My Supreme, my Supreme, my Supreme!

MY MORNING SOUL-BODY PRAYERS

15 FEBRUARY 2006

1462

My Supreme, my Supreme, my Supreme!
At every moment God whispers,
"Your God-obedience
Is indispensable."
My Supreme, my Supreme, my Supreme!

SRI CHINMOY

16 FEBRUARY 2006

1463

My Supreme, my Supreme, my Supreme!
God, my heart loves You only,
My life needs You only.
In my outer life,
I am all for You.
In my inner life,
You are my All.
My Supreme, my Supreme, my Supreme!

MY MORNING SOUL-BODY PRAYERS

17 FEBRUARY 2006

1464

My Supreme, my Supreme, my Supreme!
I love, adore and treasure
Your unexpected Visits
At my heart-door.
My Supreme, my Supreme, my Supreme!

SRI CHINMOY

18 FEBRUARY 2006

1465

My Supreme, my Supreme, my Supreme!
Singers and musicians
Intensify and multiply
The aspiration-heart-cries
Of Mother Earth,
And they bring down
Heaven's Beauty, Fragrance and Delight
To share with humanity.
My Supreme, my Supreme, my Supreme!

MY MORNING SOUL-BODY PRAYERS

19 FEBRUARY 2006

1466

My Supreme, my Supreme, my Supreme!
My life cries for happiness,
My heart cries for God-oneness,
And I cry for God-manifestation-fulness.
My Supreme, my Supreme, my Supreme!

SRI CHINMOY

20 FEBRUARY 2006

1467

My Supreme, my Supreme, my Supreme!
A real God-seeker and God-lover
Is at once his heart-beauty
And his soul-fragrance.
My Supreme, my Supreme, my Supreme!

MY MORNING SOUL-BODY PRAYERS

21 FEBRUARY 2006

1468

My Supreme, my Supreme, my Supreme!
I wake and rise
In the beauty and fragrance
Of my heart-garden
To build a special temple
Of God-worship.
My Supreme, my Supreme, my Supreme!

SRI CHINMOY

22 FEBRUARY 2006

1469

My Supreme, my Supreme, my Supreme!
My love of God
Is the sleepless song
Of my heart-tears.
My Supreme, my Supreme, my Supreme!

MY MORNING SOUL-BODY PRAYERS

23 FEBRUARY 2006

1470

My Supreme, my Supreme, my Supreme!
Heaven's Eye
And earth's heart
Constantly communicate.
My Supreme, my Supreme, my Supreme!

24 FEBRUARY 2006

1471

My Supreme, my Supreme, my Supreme!
The outer journey begins
Full of enthusiasm;
It ends full of peace.
The inner journey begins
Full of soulfulness,
And it never ends.
My Supreme, my Supreme, my Supreme!

NOTES

1. See also appendix "Prefaces to original edition".
2. 30 September 1998, 4:53 a.m. Before lifting 127 lbs with each arm once.
3. 1 October 1998, 2:33 a.m. Before lifting 83 lbs with both arms simultaneously.
4. 1 October 1998, 8:40 a.m. Before lifting 140 lbs with each arm twice.
5. 2 October 1998, 3:02 a.m. Before lifting 150 lbs with each arm once.
6. 2 October 1998, 7:08 p.m. Before lifting 160 lbs with each arm twice.
7. 3 October 1998, 4:27 a.m. Before lifting 93 lbs with both arms simultaneously.
8. 5 October 1998, 1:31 a.m. Before lifting 180 lbs with each arm three times.
9. 5 October 1998, 1:42 a.m. Before lifting 100 lbs with both arms simultaneously.
10. 5 October 1998, 1:50 a.m. Before lifting 131 lbs fifty times (25 right, 25 left).
11. 6 October 1998, 7:00 a.m. Before lifting 190 lbs with each arm once.
12. 6 October 1998, 7:10 a.m. Before lifting 110 lbs with both arms simultaneously.
13. 6 October 1998, 7:20 a.m. Before lifting 137 lbs fifty times (25 right, 25 left).
14. 6 October 1998, 8:27 p.m. Before lifting 200 lbs nine times (5 right, 4 left).
15. 10 October 1998, 3:57 a.m. Before lifting 210 lbs with left arm eight times.
16. 10 October 1998, 4:07 a.m. Before unsuccessfully attempting to lift 120 lbs with both arms simultaneously.
17. 10 October 1998, 4:17 a.m. Before lifting 120 lbs fifty times with left arm only.
18. 15 October 1998, 3:27 a.m. Before lifting 220 lbs with each arm five times.
19. 15 October 1998, 3:40 a.m. Before unsuccessfully attempting to lift 120 lbs with both arms simultaneously.
20. 15 October 1998, 3:53 a.m. Before lifting 120 lbs fifty times (25 right, 25 left).
21. 16 October 1998, 8:18 a.m. Before lifting 230 lbs with each arm four times.
22. 18 October 1998, 10:40 a.m. Before lifting 240 lbs with each arm four times.
23. 18 October 1998, 10:50 a.m. Before unsuccessfully attempting to lift 120 lbs with both arms simultaneously.
24. 18 October 1998, 10:55 a.m. Before lifting 145 lbs one hundred times (50 right, 50 left in 2 sets) for a new record of 2 mins 45.07 secs.
25. 20 October 1998, 4:01 a.m. Before lifting 250 lbs with each arm four times.
26. 20 October 1998, 4:17 a.m. Before unsuccessfully attempting to lift 120 lbs with both arms simultaneously.
27. 20 October 1998, 11:25 p.m. Before successfully lifting 120 lbs with both arms simultaneously.
28. 21 October 1998, 8:02 p.m. Before lifting 250 lbs with each arm four times.
29. 21 October 1998, 8:11 p.m. Before lifting 125 lbs with both arms simultaneously.
30. 23 October 1998, 5:15 a.m. Before lifting 270 lbs with each arm four times.
31. 23 October 1998, 5:23 a.m. Before lifting 130 lbs with both arms simultaneously.
32. 23 October 1998, 5:29 a.m. Before lifting 145 lbs one hundred times (50 right, 50 left) for a new record of 2 mins 40 secs.
33. 24 October 1998, 7:10 a.m. Before lifting 300 lbs with each arm four times.
34. 24 October 1998, 7:19 a.m. Before lifting 130 lbs with both arms simultaneously.
35. 24 October 1998, 7:28 a.m. Before lifting 145 lbs one hundred times (50 right, 50 left).
36. 24 October 1998, 11:37 p.m. Before lifting 300 lbs with each arm four times.
37. 24 October 1998, 11:45 p.m. Before lifting 130 lbs with both arms simultaneously.
38. 27 October 1998, 7:26 a.m. Before lifting 300 lbs with each arm four times.
39. 28 October 1998, 2:11 a.m. Before lifting 300 lbs with each arm four times.
40. 30 October 1998, 6:24 a.m. Before lifting 300 lbs with each arm four times.
41. 1 November 1998, 6:20 a.m. Before lifting 300 lbs with each arm four times. (The morning of the New York City Marathon.)
42. 2 November 1998, 6:19 a.m. Before lifting 300 lbs with each arm five times.
43. 3 November 1998, 5:02 a.m. Before lifting 300 lbs with each arm four times.
44. 4 November 1998, 4:02 a.m. Before lifting 300 lbs with each arm four times.

45. 6 November 1998, 4:23 a.m. Before lifting 300 lbs with each arm four times.
46. 7 November 1998, 4:03 a.m. Before lifting 300 lbs with each arm four times.
47. 8 November 1998, 5:37 a.m. Before lifting 300 lbs with each arm four times.
48. 9 November 1998, 4:24 a.m. Before lifting 300 lbs with each arm four times.
49. 9 November 1998, 4:32 a.m. Before lifting 200 lbs with each arm two times.
50. 9 November 1998, 4:40 a.m. Before lifting 140 lbs with both arms simultaneously.
51. 9 November 1998, 4:48 a.m. Before lifting 145 lbs one hundred times (50 right, 50 left).
52. 15 November 1998, 1:58 a.m. Before lifting 300 lbs with each arm four times.
53. 15 November 1998, 2:09 a.m. Before lifting 200 lbs with each arm once.
54. 15 November 1998, 2:18 a.m. Before lifting 140 lbs with both arms simultaneously two times.
55. 15 November 1998, 2:25 a.m. Before lifting 145 lbs one hundred times (50 right, 50 left).
56. 15 November 1998, 6:28 p.m. Before lifting 300 lbs with each arm four times.
57. 15 November 1998, 6:37 p.m. Before lifting 200 lbs with each arm once.
58. 15 November 1998, 6:43 p.m. Before lifting 145 lbs with both arms simultaneously.
59. 16 November 1998, 6:52 a.m. Before lifting 300 lbs with each arm four times.
60. 16 November 1998, 7:02 a.m. Before lifting 200 lbs with each arm once.
61. 16 November 1998, 7:06 a.m. Before lifting 145 lbs with both arms simultaneously.
62. 16 November 1998, 7:11 a.m. Before lifting 145 lbs one hundred times (50 right, 50 left).
63. 17 November 1998, 6:06 a.m. Before lifting 300 lbs with each arm four times.
64. 17 November 1998, 6:14 a.m. Before lifting 200 lbs with each arm once.
65. 17 November 1998, 6:19 a.m. Before lifting 145 lbs with both arms simultaneously.
66. 17 November 1998, 6:24 a.m. Before lifting 145 lbs one hundred times (50 right, 50 left).
67. 18 November 1998, 6:33 a.m. Before lifting 300 lbs with each arm four times.
68. 18 November 1998, 6:40 a.m. Before lifting 200 lbs with each arm once.
69. 18 November 1998, 6:48 a.m. Before lifting 145 lbs with both arms simultaneously.
70. 18 November 1998, 6:54 a.m. Before lifting 145 lbs one hundred times (50 right, 50 left).
71. 21 November 1998, 4:45 a.m. Before lifting 300 lbs with each arm four times.
72. 21 November 1998, 4:52 a.m. Before lifting 200 lbs with each arm once.
73. 21 November 1998, 4:57 a.m. Before lifting 145 lbs with both arms simultaneously.
74. 21 November 1998, 5:03 a.m. Before lifting 145 lbs one hundred times (50 right, 50 left) for a new record of 2 mins 13 secs.
75. 22 November 1998, 5:21 a.m. Before lifting 300 lbs with each arm twelve times (in three sets).
76. 22 November 1998, 5:28 a.m. Before lifting 200 lbs with each arm once.
77. 22 November 1998, 5:34 a.m. Before lifting 145 lbs with both arms simultaneously.
78. 22 November 1998, 5:41 a.m. Before lifting 145 lbs one hundred times (50 right, 50 left) for a new record of 2 mins 6.36 secs.
79. 23 November 1998, 6:01 a.m. Before lifting 300 lbs with each arm twenty-nine times (in four sets).
80. 23 November 1998, 6:07 a.m. Before lifting 200 lbs with each arm once.
81. 23 November 1998, 6:13 a.m. Before lifting 145 lbs with both arms simultaneously.
82. 23 November 1998, 6:18 a.m. Before lifting 145 lbs one hundred and one times (49 right, 52 left).
83. 24 November 1998, 5:15 a.m. Before lifting 300 lbs eighty times (40 right, 40 left in four sets).
84. 24 November 1998, 5:23 a.m. Before lifting 200 lbs with each arm once.
85. 24 November 1998, 5:31 a.m. Before lifting 145 lbs with both arms simultaneously.
86. 24 November 1998, 5:37 a.m. Before lifting 145 lbs one hundred times (50 right, 50 left) for a new record of 1 min 32.07 secs.

87. 25 November 1998, 4:59 a.m. Before lifting 300 lbs one hundred times (50 right, 50 left in five sets).
88. 25 November 1998, 5:07 a.m. Before lifting 200 lbs with each arm once.
89. 25 November 1998, 5:14 a.m. Before lifting 145 lbs with both arms simultaneously.
90. 25 November 1998, 5:21 a.m. Before lifting 145 lbs one hundred times (50 right, 50 left).
91. 27 November 1998, 4:46 a.m. Before lifting 300 lbs one hundred and four times (50 right, 50 left in five sets, plus two extra, higher lifts with each arm). The morning of Sri Chinmoys weightlifting demonstration at York College, in which he performed thirty-three feats of strength.
92. 27 November 1998, 5:03 a.m. Before lifting 145 lbs with both arms simultaneously.
93. 27 November 1998, 5:09 a.m. Before lifting 145 lbs ninety-seven times (48 right, 49 left).
94. 30 November 1998, 6:14 a.m. Before lifting 400 lbs one hundred times with two arms and one hundred times with one arm (50 right, 50 left in five sets).
95. 1 December 1998, 4:42 a.m. Before lifting 400 lbs one hundred times with two arms and one hundred times with one arm (50 right, 50 left in five sets).
96. 2 December 1998, 8:31 a.m. Before lifting 400 lbs one hundred times with two arms and one hundred times with one arm (50 right, 50 left in five sets).
97. 5 December 1998, 6:16 a.m. Hawaii. Before lifting 400 lbs one hundred times with two arms and one hundred and one times with one arm (50 right, 51 left in five sets).
98. 6 December 1998, 5:20 a.m. Hawaii. Before lifting 400 lbs one hundred times with two arms and one hundred times with one arm (50 right, 50 left in five sets).
99. 7 December 1998, 5:22 a.m. Hawaii. Before lifting 400 lbs one hundred times with two arms and one hundred and four times with one arm (51 right, 53 left in five sets).
100. 8 December 1998, 5:24 a.m. Hawaii. Before lifting 400 lbs one hundred and one times with two arms and one hundred times with one arm (50 right, 50 left in five sets).
101. 10 December 1998, 5:18 a.m. Hawaii. Before lifting 400 lbs fifty times with two arms and one hundred and thirteen times with one arm (55 right, 58 left in six sets).
102. 11 December 1998, 5:19 a.m. Hawaii. Before lifting 400 lbs fifty times with two arms and one hundred and twenty-eight times with one arm (57 right, 71 left in six sets).
103. 12 December 1998, 5:16 a.m. Hawaii. Before lifting 400 lbs fifty times with two arms and one hundred and eighteen times with one arm (59 right, 59 left in six sets).
104. 13 December 1998, 5:17 a.m. Hawaii. Before lifting 400 lbs fifty times with two arms and one hundred and fourteen times with one arm (55 right, 59 left in six sets).
105. 14 December 1998, 5:20 a.m. Hawaii. Before lifting 400 lbs fifty times with two arms and one hundred and twenty-four times with one arm (59 right, 65 left in six sets).
106. 18 December 1998, 5:37 a.m. Singapore. Before lifting 400 lbs fifty times with two arms and one hundred times with one arm (50 right, 50 left in five sets).
107. 19 December 1998, 3:50 a.m. Singapore. Before lifting 400 lbs fifty times with two arms and one hundred and two times with one arm (52 right, 50 left in five sets).
108. 20 December 1998, 4:43 a.m. Singapore. Before lifting 400 lbs fifty times with two arms and one hundred times with one arm (50 right, 50 left in five sets).
109. 21 December 1998, 5:30 a.m. Singapore. Before using double-arm machine. New record: 110 lbs with both arms simultaneously from a seated position. Note: This double-arm machine can be used from a seated or standing position. During his workouts, Sri Chinmoy gradually increases the poundage using a selector pin. This lift is completely different from that in which two independent dumbbells are lifted overhead simultaneously.
110. 22 December 1998, 4:13 a.m. Singapore. Before lifting 400 lbs one hundred and one times with one arm (53 right, 48 left in three sets).
111. 22 December 1998, 4:31 a.m. Singapore. Before using double-arm machine.
112. 23 December 1998, 8:23 a.m. Singapore. Before lifting 400 lbs one hundred and one times with one arm (48 right, 53 left in three sets).

113. 29 December 1998, 6:54 a.m. Kuala Lumpur, Malaysia (after returning from a three-day trip to India). Before lifting 400 lbs one hundred and ninety-four times with one arm (96 right, 98 left in five sets).
114. 29 December 1998, 7:11 a.m. Kuala Lumpur, Malaysia. Before using double-arm machine up to 140 lbs with both arms simultaneously from a standing position.
115. 30 December 1998, 7:00 a.m. Kuala Lumpur, Malaysia. Before lifting 400 lbs.
116. 30 December 1998, 7:16 a.m. Kuala Lumpur, Malaysia. Before using double-arm machine up to 130 lbs with both arms simultaneously from a standing position.
117. 31 December 1998, 6:36 a.m. Kuala Lumpur, Malaysia. Before lifting 400 lbs two hundred and two times with one arm (99 right, 103 left in five sets).
118. 31 December 1998, 6:53 a.m. Kuala Lumpur, Malaysia. Before using double-arm machine up to 140 lbs with both arms simultaneously from a standing position.
119. 1 January 1999, 8:44 a.m. Kuala Lumpur, Malaysia. Before lifting 210 lbs twice (once with each arm).
120. 1 January 1999, 8:58 a.m. Kuala Lumpur, Malaysia. Before using double-arm machine.
121. 2 January 1999, 7:33 a.m. Kuala Lumpur, Malaysia. Before lifting 210 lbs twice (once with each arm).
122. 2 January 1999, 7:46 a.m. Kuala Lumpur, Malaysia. Before using double-arm machine up to 140 lbs with both arms simultaneously from a standing position.
123. 3 January 1999, 7:33 a.m. Kuala Lumpur, Malaysia. Before lifting 210 lbs.
124. 3 January 1999, 7:51 a.m. Kuala Lumpur, Malaysia. Before using double-arm machine up to 140 lbs with both arms simultaneously from a standing position.
125. 5 January 1999, 8:17 a.m. Penang, Malaysia. Before lifting 220 lbs six times (3 right, 3 left).
126. 5 January 1999, 8:29 a.m. Penang, Malaysia. Before using double-arm machine up to 130 lbs with both arms simultaneously from a standing position.
127. 6 January 1999, 8:58 a.m. Penang, Malaysia. Before lifting 220 lbs thirty-two times with one arm (16 right, 16 left).
128. 6 January 1999, 9:17 a.m. Penang, Malaysia. Before using double-arm machine. New record: 120 lbs with both arms simultaneously from a seated position; and up to 140 lbs with both arms simultaneously from a standing position.
129. 7 January 1999, 10:53 a.m. Penang, Malaysia. Before using double-arm machine up to 130 lbs with both arms simultaneously from a standing position.
130. 7 January 1999, 11:05 a.m. Penang, Malaysia. Before lifting 220 lbs twenty times with one arm (10 right, 10 left).
131. 8 January 1999, 8:17 a.m. Penang, Malaysia. Before lifting 220 lbs twenty-four times with one arm (12 right, 12 left).
132. 8 January 1999, 8:32 a.m. Penang, Malaysia. Before using double-arm machine. New record: 130 lbs with both arms simultaneously from a seated position.
133. 9 January 1999, 5:46 a.m. Penang, Malaysia. Before lifting 220 lbs twenty-two times with one arm (10 right, 10 left, plus once each arm to maximum extension).
134. 9 January 1999, 5:59 a.m. Penang, Malaysia. Before using double-arm machine up to 130 lbs with both arms simultaneously from a standing position.
135. 10 January 1999, 7:18 a.m. Penang, Malaysia. Before lifting 230 lbs twenty-five times with one arm (10 right, 13 left, plus once each arm to maximum extension).
136. 10 January 1999, 7:34 a.m. Penang, Malaysia. Before using double-arm machine up to 140 lbs with both arms simultaneously from a standing position.
137. 11 January 1999, 5:43 a.m. Penang, Malaysia. Before lifting 230 lbs twice (once with each arm).
138. 11 January 1999, 5:56 a.m. Penang, Malaysia. Before using double-arm machine up to 130 lbs with both arms simultaneously from a standing position.
139. 12 January 1999, 5:36 a.m. Penang, Malaysia. Before lifting 230 lbs twenty-four times with one arm (10 right, 12 left, plus once each arm to maximum extension).

MY MORNING SOUL-BODY PRAYERS

140. 12 January 1999, 5:49 a.m. Penang, Malaysia. Before using double-arm machine up to 130 lbs with both arms simultaneously from a seated position and 140 lbs with both arms simultaneously from a standing position.
141. 14 January 1999, 5:56 a.m. Surabaya, Indonesia. Before lifting 230 lbs twenty-four times with one arm (10 right, 10 left, plus twice each arm to maximum extension).
142. 14 January 1999, 6:12 a.m. Surabaya, Indonesia. Before using double-arm machine up to 130 lbs with both arms simultaneously from a standing position.
143. 15 January 1999, 4:42 a.m. Surabaya, Indonesia. Before lifting 400 lbs one hundred and two times with one arm (49 right, 53 left in four sets).
144. 15 January 1999, 4:55 a.m. Surabaya, Indonesia. Before using double-arm machine up to 150 lbs with each arm separately from a standing position.
145. 16 January 1999, 8:43 a.m. Surabaya, Indonesia. Before lifting 400 lbs two hundred and three times with one arm (97 right, 106 left in five sets).
146. 16 January 1999, 9:00 a.m. Surabaya, Indonesia. Before using double-arm machine up to 140 lbs with both arms simultaneously from a standing position and 140 lbs with each arm separately from a seated position.
147. 17 January 1999, 7:29 a.m. Surabaya, Indonesia. Before lifting 400 lbs one hundred and ninety-four times with one arm (103 right, 91 left in five sets).
148. Surabaya, Indonesia. 17 January 1999, 7:51 a.m. Before using double-arm machine. New record: 150 lbs with both arms simultaneously from a standing position.
149. 19 January 1999. 6:43 a.m. Surabaya, Indonesia. Before lifting 400 lbs one hundred and eighty-six times with one arm (95 right, 91 left in five sets).
150. 19 January 1999, 7:05 a.m. Surabaya, Indonesia. Before using double-arm machine. New record: 160 lbs with both arms simultaneously from a standing position.
151. 20 January 1999, 7:07 a.m. Surabaya, Indonesia. Before using double-arm machine up to 140 lbs with both arms simultaneously from a standing position.
152. 20 January 1999, 6:50 a.m. Surabaya, Indonesia. Before lifting 400 lbs two hundred and four times with one arm (101 right, 103 left in five sets).
153. 22 January 1999. Bandung, Indonesia. Before lifting 400 lbs with one arm.
154. 22 January 1999, 7:07 a.m. Bandung, Indonesia. Before using double-arm machine up to 140 lbs with both arms simultaneously from a standing position.
155. 23 January 1999, 6:50 a.m. Bandung, Indonesia. Before using double-arm machine up to 160 lbs with both arms simultaneously from a standing position.
156. 23 January 1999, 7:04 a.m. Bandung, Indonesia. Before lifting 400 lbs two hundred and sixteen times with one arm (109 right, 107 left in five sets).
157. 24 January 1999, 4:51 a.m. Bandung, Indonesia. Before lifting 400 lbs two hundred and eight times with one arm (108 right, 100 left in five sets).
158. 24 January 1999, Bandung, Indonesia. 5:05 a.m. Before using double-arm machine up to 160 lbs with both arms simultaneously from a standing position.
159. 5 February 1999, 4:44 a.m. Before lifting 300 lbs fifty-eight times with one arm (27 right, 31 left).
160. 5 February 1999.
161. 6 February 1999, 4:28 a.m. Before using double-arm machine up to 110 lbs with both arms simultaneously from a seated position.
162. 6 February 1999, 4:54 a.m. Before lifting 200 lbs twelve times with one arm (5 right, 5 left plus once each arm to maximum extension).
163. 8 February 1999, 6:09 a.m. Before lifting 300 lbs fifty-three times with one arm (27 right, 26 left).
164. 8 February 1999, 6:24 a.m. Before using double-arm machine up to 120 lbs with both arms simultaneously from a seated position.
165. 9 February 1999, 5:28 a.m. Before lifting 300 lbs fifty-one times with one arm (25 right, 26 left).
166. 9 February 1999, 5:40 a.m. Before lifting 200 lbs twelve times with one arm (5 right, 5 left plus once each arm to maximum extension).

167. 9 February 1999, 5:48 a.m. Before lifting 130 lbs with both arms simultaneously. (Total: 260 lbs)
168. 9 February 1999, 5:51 a.m. Before using double-arm machine.
169. 10 February 1999, 6:37 a.m. Before lifting 300 lbs fifty-one times with one arm (25 right, 26 left).
170. 10 February 1999, 6:48 a.m. Before lifting 200 lbs twelve times with one arm (5 right, 5 left plus once each arm to maximum extension).
171. 10 February 1999, 6:54 a.m. Before lifting 130 lbs with both arms simultaneously. (Total: 260 lbs)
172. 10 February 1999, 6:57 a.m. Before using double-arm machine up to 130 lbs with both arms simultaneously from a seated position.
173. 15 February 1999, 3:30 a.m. Before using double-arm machine up to 130 lbs with both arms simultaneously from a seated position.
174. 15 February 1999, 3:42 a.m. Before lifting 300 lbs sixty-three times with one arm (29 right, 34 left).
175. 15 February 1999, 3:54 a.m. Before lifting 200 lbs thirteen times with one arm (6 right, 5 left plus once each arm to maximum extension).
176. 15 February 1999, 4:01 a.m. Before lifting 130 lbs with both arms simultaneously. (Total: 260 lbs)
177. 16 February 1999, 5:42 a.m. Before using double-arm machine.
178. 16 February 1999, 6:04 a.m. Before lifting 200 lbs twelve times with one arm (5 right, 5 left plus once each arm to maximum extension).
179. 16 February 1999, 6:10 a.m. Before lifting 130 lbs with both arms simultaneously. (Total: 260 lbs)
180. 20 February 1999, 7:39 a.m. Before using double-arm machine.
181. 20 February 1999, 7:57 a.m. Before lifting 210 lbs twelve times with one arm (5 right, 5 left plus once each arm to maximum extension).
182. 20 February 1999, 8:04 a.m. Before lifting 140 lbs with both arms simultaneously. (Total: 280 lbs)
183. 21 February 1999, 7:49 a.m. Before using double-arm machine up to 130 lbs with both arms simultaneously from a seated position (four repetitions).
184. 21 February 1999, 8:05 a.m. Before lifting 210 lbs sixty-five times with one arm (30 right, 33 left plus once each arm to maximum extension).
185. 21 February 1999, 8:16 a.m. Before lifting 140 lbs with both arms simultaneously. (Total: 280 lbs)
186. 22 February 1999, 7:08 a.m. Before using double-arm machine.
187. 22 February 1999, 7:32 a.m. Before lifting 200 lbs forty-seven times with one arm (21 right, 24 left plus once each arm to maximum extension).
188. 22 February 1999, 7:43 a.m. Before lifting 140 lbs with both arms simultaneously. (Total: 280 lbs)
189. 22 February 1999, 7:46 p.m. Before using double-arm machine. New record: 140 lbs with each arm separately from a seated position.
190. 23 February 1999, 8:31 a.m. Before lifting 200 lbs one hundred and three times with one arm (50 right, 51 left in three sets, plus once each arm to maximum extension).
191. 23 February 1999, 8:42 a.m. Before lifting 140 lbs with both arms simultaneously. (Total: 280 lbs)
192. 23 February 1999, 8:55 p.m. Before using double-arm machine.
193. 24 February 1999, 9:29 a.m. Before lifting 200 lbs fifty-two times with one arm (25 right, 25 left plus once each arm to maximum extension).
194. 24 February 1999, 9:41 a.m. Before lifting 150 lbs with both arms simultaneously. (Total: 300 lbs) Equal to personal best set on 13 June 1988 at age 56.
195. 26 February 1999, 8:01 a.m. Before using double-arm machine up to 130 lbs with both arms simultaneously from a seated position.
196. 26 February 1999, 8:20 a.m. Before lifting 200 lbs fifty-two times with one arm (25 right, 25 left plus once each arm to maximum extension).

197. 26 February 1999, 8:33 a.m. Before lifting 150 lbs with both arms simultaneously. (Total: 300 lbs)
198. 15 March 1999, 5:02 a.m. Before using double-arm machine up to 140 lbs with both arms simultaneously from a seated position (after returning from an 11-day trip to France, Slovakia, the Czech Republic, Hungary and South Africa).
199. 15 March 1999, 5:21 a.m. Before lifting 200 lbs fifty-two times with one arm (25 right, 25 left plus once each arm to maximum extension).
200. 15 March 1999, 5:37 a.m. Before lifting 155 lbs with both arms simultaneously. (Total: 310 lbs) New record.
201. 16 March 1999, 6:03 a.m. Before lifting 200 lbs with one arm (multiple repetitions plus once each arm to maximum extension).
202. 16 March 1999, 6:19 a.m. Before lifting 160 lbs with both arms simultaneously. (Total: 320 lbs) New record.
203. 16 March 1999, 6:52 a.m. Before using double-arm machine.
204. 17 March 1999, 5:10 a.m. Before using double-arm machine up to 140 lbs with both arms simultaneously from a seated position.
205. 17 March 1999, 5:26 a.m. Before lifting 200 lbs fifty-two times with one arm (25 right, 25 left plus once each arm to maximum extension).
206. 17 March 1999, 5:45 a.m. Before lifting 160 lbs with both arms simultaneously for the second time. (Total: 320 lbs)
207. 18 March 1999, 6:04 a.m. Before lifting 200 lbs fifty-two times with each arm (25 right, 25 left in three sets, plus once each arm to maximum extension).
208. 18 March 1999, 5:52 a.m. Before using double-arm machine.
209. 18 March 1999, 6:22 a.m. Before lifting 170 lbs with both arms simultaneously (Total: 340 lbs) New record.
210. 19 March 1999, 6:02 a.m. Before using double-arm machine up to 150 lbs with both arms simultaneously from a seated position. New record.
211. 19 March 1999, 6:18 a.m. Before lifting 200 lbs fifty-two times with each arm (25 right, 25 left in three sets plus once each arm to maximum extension).
212. 19 March 1999, 6:38 a.m. Before lifting 170 lbs (13 lbs over bodyweight) with both arms simultaneously for the second time. (Total: 340 lbs)
213. 21 March 1999, 7:45 a.m. Before using double-arm machine.
214. 21 March 1999, 7:56 a.m. Before lifting 200 lbs fifty-two times with one arm (25 right, 25 left plus once each arm to maximum extension).
215. 21 March 1999, 8:10 a.m. Before lifting 180 lbs with both arms simultaneously. (Total: 360 lbs) New record.
216. 22 March 1999, 5:23 a.m. Before using double-arm machine up to 150 lbs with both arms simultaneously from a seated position.
217. 22 March 1999, 5:42 a.m. Before lifting 200 lbs with each arm. (multiple repetitions plus once each arm to maximum extension)
218. 22 March 1999, 5:53 a.m. Before lifting 200 lbs with both arms simultaneously (Total: 400 lbs) New record.
219. 26 March 1999, 2:45 a.m. Before using double-arm machine up to 150 lbs with both arms simultaneously from a seated position.
220. 26 March 1999, 3:00 a.m. Before lifting 200 lbs fifty-two times with one arm (25 right, 25 left plus once each arm to maximum extension).
221. 26 March 1999, 3:12 a.m. Before lifting 200 lbs with both arms simultaneously (Total: 400 lbs) Lift number 5 (interim lifts not videoed) of the 200 lbs double-arm series.
222. 28 March 1999, 10:01 p.m. Before using double-arm machine up to 150 lbs with both arms simultaneously from a seated position.
223. 28 March 1999, 10:15 p.m. Before lifting 200 lbs fifty-two times with one arm (25 right, 25 left plus once each arm to maximum extension).
224. 28 March 1999, 10:30 p.m. Before lifting 200 lbs with both arms simultaneously (Total: 400 lbs) Lift number seven.

225. 31 March 1999, 7:59 a.m. Before using double-arm machine up to 150 lbs with both arms simultaneously from a seated position.
226. 31 March 1999, 8:12 a.m. Before using new standing double-arm machine up to 160 lbs with both arms simultaneously. Note: This apparatus stacks the weights vertically overhead instead of horizontally along the dumbbell. The amount to be lifted can be varied using a selector pin.
227. 31 March 1999, 8:24 a.m. Before lifting 200 lbs three times with both arms simultaneously. (Total: 400 lbs) Lifts number 8, 9 and 10.
228. 1 April 1999, 8:23 a.m. Before using seated double-arm machine.
229. 1 April 1999, 8:34 a.m. Before using standing double-arm machine up to 180 lbs with both arms simultaneously.
230. 1 April 1999, 8:50 a.m. Before lifting 200 lbs twice with both arms simultaneously. (Total: 400 lbs) Lifts number 11 and 12.
231. 2 April 1999, 8:19 a.m. Before using seated double-arm machine up to 150 lbs with both arms simultaneously.
232. 2 April 1999, 8:31 a.m. Before using standing double-arm machine up to 160 lbs with both arms simultaneously.
233. 2 April 1999, 8:47 a.m. Before lifting 200 lbs twice with both arms simultaneously. (Total: 400 lbs) Lifts number thirteen and fourteen.
234. 3 April 1999, 7:54 a.m. Before lifting 200 lbs three times with both arms simultaneously. (Total: 400 lbs) Lifts number fifteen, sixteen and seventeen.
235. 5 April 1999, 5:34 a.m. Before using seated double-arm machine.
236. 5 April 1999, 5:43 a.m. Before using standing double-arm machine up to 160 lbs with both arms simultaneously.
237. 5 April 1999, 6:00 a.m. Before lifting 200 lbs twice with both arms simultaneously. (Total: 400 lbs) Lifts number eighteen and nineteen.
238. 5 April 1999, 6:23 a.m. Before lifting 200 lbs fifty-two times with one arm (25 right, 25 left plus once each arm to maximum extension).
239. 6 April 1999, 9:07 a.m. Before using seated double-arm machine up to 150 lbs with both arms simultaneously.
240. 6 April 1999, 9:19 a.m. Before using standing double-arm machine up to 160 lbs with both arms simultaneously.
241. 6 April 1999, 9:32 a.m. Before lifting 200 lbs with both arms simultaneously. (Total: 400 lbs) Lift number twenty.
242. 6 April 1999, 9:43 a.m. Before lifting 200 lbs fifty-two times with one arm (25 right, 25 left plus once each arm to maximum extension).
243. 7 April 1999, 3:26 a.m. Before using seated double-arm machine up to 150 lbs with both arms simultaneously.
244. 7 April 1999, 3:30 a.m. Before using standing double-arm machine up to 160 lbs with both arms simultaneously.
245. 7 April 1999, 3:54 a.m. Before lifting 200 lbs with both arms simultaneously. (Total: 400 lbs) Lift number twenty-one.
246. 7 April 1999, 4:05 a.m. Before lifting 200 lbs forty-two times with one arm (20 right, 20 left plus once each arm to maximum extension).
247. 8 April 1999, 8:03 a.m. Before using seated double-arm machine.
248. 8 April 1999, 8:10 a.m. Before lifting 210 lbs forty-nine times with one arm (23 right, 24 left plus once each arm to greater extension).
249. 8 April 1999, 8:22 a.m. Before lifting 200 lbs twice with both arms simultaneously. (Total: 400 lbs) Lifts number twenty-two and twenty-three.
250. 9 April 1999, 8:29 a.m. Before using seated double-arm machine.
251. 9 April 1999, 8:41 a.m. Before lifting 220 lbs fifty times with one arm (24 right, 24 left plus once each arm to maximum extension).
252. 9 April 1999, 8:54 a.m. Before lifting 200 lbs with both arms simultaneously. (Total: 400 lbs) Lift number twenty-four.

253. 9 April 1999, 9:07 a.m. Before using standing double-arm machine up to 180 lbs with both arms simultaneously.
254. 10 April 1999, 7:57 a.m. Before using seated double-arm machine up to 160 lbs with both arms simultaneously. New record.
255. 10 April 1999, 8:10 a.m. Before using standing double-arm machine up to 160 lbs with both arms simultaneously.
256. 10 April 1999, 8:19 a.m. Before lifting 220 lbs forty-two times with one arm (21 right, 19 left plus once each arm to maximum extension).
257. 10 April 1999, 8:31 a.m. Before lifting 200 lbs with both arms simultaneously. (Total: 400 lbs) Lift number twenty-five.
258. 12 April 1999, 9:43 a.m. Before using seated double-arm machine.
259. 12 April 1999, 9:55 a.m. Before using standing double-arm machine up to 140 lbs with both arms simultaneously.
260. 12 April 1999, 10:12 a.m. Before lifting 230 lbs fifty-two times with one arm (25 right, 25 left plus once each arm to maximum extension).
261. 12 April 1999, 10:26 a.m. Before lifting 200 lbs with both arms simultaneously. (Total: 400 lbs) Lift number twenty-six.
262. 13 April 1999, 7:10 a.m. Before using seated double-arm machine up to 160 lbs five times with both arms simultaneously.
263. 13 April 1999, 7:25 a.m. Before using standing double-arm machine up to 160 lbs with both arms simultaneously.
264. 13 April 1999, 7:37 a.m. Before lifting 230 lbs forty-three times with one arm (20 right, 21 left plus once each arm to maximum extension).
265. 13 April 1999, 7:48 a.m. Before lifting 200 lbs with both arms simultaneously. (Total: 400 lbs) Lift number twenty-seven.
266. 18 April 1999, 6:19 a.m. Before using seated double-arm machine up to 160 lbs with both arms simultaneously.
267. 18 April 1999, 6:29 a.m. Before using standing double-arm machine up to 160 lbs with both arms simultaneously.
268. 18 April 1999, 6:40 a.m. Before lifting 230 lbs fifty-two times with one arm (25 right, 25 left plus once each arm to maximum extension).
269. 18 April 1999, 6:47 a.m. Before lifting 200 lbs with both arms simultaneously. (Total: 400 lbs) Lift number thirty-two.
270. 21 April 1999, 7:15 a.m. Before using seated double-arm machine up to 160 lbs with both arms simultaneously.
271. 21 April 1999, 7:25 a.m. Before using standing double-arm machine up to 160 lbs with both arms simultaneously.
272. 21 April 1999, 7:34 a.m. Before lifting 230 lbs fifty-two times with one arm (25 right, 25 left plus once each arm to maximum extension).
273. 21 April 1999, 7:45 a.m. Before lifting 200 lbs twice with both arms simultaneously. (Total: 400 lbs) Lifts number thirty-four and thirty-five.
274. 22 April 1999, 6:28 a.m. Before using seated double-arm machine.
275. 22 April 1999, 6:37 a.m. Before lifting 240 lbs fifty-five times with one arm (26 right, 27 left plus once each arm to maximum extension).
276. 22 April 1999, 6:51 a.m. Before lifting 200 lbs twice with both arms simultaneously. (Total: 400 lbs) Lifts number thirty-six and thirty-seven.
277. 25 April 1999, 8:24 p.m. Before using seated double-arm machine up to 160 lbs with both arms simultaneously.
278. 25 April 1999, 8:34 p.m. Before using standing double-arm machine up to 160 lbs with both arms simultaneously and 200 lbs with each arm separately.
279. 25 April 1999, 8:46 p.m. Before lifting 240 lbs fifty-five times with one arm (27 right, 26 left plus once each arm to maximum extension).
280. 25 April 1999, 8:59 p.m. Before lifting 200 lbs with both arms simultaneously. (Total: 400 lbs) Lift number thirty-eight.
281. 27 April 1999, 7:21 a.m. Before using seated double-arm machine.

282. 27 April 1999, 7:31 a.m. Before using standing double-arm machine up to 180 lbs with both arms simultaneously.
283. 27 April 1999, 7:45 a.m. Before lifting 220 lbs three times with both arms simultaneously. (Total: 440 lbs) New record.
284. 27 April 1999, 8:40 p.m. Before using seated double-arm machine up to 160 lbs with both arms simultaneously.
285. 27 April 1999, 8:49 p.m. Before using standing double-arm machine up to 180 lbs with both arms simultaneously and 210 lbs with each arm separately.
286. 27 April 1999, 9:01 p.m. Before lifting 250 lbs fifty-two times with one arm (25 right, 25 left plus once each arm to maximum extension).
287. 27 April 1999, 9:12 p.m. Before lifting 230 lbs three times with both arms simultaneously. (Total: 460 lbs) New record.
288. 29 April 1999, 7:17 a.m. Before using seated double-arm machine.
289. 29 April 1999, 7:25 a.m. Before using standing double-arm machine up to 200 lbs with both arms simultaneously and 230 lbs with each arm separately.
290. 1 May 1999, 7:33 a.m. Before using seated double-arm machine.
291. 1 May 1999, 7:41 a.m. Before using standing double-arm machine up to 160 lbs with both arms simultaneously.
292. 1 May 1999, 7:56 a.m. Before lifting 250 lbs three times with both arms simultaneously. (Total: 500 lbs)
293. 3 May 1999, 6:08 a.m. Before using seated double-arm machine up to 160 lbs with both arms simultaneously.
294. 3 May 1999, 6:20 a.m. Before using standing double-arm machine up to 200 lbs with both arms simultaneously and 240 lbs with each arm separately.
295. 3 May 1999, 6:37 a.m. Before lifting 270 lbs seven times with both arms simultaneously. (Total: 540 lbs) New record.
296. 4 May 1999, 6:02 a.m. Before using seated double-arm machine.
297. 4 May 1999, 6:10 a.m. Before using standing double-arm machine up to 200 lbs with both arms simultaneously and 240 lbs with each arm separately.
298. 4 May 1999, 6:27 a.m. Before lifting 270 lbs fifty-six times with one arm (27 right, 27 left plus once each arm to maximum extension).
299. 4 May 1999, 6:41 a.m. Before lifting 270 lbs four times with both arms simultaneously. (Total: 540 lbs)
300. 5 May 1999, 6:34 a.m. Before using seated double-arm machine.
301. 5 May 1999, 6:44 a.m. Before using standing double-arm machine up to 210 lbs with both arms simultaneously and 240 lbs with each arm separately.
302. 5 May 1999, 7:01 a.m. Before lifting 280 lbs three times with both arms simultaneously. (Total: 560 lbs) New record.
303. 7 May 1999, 4:13 a.m. Before using seated double-arm machine.
304. 7 May 1999, 4:24 a.m. Before using standing double-arm machine up to 210 lbs with both arms simultaneously and 240 lbs with each arm separately.
305. 7 May 1999, 4:43 a.m.
306. 9 May 1999, 7:12 a.m. Before using seated double-arm machine up to 160 lbs with both arms simultaneously.
307. 9 May 1999, 7:22 a.m. Before using standing double-arm machine up to 210 lbs with both arms simultaneously and 240 lbs with each arm separately.
308. 9 May 1999, 7:38 a.m.
309. 10 May 1999, 3:54 a.m. Before lifting 280 lbs fifty-eight times with one arm (26 right, 26 left plus three times each arm to maximum extension).
310. 10 May 1999, 3:54 a.m.
311. 11 May 1999, 8:18 a.m. Before using seated double-arm machine.
312. 11 May 1999, 8:27 a.m. Before using standing double-arm machine up to 210 lbs with both arms simultaneously and 240 lbs with each arm separately.
313. 11 May 1999, 8:45 a.m.
314. 12 May 1999, 6:33 a.m. Before using seated double-arm machine.

MY MORNING SOUL-BODY PRAYERS

315. 12 May 1999, 6:40 a.m. Before using standing double-arm machine up to 210 lbs with both arms simultaneously and 240 lbs with each arm separately.
316. 12 May 1999, 6:59 a.m.
317. 13 May 1999, 7:08 a.m. Before using standing double-arm machine up to 210 lbs with both arms simultaneously and 250 lbs with each arm separately.
318. 13 May 1999, 7:21 a.m.
319. 13 May 1999, 7:54 a.m. Before lifting 280 lbs seventy-eight times with one arm (38 right, 40 left).
320. 14 May 1999, 7:16 a.m. Before using standing double-arm machine up to 210 lbs with both arms simultaneously and 250 lbs with each arm separately.
321. 14 May 1999, 7:28 a.m. Before lifting 300 lbs fifty-six times with one arm (28 right, 28 left).
322. 14 May 1999, 7:45 a.m.
323. 16 May 1999, 5:28 a.m. Before using standing double-arm machine up to 230 lbs with both arms simultaneously and 250 lbs with each arm separately.
324. 16 May 1999, 5:45 a.m. Before lifting 300 lbs with one arm sixty-one times (29 right, 32 left).
325. 16 May 1999, 6:10 a.m. Before using seated double-arm machine up to 160 lbs with both arms simultaneously and 180 lbs with each arm separately.
326. 17 May 1999, 7:28 a.m. Before using standing double-arm machine up to 230 lbs with both arms simultaneously and 250 lbs with each arm separately. The morning after the passing of Sri Chinmoys beloved sister Lily.
327. 17 May 1999, 7:47 a.m.
328. 18 May 1999, 7:06 a.m. Before using standing double-arm machine up to 230 lbs with both arms simultaneously and 250 lbs with each arm separately.
329. 18 May 1999, 7:25 a.m.
330. 18 May 1999, 7:39 a.m. Before lifting 300 lbs sixty-four times with one arm (32 right, 32 left).
331. 19 May 1999, 5:51 a.m. Before using standing double-arm machine up to 230 lbs with both arms simultaneously and 250 lbs with each arm separately.
332. 19 May 1999, 6:10 a.m.
333. 19 May 1999, 6:32 a.m. Before lifting 210 lbs four times with one arm (2 right, 2 left).
334. 19 May 1999, 6:39 a.m. Before using seated double-arm machine up to 160 lbs with both arms simultaneously and 190 lbs with each arm separately.
335. 21 May 1999, 7:06 a.m. Before using standing double-arm machine up to 230 lbs with both arms simultaneously and 260 lbs with each arm separately.
336. 21 May 1999, 7:24 a.m.
337. 23 May 1999, 6:18 a.m.
338. 23 May 1999, 6:42 a.m. Before lifting 300 lbs fifty-two times with one arm (26 right, 26 left).
339. 23 May 1999, 6:00 a.m. Before using standing double-arm machine up to 250 lbs with both arms simultaneously.
340. 23 May 1999, 8:48 p.m. Before using standing double-arm machine up to 230 lbs with both arms simultaneously and 250 lbs with each arm separately.
341. 23 May 1999, 9:00 p.m.
342. 23 May 1999, 9:21 p.m. Before lifting 300 lbs fifty-six times with one arm (28 right, 28 left).
343. 23 May 1999, 9:26 p.m. Before using seated double-arm machine up to 160 lbs with both arms simultaneously and 190 lbs with each arm separately.
344. 25 May 1999, 6:07 a.m. Before using standing double-arm machine up to 230 lbs with both arms simultaneously and 250 lbs with each arm separately.
345. 25 May 1999, 6:28 a.m. Before lifting 300 lbs with one arm sixty times (29 right, 31 left).
346. 25 May 1999, 6:39 a.m.
347. 25 May 1999, 6:59 a.m. Before using seated double-arm machine.

348. 26 May 1999, 7:29 a.m. Before using standing double-arm machine up to 230 lbs with both arms simultaneously and 250 lbs with each arm separately.
349. 26 May 1999, 7:57 a.m.
350. 27 May 1999, 7:35 a.m. Before using seated double-arm machine.
351. 27 May 1999, 7:40 a.m. Before using standing double-arm machine up to 210 lbs with both arms simultaneously and 250 lbs with each arm separately.
352. 27 May 1999, 8:08 a.m.
353. 28 May 1999, 6:48 a.m. Before using seated double-arm machine.
354. 28 May 1999, 6:55 a.m. Before using standing double-arm machine up to 210 lbs with both arms simultaneously and 250 lbs with each arm separately.
355. 28 May 1999, 7:11 a.m.
356. 28 May 1999, 7:32 a.m. Before lifting 300 lbs with one arm fifty-three times (27 right, 26 left).
357. 29 May 1999, 7:25 a.m.
358. 31 May 1999, 5:45 a.m. Before using seated double-arm machine up to 160 lbs with both arms simultaneously.
359. 31 May 1999, 5:50 a.m. Before using standing double-arm machine up to 210 lbs with both arms simultaneously and 250 lbs with each arm separately.
360. 31 May 1999, 6:09 a.m.
361. 31 May 1999, 6:29 a.m. Before lifting 300 lbs with one arm fifty-four times (27 right, 27 left).
362. 1 June 1999, 6:38 a.m. Before using seated double-arm machine up to 120 lbs with both arms simultaneously and 190 lbs with each arm separately.
363. 1 June 1999, 6:48 a.m.
364. 1 June 1999, 7:07 a.m. Before lifting 300 lbs fifty-seven times with one arm (28 right, 29 left).
365. 2 June 1999, 7:22 a.m. Before using seated double-arm machine up to 120 lbs with both arms simultaneously and 190 lbs with each arm separately.
366. 2 June 1999, 7:36 a.m.
367. 3 June 1999, 6:29 a.m. Before using seated double-arm machine up to 160 lbs with both arms simultaneously.
368. 3 June 1999, 6:40 a.m.
369. 3 June 1999, 7:12 a.m. Before lifting 300 lbs fifty-seven times with one arm (28 right, 29 left).
370. 4 June 1999, 8:43 a.m. Before using seated double-arm machine up to 120 lbs with both arms simultaneously and 190 lbs with each arm separately.
371. 4 June 1999, 8:53 a.m.
372. 4 June 1999, 9:15 a.m. Before lifting 250 lbs five times with both arms simultaneously. (Total: 500 lbs)
373. 4 June 1999, 9:25 a.m. Before lifting 300 lbs fifty-one times with one arm (25 right, 26 left).
374. 15 June 1999, 8:25 a.m. Before using seated double-arm machine. Note: This was Sri Chinmoys first day of lifting since June 4th, when he left New York to visit his brother Mantu in India. He returned on June 11th.
375. 15 June 1999, 8:29 a.m. Before using standing double-arm machine up to 210 lbs with both arms simultaneously and 250 lbs with each arm separately.
376. 15 June 1999, 8:45 a.m.
377. 15 June 1999, 9:07 a.m. Before lifting 250 lbs three times with both arms simultaneously. (Total: 500 lbs)
378. 15 June 1999, 9:10 a.m. Before lifting 300 lbs fifty-two times with one arm (26 right, 26 left).
379. 17 June 1999, 8:41 a.m. Before using seated double-arm machine.
380. 17 June 1999, 8:58 a.m. Before lifting 250 lbs with both arms simultaneously. (Total: 500 lbs)

381. 17 June 1999, 9:05 a.m. Before lifting 300 lbs fifty-two times with one arm (25 right, 27 left).
382. 17 June 1999, 9:17 a.m. Before using standing double-arm machine up to 210 lbs with both arms simultaneously and 250 lbs with each arm separately.
383. 19 June 1999, 8:32 a.m. Before using seated double-arm machine.
384. 19 June 1999, 8:41 a.m.
385. 19 June 1999, 9:00 a.m. Before lifting 250 lbs three times with both arms simultaneously. (Total: 500 lbs)
386. 19 June 1999, 9:07 a.m. Before lifting 300 lbs fifty-three times with one arm (26 right, 27 left).
387. 21 June 1999, 9:17 a.m. Before using seated double-arm machine.
388. 21 June 1999, 9:25 a.m.
389. 21 June 1999, 9:48 a.m. Before lifting 250 lbs four times with both arms simultaneously. (Total: 500 lbs)
390. 21 June 1999, 9:51 a.m. Before lifting 300 lbs fifty-five times with one arm (28 right, 27 left).
391. 22 June 1999, 7:01 a.m. Before using seated double-arm machine.
392. 22 June 1999, 7:08 a.m. Before using standing double-arm machine up to 210 lbs with both arms simultaneously and 250 lbs with each arm separately.
393. 22 June 1999, 7:20 a.m. Before lifting 250 lbs four times with both arms simultaneously. (Total: 500 lbs)
394. 22 June 1999, 7:31 a.m. Before lifting 300 lbs fifty-six times with one arm (27 right, 29 left).
395. 23 June 1999, 7:24 a.m. Before using seated double-arm machine up to 160 lbs with both arms simultaneously and 190 lbs with each arm separately.
396. 23 June 1999, 7:35 a.m. Before lifting 250 lbs three times with both arms simultaneously. (Total: 500 lbs)
397. 23 June 1999, 7:47 a.m. Before lifting 300 lbs fifty-six times with one arm (29 right, 27 left).
398. 24 June 1999, 4:28 a.m. Before using seated double-arm machine.
399. 24 June 1999, 4:35 a.m. Before lifting 250 lbs four times with both arms simultaneously. (Total: 500 lbs)
400. 24 June 1999, 4:46 a.m. Before lifting 300 lbs fifty-two times with one arm (26 right, 26 left).
401. 25 June 1999, 7:42 a.m. Before using seated double-arm machine up to 160 lbs with both arms simultaneously.
402. 25 June 1999, 7:52 a.m. Before lifting 250 lbs three times with both arms simultaneously. (Total: 500 lbs)
25. June 1999, 8:04 a.m. Before lifting 300 lbs fifty-six times with one arm (27 right, 29 left).
404. 26 June 1999, 7:34 a.m. 14th Weightlifting Anniversary. Before using seated double-arm machine.
405. 26 June 1999, 7:41 a.m. Before lifting 250 lbs three times with both arms simultaneously. (Total: 500 lbs)
406. 26 June 1999, 7:57 a.m. Before lifting 300 lbs fifty-four times with one arm (28 right, 26 left).
407. 28 June 1999, 7:38 a.m. Before using seated double-arm machine up to 160 lbs with both arms simultaneously.
408. 28 June 1999, 7:46 a.m. Before lifting 250 lbs three times with both arms simultaneously. (Total: 500 lbs)
409. 28 June 1999, 8:01 a.m. Before lifting 350 lbs fifty-eight times with one arm (29 right, 29 left).
410. 30 June 1999, 8:42 a.m. Before using seated double-arm machine up to 160 lbs with both arms simultaneously and 190 lbs with each arm separately.

411. 30 June 1999, 8:52 a.m. Before lifting 250 lbs three times with both arms simultaneously. (Total: 500 lbs)
412. 30 June 1999, 9:04 a.m. Before lifting 350 lbs with one arm.
413. 1 July 1999, 8:07 a.m. Before using seated double-arm machine.
414. 1 July 1999, 8:14 a.m. Before lifting 250 lbs three times with both arms simultaneously. (Total: 500 lbs)
415. 1 July 1999, 8:27 a.m. Before lifting 350 lbs fifty-seven times with one arm (28 right, 29 left).
416. 5 July 1999, 8:20 a.m. Before using seated double-arm machine up to 160 lbs with both arms simultaneously and 190 lbs with each arm separately.
417. 5 July 1999, 8:33 a.m. Before lifting 250 lbs twice with both arms simultaneously. (Total: 500 lbs)
418. 5 July 1999, 8:43 a.m. Before lifting 350 lbs fifty-six times with one arm (27 right, 29 left).
419. 6 July 1999, 7:17 a.m. Before using seated double-arm machine up to 120 lbs with both arms simultaneously and 160 lbs with each arm separately.
420. 6 July 1999, 7:26 a.m. Before lifting 250 lbs twice with both arms simultaneously. (Total: 500 lbs)
421. 6 July 1999, 7:34 a.m. Before lifting 350 lbs fifty-seven times with one arm (29 right, 28 left).
422. 7 July 1999, 4:48 a.m. Before using seated double-arm machine up to 160 lbs with both arms simultaneously and 190 lbs with each arm separately.
423. 7 July 1999, 4:58 a.m. Before lifting 250 lbs three times with both arms simultaneously (Total: 500 lbs)
424. 7 July 1999, 5:07 a.m. Before lifting 350 lbs fifty-four times with one arm (25 right, 29 left).
425. 8 July 1999, 7:48 a.m. Before doing clean and press from the ground up to 35 lbs with both arms simultaneously and 80 lbs with right arm.
426. 8 July 1999, 8:05 a.m. Before using seated calf raise machine up to 900 lbs.
427. 8 July 1999, 8:48 a.m. Before using standing double-arm machine up to 210 lbs with both arms simultaneously.
428. 9 July 1999, 8:25 a.m. Before using seated double-arm machine up to 160 lbs with both arms simultaneously and 190 lbs with each arm separately.
429. 9 July 1999, 8:39 a.m. Before lifting 250 lbs twice with both arms simultaneously. (Total: 500 lbs)
430. 9 July 1999, 8:49 a.m. Before lifting 350 lbs sixty times with one arm (29 right, 31 left).
431. 10 July 1999, 8:16 a.m. Before using seated double-arm machine up to 120 lbs with both arms simultaneously and 160 lbs with each arm separately.
432. 10 July 1999, 8:24 a.m. Before lifting 250 lbs twice with both arms simultaneously. (Total: 500 lbs)
433. 10 July 1999, 8:35 a.m. Before lifting 350 lbs fifty-four times with one arm (27 right, 27 left).
434. 10 July 1999, 9:21 a.m. Before doing clean and press from the ground up to 40 lbs with both arms simultaneously.
435. 11 July 1999, 8:34 a.m. Before doing clean and press from the ground up to 85 lbs with one arm.
436. 11 July 1999, 8:56 a.m. Before using seated calf raise machine up to 900 lbs.
437. 11 July 1999, 9:32 a.m. Before lifting 400 lbs sixty-six times with one arm (33 right, 33 left).
438. 12 July 1999, 8:36 a.m. Before using seated double-arm machine up to 160 lbs with both arms simultaneously and 190 lbs with each arm separately.
439. 12 July 1999, 8:48 a.m. Before lifting 250 lbs twice with both arms simultaneously. (Total: 500 lbs)
440. 12 July 1999, 8:59 a.m. Before lifting 400 lbs fifty-seven times with one arm (27 right, 30 left).

MY MORNING SOUL-BODY PRAYERS

441. 13 July 1999, 10:00 a.m. Before doing clean and press from the ground up to 40 lbs with both arms simultaneously.
442. 14 July 1999, 6:55 a.m. Before using seated double-arm machine up to 160 lbs with both arms simultaneously.
443. 14 July 1999, 7:07 a.m. Before lifting 250 lbs twice with both arms simultaneously. (Total: 500 lbs)
444. 14 July 1999, 7:21 a.m. Before lifting 400 lbs seventy-two times with one arm (36 right, 36 left).
445. 14 July 1999, 9:09 a.m. Before using seated calf raise machine up to 1,000 lbs New record.
446. 15 July 1999, 8:29 a.m. Before doing clean and press from the ground up to 45 lbs with both arms simultaneously.
447. 15 July 1999, 8:57 a.m. Before using standing double-arm machine up to 210 lbs with both arms simultaneously and 230 lbs with each arm separately.
448. 15 July 1999, 9:12 a.m. Before lifting 400 lbs one hundred and nine times with one arm (56 right, 53 left).
449. 16 July 1999, 9:09 a.m. Before using seated double-arm machine up to 120 lbs with both arms simultaneously and 160 lbs with each arm separately.
450. 16 July 1999, 9:17 a.m. Before lifting 250 lbs three times with both arms simultaneously. (Total: 500 lbs)
451. 16 July 1999, 9:27 a.m. Before lifting 400 lbs one hundred and seven times with one arm (52 right, 55 left).
452. 17 July 1999, 8:50 a.m. Before lifting 250 lbs twice with both arms simultaneously. (Total: 500 lbs)
453. 17 July 1999, 8:34 a.m. Before using seated double-arm machine up to 160 lbs with both arms simultaneously.
454. 17 July 1999, 9:08 a.m. Before doing clean and press from the ground up to 70 lbs with one arm.
455. 17 July 1999, 9:39 a.m. Before using seated calf raise machine up to 900 lbs.
456. 19 July 1999, 7:21 a.m. Before using seated double-arm machine up to 160 lbs with both arms simultaneously and 190 lbs with each arm separately.
457. 19 July 1999, 7:35 a.m. Before lifting 250 lbs four times with both arms simultaneously. (Total 500 lbs)
458. 19 July 1999, 7:50 a.m. Before lifting 400 lbs one hundred and nine times with one arm (55 right, 54 left).
459. 21 July 1999, 8:11 a.m. Before using seated double-arm machine.
460. 21 July 1999, 8:20 a.m. Before lifting 250 lbs twice with both arms simultaneously. (Total: 500 lbs)
461. 21 July 1999, 8:32 a.m. Before lifting 400 lbs ninety-eight times with one arm (48 right, 50 left).
462. 22 July 1999, 6:46 a.m. Before lifting 250 lbs twice with both arms simultaneously. (Total: 500 lbs)
463. 22 July 1999, 7:12 a.m. Before doing clean and press from the ground up to 85 lbs with one arm.
464. 22 July 1999, 8:24 a.m. Before using seated double-arm machine up to 160 lbs with both arms simultaneously and 200 lbs with each arm separately. New record.
465. 23 July 1999, 8:39 a.m. Before using seated double-arm machine up to 120 lbs with both arms simultaneously and 160 lbs with each arm separately.
466. 23 July 1999, 8:47 a.m. Before lifting 250 lbs twice with both arms simultaneously. (Total: 500 lbs)
467. 23 July 1999, 8:56 a.m. Before lifting 400 lbs with one arm.
468. 24 July 1999, 7:56 a.m. Before using seated double-arm machine up to 120 lbs with both arms simultaneously and 160 lbs with each arm separately.
469. 24 July 1999, 8:06 a.m. Before lifting 250 lbs twice with both arms simultaneously. (Total: 500 lbs)

470. 24 July 1999, 8:34 a.m. Before doing clean and press from the ground up to 45 lbs with both arms simultaneously.
471. 24 July 1999, 9:15 a.m. Before using seated calf raise machine up to 1,000 lbs.
472. 26 July 1999, 1:31 a.m. Before using seated double-arm machine up to 120 lbs with both arms simultaneously and 160 lbs with each arm separately.
473. 26 July 1999, 1:42 a.m. Before lifting 250 lbs three times with both arms simultaneously. (Total: 500 lbs)
474. 26 July 1999, 2:00 a.m. Before lifting 400 lbs ninety-nine times with one arm (50 right, 49 left).
475. 27 July 1999, 1:08 a.m. Before using seated double-arm machine up to 160 lbs with both arms simultaneously and 200 lbs with each arm separately.
476. 27 July 1999, 1:22 a.m. Before lifting 260 lbs three times with both arms simultaneously. (Total: 520 lbs)
477. 27 July 1999, 1:31 a.m. Before lifting 400 lbs one hundred and two times with one arm (50 right, 52 left).
478. 27 July 1999, 1:45 a.m. Before doing clean and press from the ground up to 45 lbs with both arms simultaneously.
479. 27 July 1999, 2:02 a.m. Before using seated calf raise machine.
480. 28 July 1999, 7:18 a.m. Before using seated double-arm machine up to 120 lbs with both arms simultaneously and 160 lbs with each arm separately.
481. 28 July 1999, 7:24 a.m. Before lifting 260 lbs three times with both arms simultaneously. (Total: 520 lbs)
482. 28 July 1999, 7:34 a.m. Before lifting 400 lbs one hundred and five times with one arm (52 right, 53 left).
483. 30 July 1999, 8:43 a.m. Before doing clean and press from the ground up to 85 lbs with one arm.
484. 30 July 1999, 9:12 a.m. Before lifting 260 lbs twice with both arms simultaneously. (Total: 520 lbs)
485. 31 July 1999, 8:59 a.m. Before using seated calf raise machine up to 1,000 lbs.
486. 31 July 1999, 10:05 a.m. Before lifting 260 lbs twice with both arms simultaneously. (Total: 520 lbs)
487. 31 July 1999, 10:15 a.m. Before lifting 400 lbs one hundred and three times with one arm (51 right, 52 left).
488. 1 August 1999, 9:18 a.m. Before lifting 270 lbs three times with both arms simultaneously. (Total: 540 lbs)
489. 1 August 1999, 9:26 a.m. Before lifting 400 lbs one hundred and four times with one arm (53 right, 51 left).
490. 2 August 1999, 10:11 a.m. Before lifting 270 lbs twice with both arms simultaneously. (Total: 540 lbs)
491. 2 August 1999, 10:18 a.m. Before lifting 400 lbs one hundred and eleven times with one arm (55 right, 56 left).
492. 3 August 1999, 12:49 a.m. Before doing clean and press from the ground up to 45 lbs with both arms simultaneously (25 reps).
493. 3 August 1999, 1:00 a.m. Before using seated calf raise machine up to 1,000 lbs.
494. 3 August 1999, 1:22 a.m. Before lifting 270 lbs twice with both arms simultaneously. (Total: 540 lbs)
495. 3 August 1999, 1:32 a.m. Before lifting 400 lbs one hundred and nine times with one arm (54 right, 55 left).
496. 3 August 1999, 1:42 a.m. Before using seated double-arm machine up to 160 lbs with both arms simultaneously and 200 lbs with each arm separately.
497. 6 August 1999, 6:16 a.m. Before lifting 270 lbs twice with both arms simultaneously. (Total: 540 lbs)
498. 6 August 1999, 6:41 a.m. Before doing clean and press from the ground up to 90 lbs (10 reps).
499. 6 August 1999, 7:15 a.m. Before using seated calf raise machine up to 1,000 lbs (2 lifts).

MY MORNING SOUL-BODY PRAYERS

500. 10 August 1999, 1:52 a.m. Before lifting 270 lbs three times with both arms simultaneously. (Total: 540 lbs)
501. 10 August 1999. 2:00 a.m. Before lifting 400 lbs one hundred and three times with one arm (49 right, 54 left).
502. 10 August 1999, 2:21 a.m. Before doing clean and press from the ground up to 45 lbs with both arms simultaneously (22 reps).
503. 10 August 1999, 2:36 a.m. Before using seated calf raise machine up to 1,000 lbs.
504. 10 August 1999, 8:22 a.m. Before using seated double-arm machine up to 120 lbs with both arms simultaneously and 160 lbs with each arm separately.
505. 11 August 1999, 9:09 a.m. Before lifting 270 lbs three times with both arms simultaneously. (Total: 540 lbs)
506. 11 August 1999, 9:18 a.m. Before lifting 400 lbs one hundred and eight times with one arm (52 right, 56 left).
507. 11 August 1999, 9:39 a.m. Before using seated double-arm machine up to 120 lbs with both arms simultaneously and 160 lbs with each arm separately.
508. 12 August 1999, 6:26 a.m. Before lifting 270 lbs twice with both arms simultaneously. (Total: 540 lbs)
509. 12 August 1999, 6:44 a.m. Before doing clean and press from the ground up to 90 lbs (10 reps).
510. 12 August 1999, 7:04 a.m. Before lifting 400 lbs one hundred and twenty times with one arm (58 right, 62 left).
511. 14 August 1999, 6:26 a.m. Before lifting 270 lbs three times with both arms simultaneously. (Total: 540 lbs)
512. 14 August 1999, 6:35 a.m. Before lifting 400 lbs one hundred and twenty-two times with one arm (53 right, 69 left).
513. 14 August 1999, 6:47 a.m. Before lifting 300 lbs seventeen times with one arm (9 right, 8 left).
514. 14 August 1999, 7:04 a.m. Before using seated double-arm machine up to 200 lbs with both arms simultaneously. New record.
515. 14 August 1999, 7:34 a.m. Before doing clean and press from the ground up to 45 lbs with both arms simultaneously.
516. 15 August 1999, 7:33 a.m. Before doing clean and press from the ground up to 45 lbs with both arms simultaneously (21 reps).
517. 15 August 1999, 7:46 a.m. Before using seated calf raise machine up to 1,000 lbs.
518. 15 August 1999 8:16 a.m. Before lifting 270 lbs with both arms simultaneously. (Total: 540 lbs)
519. 15 August 1999, 8:21 a.m. Before lifting 400 lbs one hundred and nineteen times with one arm (54 right, 65 left).
520. 16 August 1999, 7:12 a.m. Before lifting 400 lbs one hundred and twenty-one times with one arm (56 right, 65 left).
521. 16 August 1999, 7:29 a.m. Before lifting 270 lbs twice with both arms simultaneously. (Total: 540 lbs)
522. 16 August 1999, 7:44 a.m. Before lifting 300 lbs nineteen times with one arm. (7 right, 12 left).
523. 16 August 1999, 7:58 a.m. Before using seated double-arm machine up to 200 lbs with both arms simultaneously.
524. 17 August 1999, 8:23 a.m. Before doing clean and press from the ground up to 90 lbs (18 reps).
525. 17 August 1999, 8:45 a.m. Before using seated calf raise machine up to 1,000 lbs.
526. 17 August 1999, 9:10 a.m. Before lifting 270 lbs three times with both arms simultaneously. (Total: 540 lbs)
527. 17 August 1999, 9:20 a.m. Before lifting 300 lbs nineteen times with one arm (7 right, 12 left).
528. 18 August 1999, 8:12 a.m. Before lifting 270 lbs three times with both arms simultaneously. (Total: 540 lbs)

529. 18 August 1999, 8:20 a.m. Before lifting 300 lbs sixteen times with one arm (9 right, 7 left).
530. 18 August 1999, 8:26 a.m. Before lifting 400 lbs one hundred and eleven times with one arm (55 right, 56 left).
531. 18 August 1999, 8:42 a.m. Before using seated double-arm machine up to 140 lbs with both arms simultaneously and 160 lbs with each arm separately.
532. 19 August 1999, 8:26 a.m. Before doing clean and press from the ground up to 45 lbs with both arms simultaneously. (26 reps).
533. 19 August 1999, 8:57 a.m. Before lifting 270 lbs twice with both arms simultaneously. (Total: 540 lbs).
534. 19 August 1999, 9:05 a.m. Before lifting 300 lbs thirty-one times with one arm (13 right, 18 left).
535. 20 August 1999, 8:19 a.m. Before lifting 300 lbs forty-eight times with one arm (20 right, 28 left).
536. 20 August 1999, 8:30 a.m. Before lifting 270 lbs twice with both arms simultaneously. (Total: 540 lbs)
537. 20 August 1999, 8:40 a.m. Before lifting 400 lbs one hundred and eighteen times with one arm (57 right, 61 left).
538. 20 August 1999, 9:03 a.m. Before using seated double-arm machine up to 200 lbs with both arms simultaneously.
539. 20 August 1999, 9:40 a.m. Before using seated calf raise machine up to 1,000 lbs.
540. 21 August 1999. Before lifting 270 lbs three times with both arms simultaneously. (Total: 540 lbs)
541. 21 August 1999, 8:40 a.m. Before lifting 300 lbs twenty-seven times with one arm (14 right, 13 left).
542. 21 August 1999. Before using seated double-arm machine up to 120 lbs with both arms simultaneously and 160 lbs with each arm separately.
543. 23 August 1999, 8:01 a.m. Before lifting 300 lbs thirty-one times with one arm (16 right, 15 left).
544. 23 August 1999, 8:11 a.m. Before lifting 270 lbs three times with both arms simultaneously. (Total: 540 lbs)
545. 23 August 1999, 8:36 a.m. Before using seated double-arm machine up to 140 lbs with both arms simultaneously and 180 lbs with each arm separately.
546. 24 August 1999, 5:20 a.m. Before doing clean and press from the ground up to 90 lbs (15 reps).
547. 24 August 1999, 5:46 a.m. Before using seated calf raise machine up to 1,000 lbs.
548. 24 August 1999, 6:10 a.m. Before lifting 270 lbs twice with both arms simultaneously. (Total: 540 lbs)
549. 25 August 1999, 9:11 a.m. Before using seated double-arm machine up to 120 lbs with both arms simultaneously and 160 lbs with each arm separately.
550. 25 August 1999, 9:21 a.m. Before lifting 270 lbs with both arms simultaneously. (Total: 540 lbs)
551. 25 August 1999, 9:28 a.m. Before lifting 300 lbs twenty-seven times with one arm. (14 right, 13 left).
552. 25 August 1999, 9:33 a.m. Before lifting 400 lbs one hundred and seven times with one arm (53 right, 54 left).
553. 26 August 1999, 9:06 a.m. Before doing clean and press from the ground up to 50 lbs with both arms simultaneously (41 reps). New record.
554. 26 August 1999, 9:50 a.m. Before lifting 270 lbs with both arms simultaneously. (Total: 540 lbs)
555. 26 August 1999, 10:00 a.m. Before lifting 300 lbs thirty-one times with one arm (15 right, 16 left).
556. 26 August 1999, 10:14 a.m. Before using seated double-arm machine up to 160 lbs with both arms simultaneously and 200 lbs with each arm separately.

MY MORNING SOUL-BODY PRAYERS

557. 28 August 1999, 7:58 a.m. Before lifting 270 lbs three times with both arms simultaneously. (Total: 540 lbs)
558. 28 August 1999, 8:06 a.m. Before lifting 300 lbs thirty-four times with one arm (16 right, 18 left).
559. 28 August 1999, 8:14 a.m. Before lifting 400 lbs one hundred and four times with one arm (52 right, 52 left).
560. 28 August 1999, 8:31 a.m. Before using seated double-arm machine up to 140 lbs with both arms simultaneously and 160 lbs with each arm separately.
561. 29 August 1999, 8:24 a.m. Before lifting 270 lbs with both arms simultaneously. (Total: 540 lbs)
562. 29 August 1999, 8:33 a.m. Before lifting 300 lbs fifty times with one arm (25 right, 25 left).
563. 29 August 1999, 8:42 a.m. Before lifting 400 lbs one hundred and nine times with one arm (54 right, 55 left).
564. 29 August 1999, 8:59 a.m. Before using seated double-arm machine up to 120 lbs with both arms simultaneously and 160 lbs with each arm separately.
565. 30 August 1999, 8:24 a.m. Before lifting 300 lbs thirty-three times with one arm (16 right, 17 left).
566. 30 August 1999, 8:12 a.m. Before lifting 270 lbs four times with both arms simultaneously. (Total: 540 lbs)
567. 30 August 1999, 8:02 a.m. Before using seated double-arm machine up to 120 lbs with both arms simultaneously and 160 lbs with each arm separately.
568. 30 August 1999, 8:56 a.m. Before using seated calf raise machine up to 1,000 lbs (2 lifts).
569. 31 August 1999, 8:31 a.m. After doing clean and press from the ground up to 90 lbs (21 reps).
570. 31 August 1999, 8:43 a.m. Before lifting 270 lbs three times with both arms simultaneously. (Total: 540 lbs)
571. 31 August 1999, 8:53 a.m. Before lifting 300 lbs forty-one times with one arm (17 right, 24 left).
572. 31 August 1999, 9:02 a.m. Before lifting 400 lbs one hundred and three times with one arm (47 right, 56 left).
573. 1 September 1999, 6:54 a.m. Before lifting 270 lbs with both arms simultaneously twice. (Total: 540 lbs)
574. 1 September 1999, 7:04 a.m. Before lifting 300 lbs with one arm thirty-five times (18 right, 17 left).
575. 1 September 1999, 7:13 a.m. Before lifting 400 lbs with one arm one hundred and ten times (55 right, 55 left).
576. 1 September 1999, 7:34 a.m. Before using seated double-arm machine up to 160 lbs with both arms simultaneously and 200 lbs with each arm separately.
577. 1 September 1999. Before doing bench press.
578. 1 September 1999.
579. 1 September 1999.
580. 2 September 1999, 6:37 a.m. Before doing clean and press from the ground up to 50 lbs with both arms simultaneously (41 reps).
581. 2 September 1999, 6:56 a.m. Before lifting 270 lbs with both arms simultaneously three times. (Total: 540 lbs)
582. 2 September 1999, 7:07 a.m. Before lifting 300 lbs with one arm forty-two times (20 right, 22 left).
583. 2 September 1999, 7:17 a.m. Before lifting 400 lbs with one arm ninety-five times (56 right, 39 left).
584. 2 September 1999, 7:36 a.m. Before using seated double-arm machine up to 120 lbs with both arms simultaneously and 160 lbs with each arm separately.
585. 2 September 1999, 7:52 a.m. Before using seated calf raise machine up to 1,000 lbs.

586. 3 September 1999, 8:03 a.m. Before lifting 270 lbs with both arms simultaneously three times. (Total: 540 lbs)
587. 3 September 1999, 8:13 a.m. Before lifting 300 lbs with one arm thirty-five times (15 right, 20 left).
588. 3 September 1999, 8:21 a.m. Before lifting 400 lbs with one arm one hundred and fifteen times (55 right, 60 left).
589. 3 September 1999, 8:51 a.m. Before using seated double-arm machine.
590. 4 September 1999, 7:50 a.m. Before doing clean and press from the ground up to 90 lbs.
591. 4 September 1999, 8:06 a.m. Before lifting 270 lbs with both arms simultaneously three times. (Total: 540 lbs)
592. 4 September 1999, 8:16 a.m. Before lifting 300 lbs with one arm forty-four times (29 right, 15 left).
593. 4 September 1999, 8:25 a.m. Before lifting 400 lbs with one arm one hundred and seven times (55 right, 52 left).
594. 4 September 1999, 8:37 a.m. Before using seated double-arm machine up to 120 lbs with both arms simultaneously and 160 lbs with each arm separately.
595. 4 September 1999.
596. 5 September 1999, 7:48 a.m. Before lifting 270 lbs with both arms simultaneously three times. (Total: 540 lbs)
597. 5 September 1999, 7:57 a.m. Before lifting 300 lbs with one arm thirty-three times (16 right, 17 left).
598. 5 September 1999, 9:03 a.m. Before doing clean and press from the ground up to 40 lbs with both arms simultaneously twice (65 and 75 reps).
599. 6 September 1999, 8:02 a.m. Before lifting 270 lbs with both arms simultaneously three times. (Total: 540 lbs)
600. 6 September 1999, 8:12 a.m. Before lifting 300 lbs with one arm twenty-four times (13 right, 11 left).
601. 6 September 1999, 8:19 a.m. Before lifting 400 lbs with one arm one hundred and twenty times (61 right, 59 left).
602. 6 September 1999, 8:34 a.m. Before using seated double-arm machine up to 140 lbs with both arms simultaneously.
603. 6 September 1999, 8:57 a.m. Before doing clean and press from the ground up to 70 lbs (73 reps).
604. 6 September 1999, 10:54 a.m. Before using seated calf raise machine up to 1,000 lbs (3 lifts).
605. 8 September 1999, 8:19 a.m. Before lifting 270 lbs with both arms simultaneously four times. (Total: 540 lbs)
606. 8 September 1999, 8:30 a.m. Before lifting 300 lbs with one arm twenty-three times (12 right, 11 left).
607. 8 September 1999, 8:46 a.m. Before doing clean and press from the ground up to 50 lbs with both arms simultaneously (63 reps).
608. 9 September 1999, 8:20 a.m. Before doing clean and press from the ground up to 96 lbs (13 reps).
609. 9 September 1999, 8:37 a.m. Before lifting 270 lbs with both arms simultaneously four times. (Total: 540 lbs)
610. 9 September 1999, 8:48 a.m. Before lifting 300 lbs with one arm twenty-four times (13 right, 11 left).
611. 9 September 1999, 8:55 a.m. Before lifting 400 lbs with one arm one hundred and five times (53 right, 52 left).
612. 9 September 1999, 9:08 a.m. Before using seated double-arm machine up to 160 lbs with both arms simultaneously and 200 lbs with each arm separately.
613. 10 September 1999, 7:10 a.m. Before lifting 270 lbs with both arms simultaneously three times. (Total: 540 lbs)

MY MORNING SOUL-BODY PRAYERS

614. 10 September 1999, 7:19 a.m. Before lifting 300 lbs with one arm twenty-five times (12 right, 13 left).
615. 10 September 1999, 7:27 a.m. Before lifting 400 lbs with one arm one hundred times (50 right, 50 left).
616. 10 September 1999, 7:45 a.m. Before using seated double-arm machine up to 140 lbs with both arms simultaneously.
617. 10 September 1999, 8:22 a.m. Before doing clean and press from the ground up to 40 lbs with both arms simultaneously (87 reps).
618. 11 September 1999, 8:17 a.m. Before lifting 270 lbs with both arms simultaneously three times. (Total: 540 lbs)
619. 11 September 1999 8:27 a.m. Before lifting 300 lbs with one arm twenty-three times (12 right, 11 left).
620. 11 September 1999, 8:45 a.m. Before using seated double-arm machine up to 140 lbs with both arms simultaneously.
621. 11 September 1999, 9:05 a.m.
622. 12 September 1999, 8:15 a.m. Before lifting 300 lbs with both arms simultaneously three times. (Total: 600 lbs)
623. 12 September 1999, 8:28 a.m. Before lifting 270 lbs with both arms simultaneously twice. (Total: 540 lbs)
624. 12 September 1999, 9:06 a.m. Before using seated calf raise machine up to 1,000 lbs.
625. 13 September 1999, 8:20 a.m. Before doing clean and press from the ground up to 70 lbs.
626. 13 September 1999, 8:43 a.m. Before lifting 300 lbs with both arms simultaneously. (Total: 600 lbs)
627. 13 September 1999, 8:56 a.m. Before lifting 275 lbs with both arms simultaneously. (Total: 550 lbs)
628. 13 September 1999, 9:06 a.m. Before lifting 400 lbs with one arm.
629. 13 September 1999, 9:22 a.m. Before using seated double-arm machine up to 140 lbs with both arms simultaneously.
630. 14 September 1999, 7:56 a.m. Before lifting 300 lbs with both arms simultaneously five times. (Total: 600 lbs)
631. 14 September 1999, 8:09 a.m. Before lifting 275 lbs with both arms simultaneously three times. (Total: 550 lbs)
632. 14 September 1999, 8:30 a.m. Before using seated double-arm machine up to 160 lbs with both arms simultaneously and 200 lbs with each arm separately.
633. 14 September 1999, 9:00 a.m. Before doing clean and press from the ground up to 40 lbs with both arms simultaneously (84 reps).
634. 15 September 1999, 7:50 a.m. Before lifting 300 lbs with both arms simultaneously. (Total: 600 lbs)
635. 15 September 1999, 8:09 a.m. Before lifting 275 lbs with both arms simultaneously. (Total: 550 lbs)
636. 15 September 1999, 8:15 a.m. Before lifting 400 lbs with one arm.
637. 15 September 1999, 8:25 a.m. Before using seated double-arm machine up to 140 lbs with both arms simultaneously and 160 lbs with each arm separately.
638. 15 September 1999, 11:48 p.m. Before lifting 300 lbs with both arms simultaneously. (Total: 600 lbs)
639. 15 September 1999, 11:55 p.m. Before lifting 275 lbs with both arms simultaneously. (Total: 550 lbs)
640. 17 September 1999, 7:06 a.m. Before lifting 300 lbs with both arms simultaneously three times. (Total: 600 lbs)
641. 17 September 1999, 7:19 a.m. Before lifting 275 lbs with both arms simultaneously three times. (Total: 550 lbs)
642. 17 September 1999, 7:53 a.m. Before doing clean and press from the ground up to 70 lbs.
643. 17 September 1999, 9:40 a.m. Before using seated calf raise machine up to 1,000 lbs.

644. 18 September 1999, 8:33 a.m. Before doing clean and press from the ground up to 96 lbs (18 reps).
645. 18 September 1999, 9:15 a.m. Before lifting 275 lbs with both arms simultaneously twice. (Total: 550 lbs)
646. 18 September 1999, 9:20 a.m. Before lifting 400 lbs with one arm one hundred times (50 right, 50 left).
647. 19 September 1999, 8:04 a.m. Before doing clean and press from the ground up to 50 lbs with both arms simultaneously (67 reps).
648. 19 September 1999, 9:06 a.m. Before lifting 300 lbs with both arms simultaneously three times. (Total: 600 lbs)
649. 19 September 1999, 9:20 a.m. Before lifting 275 lbs with both arms simultaneously three times. (Total: 550 lbs)
650. 19 September 1999, 9:36 a.m. Before using seated double-arm machine up to 140 lbs with both arms simultaneously.
651. 21 September 1999, 9:13 a.m. Before lifting 300 lbs with both arms simultaneously three times. (Total: 600 lbs)
652. 21 September 1999, 9:26 a.m. Before lifting 275 lbs with both arms simultaneously twice. (Total: 550 lbs)
653. 21 September 1999, 9:32 a.m. Before lifting 400 lbs with one arm sixty-five times (33 right, 32 left).
654. 21 September 1999, 9:49 a.m. Before doing clean and press from the ground up to 40 lbs with both arms simultaneously (101 reps).
655. 22 September 1999, 8:48 a.m. Before doing clean and press from the ground up to 70 lbs (95 reps).
656. 22 September 1999, 9:07 a.m. Before lifting 300 lbs with both arms simultaneously four times. (Total: 600 lbs)
657. 22 September 1999, 9:27 a.m. Before lifting 275 lbs with both arms simultaneously twice. (Total: 550 lbs)
658. 22 September 1999, 9:46 a.m. Before using seated double-arm machine up to 140 lbs with both arms simultaneously.
659. 23 September 1999, 8:36 a.m. Before doing clean and press from the ground up to 50 lbs with both arms simultaneously (62 reps).
660. 23 September 1999, 9:21 a.m. Before lifting 300 lbs with both arms simultaneously four times. (Total: 600 lbs)
661. 23 September 1999, 9:39 a.m. Before lifting 275 lbs with both arms simultaneously three times. (Total: 550 lbs)
662. 24 September 1999, 7:30 a.m. Before lifting 300 lbs with both arms simultaneously three times. (Total: 600 lbs)
663. 24 September 1999, 7:47 a.m. Before lifting 275 lbs with both arms simultaneously twice. (Total: 550 lbs)
664. 24 September 1999, 7:57 a.m. Before lifting 400 lbs with one arm seventy-two times (36 right, 36 left).
665. 24 September 1999, 8:12 a.m. Before using seated double-arm machine up to 140 lbs with both arms simultaneously and 160 lbs with each arm separately.
666. 26 September 1999, 6:27 a.m. Before using seated double-arm machine up to 120 lbs with both arms simultaneously and 160 lbs with each arm separately.
667. 26 September 1999, 6:33 a.m. Before lifting 200 lbs with both arms simultaneously. (Total: 400 lbs)
668. 26 September 1999, 6:45 a.m. Before lifting 300 lbs with both arms simultaneously twice. (Total: 600 lbs)
669. 26 September 1999, 6:56 a.m. Before lifting 250 lbs with both arms simultaneously twice. (Total: 500 lbs)
670. 26 September 1999, 7:07 a.m. Before lifting 400 lbs with one arm seventy-one times (36 right, 35 left).
671. 26 September 1999, 7:40 a.m. Before using seated calf raise machine up to 700 lbs.

MY MORNING SOUL-BODY PRAYERS

672. 27 September 1999, 8:28 a.m. Before using seated double-arm machine up to 140 lbs with both arms simultaneously.
673. 27 September 1999, 8:34 a.m. Before lifting 200 lbs with both arms simultaneously twice. (Total: 400 lbs)
674. 27 September 1999, 8:43 a.m. Before lifting 300 lbs with both arms simultaneously twice. (Total: 600 lbs)
675. 27 September 1999, 8:56 a.m. Before lifting 250 lbs with both arms simultaneously twice. (Total: 500 lbs)
676. 27 September 1999, 9:15 a.m. Before lifting 400 lbs with one arm.
677. 27 September 1999, 9:31 a.m. Before using seated calf raise machine up to 700 lbs.
678. 27 September 1999.
679. 27 September 1999. Before using seated calf raise machine up to 800 lbs.
680. 27 September 1999. Before using seated calf raise machine.
681. 28 September 1999, 8:06 a.m. Before using seated double-arm machine up to 140 lbs with both arms simultaneously.
682. 28 September 1999, 8:16 a.m. Before lifting 200 lbs with both arms simultaneously twice. (Total: 400 lbs)
683. 28 September 1999, 8:21 a.m. Before lifting 250 lbs with both arms simultaneously twice. (Total: 500 lbs)
684. 28 September 1999, 8:29 a.m. Before lifting 300 lbs with both arms simultaneously three times. (Total: 600 lbs)
685. 28 September 1999, 8:41 a.m. Before lifting 400 lbs with one arm sixty-eight times (33 right, 35 left).
686. 28 September 1999, 9:04 a.m. Before using seated calf raise machine up to 1,000 lbs.
687. 30 September 1999, 8:29 a.m. Before lifting 200 lbs with both arms simultaneously. (Total: 400 lbs)
688. 30 September 1999, 8:34 a.m. Before lifting 250 lbs with both arms simultaneously twice. (Total: 500 lbs)
689. 30 September 1999, 8:41 a.m. Before lifting 300 lbs with both arms simultaneously twice. (Total: 600 lbs)
690. 30 September 1999, 8:49 a.m. Before lifting 400 lbs with one arm sixty-six times (33 right, 33 left).
691. 30 September 1999, 9:10 a.m. Before doing clean and press from the ground up to 70 lbs (94 reps).
692. 1 October 1999, 8:37 a.m. Before using seated double-arm machine up to 140 lbs with both arms simultaneously.
693. 1 October 1999, 8:46 a.m. Before lifting 200 lbs with both arms simultaneously. (Total: 400 lbs)
694. 1 October 1999, 8:54 a.m. Before lifting 250 lbs with both arms simultaneously. (Total: 500 lbs)
695. 1 October 1999, 9:09 a.m. Before lifting 400 lbs with one arm sixty-two times (32 right, 30 left).
696. 1 October 1999, 9:30 a.m. Before doing clean and press from the ground up to 40 lbs with both arms simultaneously. (95 reps).
697. 2 October 1999, 9:30 a.m. Before using seated calf raise machine up to 900 lbs.
698. 2 October 1999, 9:46 a.m. Before using seated double-arm machine up to 140 lbs with both arms simultaneously.
699. 2 October 1999, 10:01 a.m. Before lifting 200 lbs with both arms simultaneously twice. (Total: 400 lbs)
700. 2 October 1999, 10:12 a.m. Before lifting 250 lbs with both arms simultaneously. (Total: 500 lbs)
701. 2 October 1999, 10:17 a.m. Before lifting 300 lbs with both arms simultaneously three times. (Total: 600 lbs) 700th Prayer.
702. 2 October 1999, 10:30 a.m. Before lifting 400 lbs with one arm sixty-five times (33 right, 32 left).

703. 2 October 1999, 11:50 p.m. Before using seated calf raise machine up to 1,000 lbs.
704. 5 October 1999, 9:24 a.m. Before using seated double-arm machine up to 140 lbs with both arms simultaneously.
705. 5 October 1999, 9:30 a.m. Before lifting 400 lbs with one arm sixty-eight times (33 right, 35 left).
706. 5 October 1999, 9:42 a.m. Before lifting 200 lbs with both arms simultaneously twice. (Total: 400 lbs)
707. 5 October 1999, 10:06 a.m. Before using seated calf raise machine up to 1,000 lbs.
708. 6 October 1999, 8:01 a.m. Before using seated double-arm machine up to 150 lbs with both arms simultaneously.
709. 6 October 1999, 8:07 a.m. Before lifting 400 lbs with one arm sixty-five times (31 right, 34 left).
710. 6 October 1999, 8:21 a.m. Before lifting 200 lbs with both arms simultaneously twice. (Total: 400 lbs)
711. 6 October 1999, 8:29 a.m. Before lifting 250 lbs with both arms simultaneously. (Total: 500 lbs)
712. 6 October 1999, 8:35 a.m. Before lifting 300 lbs with both arms simultaneously twice. (Total: 600 lbs)
713. 6 October 1999, 8:54 a.m. Before doing clean and press from the ground up to 80 lbs (72 reps).
714. 9 October 1999, 8:41 a.m. Before using seated double-arm machine up to 120 lbs with both arms simultaneously and 160 lbs with each arm separately.
715. 9 October 1999, 8:47 a.m. Before lifting 400 lbs with one arm sixty times (30 right, 30 left).
716. 9 October 1999, 9:01 a.m. Before lifting 200 lbs with both arms simultaneously three times. (Total: 400 lbs)
717. 9 October 1999, 9:07 a.m. Before lifting 250 lbs with both arms simultaneously. (Total: 500 lbs)
718. 9 October 1999, 9:10 a.m. Before lifting 300 lbs with both arms simultaneously twice. (Total: 600 lbs)
719. 11 October 1999, 12:55 a.m. Before doing clean and press from the ground up to 96 lbs (18 reps).
720. 11 October 1999, 1:22 a.m. Before using seated double-arm machine up to 140 lbs with both arms simultaneously.
721. 11 October 1999, 1:39 a.m. Before lifting 200 lbs with both arms simultaneously three times. (Total: 400 lbs)
722. 11 October 1999, 1:40 a.m. Before lifting 250 lbs with both arms simultaneously. (Total: 500 lbs)
723. 11 October 1999, 1:42 a.m. Before lifting 300 lbs with both arms simultaneously twice. (Total: 600 lbs)
724. 12 October 1999, 8:41 a.m. Before doing clean and press from the ground up to 50 lbs with both arms simultaneously. (61 reps).
725. 12 October 1999, 9:04 a.m. Before using seated double-arm machine up to 140 lbs with both arms simultaneously and 160 lbs with each arm separately.
726. 12 October 1999, 9:21 a.m. Before lifting 200 lbs with both arms simultaneously twice. (Total: 400 lbs)
727. 12 October 1999, 9:24 a.m. Before lifting 400 lbs with one arm sixty-four times (31 right, 33 left).
728. 13 October 1999, 6:52 a.m. Before using seated double-arm machine up to 140 lbs with both arms simultaneously.
729. 13 October 1999, 7:07 a.m. Before lifting 200 lbs with both arms simultaneously twice. (Total: 400 lbs)
730. 13 October 1999, 7:14 a.m. Before lifting 250 lbs with both arms simultaneously. (Total: 500 lbs)

MY MORNING SOUL-BODY PRAYERS

731. 13 October 1999, 7:17 a.m. Before lifting 300 lbs with both arms simultaneously three times. (Total: 600 lbs)
732. 13 October 1999, 7:29 a.m. Before lifting 400 lbs with one arm sixty-seven times (34 right, 33 left).
733. 13 October 1999, 7:50 a.m. Before using seated calf raise machine up to 1,000 lbs.
734. 14 October 1999, 9:46 a.m. Before using seated double-arm machine up to 150 lbs with both arms simultaneously.
735. 14 October 1999, 9:53 a.m. Before lifting 400 lbs with one arm sixty-six times (31 right, 35 left).
736. 14 October 1999, 10:08 a.m. Before lifting 200 lbs with both arms simultaneously twice. (Total: 400 lbs)
737. 14 October 1999, 10:30 a.m. Before doing clean and press from the ground up to 80 lbs (77 reps).
738. 15 October 1999, 9:47 a.m. Before using seated double-arm machine up to 140 lbs with both arms simultaneously.
739. 15 October 1999, 9:58 a.m. Before lifting 200 lbs with both arms simultaneously twice. (Total: 400 lbs)
740. 15 October 1999, 10:07 a.m. Before lifting 250 lbs with both arms simultaneously. (Total: 500 lbs)
741. 15 October 1999, 10:08 a.m. Before lifting 300 lbs with both arms simultaneously twice. (Total: 600 lbs)
742. 15 October 1999, 10:29 a.m. Before doing clean and press from the ground up to 40 lbs with both arms simultaneously. (96 reps).
743. 16 October 1999, 9:24 a.m. Before using seated double-arm machine up to 140 lbs with both arms simultaneously and 160 lbs with each arm separately.
744. 16 October 1999, 9:31 a.m. Before lifting 400 lbs with one arm fifty-two times (26 right, 26 left).
745. 16 October 1999, 9:57 a.m. Before using seated calf raise machine up to 1,000 lbs.
746. 18 October 1999, 8:54 a.m. Before using seated double-arm machine up to 150 lbs with both arms simultaneously.
747. 18 October 1999, 9:03 a.m. Before lifting 200 lbs with both arms simultaneously. (Total: 400 lbs)
748. 18 October 1999, 9:13 a.m. Before lifting 250 lbs with both arms simultaneously. (Total: 500 lbs)
749. 18 October 1999, 9:14 a.m. Before lifting 300 lbs with both arms simultaneously twice. (Total: 600 lbs)
750. 18 October 1999, 9:22 a.m. Before lifting 400 lbs with one arm one hundred and six times (52 right, 54 left).
751. 19 October 1999, 7:04 a.m. Before using seated double-arm machine up to 140 lbs with both arms simultaneously and 150 lbs with each arm separately.
752. 19 October 1999, 7:20 a.m. Before lifting 200 lbs with both arms simultaneously twice. (Total: 400 lbs)
753. 19 October 1999, 7:26 a.m. Before lifting 400 lbs with one arm one hundred and nine times (54 right, 55 left).
754. 19 October 1999, 7:54 a.m. Before doing clean and press from the ground up to 80 lbs (73 reps).
755. 19 October 1999, 8:29 a.m. Before using seated calf raise machine up to 1,000 lbs.
756. 20 October 1999, 9:18 a.m. Before using seated double-arm machine up to 140 lbs with both arms simultaneously.
757. 20 October 1999, 9:30 a.m. Before lifting 200 lbs with both arms simultaneously. (Total: 400 lbs)
758. 20 October 1999, 9:37 a.m. Before lifting 250 lbs with both arms simultaneously. (Total: 500 lbs)
759. 20 October 1999, 9:40 a.m. Before lifting 300 lbs with both arms simultaneously. (Total: 600 lbs)

760. 20 October 1999, 9:49 a.m. Before lifting 400 lbs with one arm one hundred and four times (52 right, 52 left).
761. 20 October 1999, 10:14 a.m. Before doing clean and press from the ground up to 40 lbs with both arms simultaneously. (100 reps).
762. 22 October 1999, 9:15 a.m. Before using seated double-arm machine up to 140 lbs with both arms simultaneously.
763. 22 October 1999, 9:22 a.m. Before lifting 200 lbs with both arms simultaneously. (Total: 400 lbs)
764. 22 October 1999, 9:28 a.m. Before lifting 250 lbs with both arms simultaneously. (Total: 500 lbs)
765. 22 October 1999, 9:31 a.m. Before lifting 300 lbs with both arms simultaneously. (Total: 600 lbs)
766. 22 October 1999, 9:48 a.m. Before doing clean and press from the ground up to 80 lbs (89 reps).
767. 25 October 1999, 9:51 a.m. Before using seated double-arm machine up to 150 lbs with both arms simultaneously.
768. 25 October 1999, 10:03 a.m. Before lifting 200 lbs with both arms simultaneously. (Total: 400 lbs)
769. 25 October 1999, 10:07 a.m. Before lifting 250 lbs with both arms simultaneously. (Total: 500 lbs)
770. 25 October 1999, 10:11 a.m. Before lifting 300 lbs with both arms simultaneously. (Total: 600 lbs)
771. 25 October 1999, 10:14 a.m. Before lifting 400 lbs with one arm one hundred times. (50 right, 50 left).
772. 25 October 1999, 10:35 a.m. Before doing clean and press from the ground up to 40 lbs with both arms simultaneously. (104 reps).
773. 26 October 1999, 10:00 p.m. Before using seated double-arm machine up to 140 lbs with both arms simultaneously.
774. 26 October 1999, 10:08 p.m. Before lifting 200 lbs with both arms simultaneously. (Total: 400 lbs)
775. 26 October 1999, 10:14 p.m. Before lifting 250 lbs with both arms simultaneously (Total: 500 lbs)
776. 26 October 1999, 10:18 p.m. Before lifting 300 lbs with both arms simultaneously. (Total: 600 lbs)
777. 26 October 1999, 10:26 p.m. Before lifting 400 lbs with one arm one hundred and four times (52 right, 52 left).
778. 26 October 1999, 10:45 p.m. Before doing clean and press from the ground up to 80 lbs (81 reps).
779. 28 October 1999, 6:33 p.m. Before using seated double-arm machine up to 140 lbs with both arms simultaneously and 160 lbs with each arm separately.
780. 28 October 1999, 6:49 p.m. Before lifting 200 lbs with both arms simultaneously. (Total: 400 lbs)
781. 28 October 1999, 6:55 p.m. Before lifting 250 lbs with both arms simultaneously. (Total: 500 lbs)
782. 28 October 1999, 6:57 p.m. Before lifting 300 lbs with both arms simultaneously. (Total: 600 lbs)
783. 28 October 1999, 7:27 p.m. Before doing clean and press from the ground up to 40 lbs with both arms simultaneously.(94 reps).
784. 1 November 1999, 8:47 a.m. Before doing clean and press from the ground up to 80 lbs (78 reps).
785. 1 November 1999, 9:07 a.m. Before doing one hundred one-arm pushes with 400 lbs (50 right, 50 left).
786. 1 November 1999, 9:19 a.m. Before lifting 200 lbs with both arms simultaneously. (Total: 400 lbs)

MY MORNING SOUL-BODY PRAYERS

787. 1 November 1999, 9:24 a.m. Before lifting 250 lbs with both arms simultaneously. (Total: 500 lbs)
788. 1 November 1999, 9:31 a.m. Before lifting 300 lbs with both arms simultaneously. (Total: 600 lbs)
789. 1 November 1999, 9:44 a.m. Before using seated double-arm machine up to 140 lbs with both arms simultaneously.
790. 1 November 1999, 10:08 a.m. Before using seated calf raise machine up to 1,000 lbs.
791. 2 November 1999 9:22 a.m. Before using seated double-arm machine up to 150 lbs with both arms simultaneously.
792. 2 November 1999, 9:34 a.m. Before lifting 200 lbs with both arms simultaneously. (Total: 400 lbs)
793. 2 November 1999, 9:38 a.m. Before doing one hundred one-arm pushes with 400 lbs (50 right, 50 left).
794. 3 November 1999, 1:00 a.m. Before using seated double-arm machine up to 140 lbs with both arms simultaneously.
795. 3 November 1999, 1:13 a.m. Before lifting 200 lbs with both arms simultaneously. (Total: 400 lbs)
796. 3 November 1999, 1:19 a.m. Before lifting 250 lbs with both arms simultaneously. (Total: 500 lbs)
797. 3 November 1999, 1:20 a.m. Before lifting 300 lbs with both arms simultaneously. (Total: 600 lbs)
798. 3 November 1999, 1:28 a.m. Before doing one hundred one-arm pushes with 400 lbs (50 right, 50 left).
799. 4 November 1999, 8:57 a.m. Before doing clean and press from the ground up to 40 lbs with both arms simultaneously. (104 reps).
800. 4 November 1999, 9:19 a.m. Before lifting 200 lbs with both arms simultaneously. (Total: 400 lbs)
801. 4 November 1999, 9:25 a.m. Before lifting 250 lbs with both arms simultaneously. (Total: 500 lbs)
802. 4 November 1999, 9:27 a.m. Before lifting 300 lbs with both arms simultaneously. (Total: 600 lbs)
803. 4 November 1999, 9:34 a.m. Before doing one hundred one-arm pushes with 400 lbs (50 right, 50 left).
804. 6 November 1999, 6:34 a.m. Before using seated double-arm machine up to 140 lbs with both arms simultaneously.
805. 6 November 1999, 6:46 a.m. Before lifting 200 lbs with both arms simultaneously. (Total: 400 lbs)
806. 6 November 1999, 6:48 a.m. Before lifting 250 lbs with both arms simultaneously. (Total: 500 lbs)
807. 6 November 1999, 6:51 a.m. Before lifting 300 lbs with both arms simultaneously. (Total: 600 lbs)
808. 6 November 1999, 6:58 a.m. Before doing one hundred one-arm pushes with 400 lbs (50 right, 50 left).
809. 8 November 1999, 7:39 a.m. Before using seated double-arm machine up to 150 lbs with both arms simultaneously.
810. 8 November 1999, 7:47 a.m. Before lifting 200 lbs with both arms simultaneously. (Total: 400 lbs)
811. 8 November 1999, 7:52 a.m. Before lifting 250 lbs with both arms simultaneously. (Total: 500 lbs)
812. 8 November 1999, 7:56 a.m. Before lifting 300 lbs with both arms simultaneously. (Total: 600 lbs)
813. 8 November 1999, Before doing one hundred and five one-arm pushes with 400 lbs (53 right, 52 left).
814. 8 November 1999, 8:37 a.m. Before using seated calf raise machine up to 1,000 lbs.

815. 14 November 1999, 8:36 a.m. Before using seated double-arm machine up to 140 lbs with both arms simultaneously.
816. 14 November 1999, 8:45 a.m. Before lifting 200 lbs with both arms simultaneously. (Total: 400 lbs)
817. 14 November 1999, 8:52 a.m. Before lifting 250 lbs with both arms simultaneously. (Total: 500 lbs)
818. 14 November 1999, 8:55 a.m. Before lifting 300 lbs with both arms simultaneously. (Total: 600 lbs)
819. 14 November 1999, 9:03 a.m. Before doing sixty-four one-arm pushes with 400 lbs (32 right, 32 left).
820. 14 November 1999, 9:27 a.m. Before using seated calf raise machine up to 800 lbs.
821. 15 November 1999, 7:57 a.m. Before using seated double-arm machine up to 140 lbs with both arms simultaneously.
822. 15 November 1999, 8:06 a.m. Before lifting 200 lbs with both arms simultaneously. (Total: 400 lbs)
823. 15 November 1999, 8:11 a.m. Before lifting 250 lbs with both arms simultaneously. (Total: 500 lbs)
824. 15 November 1999, 8:14 a.m. Before lifting 300 lbs with both arms simultaneously. (Total: 600 lbs)
825. 15 November 1999, 8:21 a.m. Before doing fifty one-arm pushes with 400 lbs (25 right, 25 left).
831. 29 November 1999, 4:17 a.m. Before lifting 350 lbs with both arms simultaneously three times. (Total: 700 lbs) New record.
832. 30 November 1999, 8:52 a.m. Before using seated double-arm machine up to 140 lbs with both arms simultaneously.
833. 30 November 1999, 9:01 a.m. Before lifting 250 lbs with both arms simultaneously. (Total: 500 lbs)
834. 30 November 1999, 9:05 a.m. Before lifting 300 lbs with both arms simultaneously. (Total: 600 lbs)
835. 30 November 1999, 9:11 a.m. Before lifting 350 lbs with both arms simultaneously. (Total: 700 lbs)
836. 30 November 1999, 9:21 a.m. Before doing forty-six one-arm pushes with 500 lbs.
837. 5 December 1999, 9:11 a.m. Sao Paulo, Brazil. Before using seated double-arm machine up to 140 lbs with both arms simultaneously.
838. 5 December 1999, 9:24 a.m. Sao Paulo, Brazil. Before lifting 350 lbs with both arms simultaneously eight times. (Total: 700 lbs)
839. 5 December 1999, 9:38 a.m. Sao Paulo, Brazil. Before doing fifty one-arm pushes with 500 lbs (25 right, 25 left).
840. 6 December 1999, 8:57 a.m. Sao Paulo, Brazil. Before using seated double-arm machine up to 150 lbs with both arms simultaneously.
841. 6 December 1999, 9:08 a.m. Sao Paulo, Brazil. Before lifting 350 lbs with both arms simultaneously four times. (Total: 700 lbs)
842. 6 December 1999, 9:20 a.m. Sao Paulo, Brazil. Before doing sixty-four one-arm pushes with 500 lbs (29 right, 35 left).
843. 8 December 1999, 8:14 a.m. Nova Friburgo, Brazil. Before using seated double-arm machine up to 140 lbs with both arms simultaneously.
844. 8 December 1999, 8:32 a.m. Nova Friburgo, Brazil. Before lifting 350 lbs with both arms simultaneously five times. (Total: 700 lbs)
845. 8 December 1999, 8:44 a.m. Nova Friburgo, Brazil. Before doing one-arm pushes with 500 lbs.
846. 9 December 1999, 6:37 a.m. Nova Friburgo, Brazil. Before using seated double-arm machine up to 150 lbs with both arms simultaneously.
847. 9 December 1999, 6:44 a.m. Nova Friburgo, Brazil. Before lifting 350 lbs with both arms simultaneously twice. (Total: 700 lbs)

MY MORNING SOUL-BODY PRAYERS

848. 9 December 1999, 6:51 a.m. Nova Friburgo, Brazil. Before doing one-arm pushes with 500 lbs.
849. 13 December 1999, 8:13 a.m. Nova Friburgo, Brazil. Before using seated double-arm machine.
850. 13 December 1999, 8:20 a.m. Nova Friburgo, Brazil. Before lifting 350 lbs with both arms simultaneously five times. (Total: 700 lbs)
851. 13 December 1999, 8:27 a.m. Nova Friburgo, Brazil. Before doing seventy one-arm pushes with 500 lbs (29 right, 41 left).
852. 13 December 1999, 8:30 a.m. Nova Friburgo, Brazil.
853. 14 December 1999, 6:29 a.m. Nova Friburgo, Brazil. Before using seated double-arm machine.
854. 14 December 1999, 6:45 a.m. Nova Friburgo, Brazil. Before lifting 350 lbs with both arms simultaneously four times. (Total: 700 lbs)
855. 14 December 1999, 6:53 a.m. Nova Friburgo, Brazil. Before doing fifty one-arm pushes with 500 lbs (25 right, 25 left).
856. 15 December 1999, 7:30 a.m. Rio de Janeiro, Brazil. Before using seated double-arm machine up to 140 lbs with both arms simultaneously.
857. 15 December 1999, 7:42 a.m. Rio de Janeiro, Brazil. Before lifting 350 lbs with both arms simultaneously four times. (Total: 700 lbs)
858. 15 December 1999, 7:52 a.m. Rio de Janeiro, Brazil. Before doing sixty-three one-arm pushes with 500 lbs (29 right, 34 left).
859. 16 December 1999, 7:47 a.m. Rio de Janeiro, Brazil. Before using seated double-arm machine up to 150 lbs with both arms simultaneously.
860. 16 December 1999, 8:01 a.m. Rio de Janeiro, Brazil. Before lifting 350 lbs with both arms simultaneously. (Total: 700 lbs)
861. 16 December 1999, 8:06 a.m. Rio de Janeiro, Brazil. Before doing sixty-eight one-arm pushes with 500 lbs (30 right, 38 left).
862. 17 December 1999, 7:17 a.m. Rio de Janeiro, Brazil. Before using seated double-arm machine up to 140 lbs with both arms simultaneously.
863. 17 December 1999, 7:22 a.m. Rio de Janeiro, Brazil. Before using bench press machine up to 100 lbs with both arms simultaneously.
864. 17 December 1999, 7:37 a.m. Rio de Janeiro, Brazil. Before lifting 350 lbs with both arms simultaneously four times. (Total: 700 lbs)
865. 17 December 1999, 7:43 a.m. Rio de Janeiro, Brazil. Before doing sixty-one one-arm pushes with 500 lbs (28 right, 33 left).
866. 20 December 1999, 6:10 a.m. Rio de Janeiro, Brazil. Before using seated double-arm machine up to 140 lbs with both arms simultaneously.
867. 20 December 1999, 6:21 a.m. Rio de Janeiro, Brazil. Before lifting 350 lbs with both arms simultaneously five times. (Total: 700 lbs)
868. 20 December 1999, 6:30 a.m. Rio de Janeiro, Brazil. Before doing fifty-two one-arm pushes with 500 lbs (26 right, 26 left).
869. 21 December 1999, 6:41 a.m. Rio de Janeiro, Brazil. Before using seated double-arm machine up to 140 lbs with both arms simultaneously.
870. 21 December 1999, 7:44 a.m. Rio de Janeiro, Brazil. Before lifting 350 lbs with both arms simultaneously. (Total: 700 lbs)
871. 21 December 1999, 7:52 a.m. Rio de Janeiro, Brazil. Before doing fifty-five one-arm pushes with 500 lbs (27 right, 28 left).
872. 22 December 1999, 7:11 a.m. Rio de Janeiro, Brazil. Before using seated double-arm machine.
873. 22 December 1999, 7:23 a.m. Rio de Janeiro, Brazil. Before lifting 350 lbs with both arms simultaneously twice. (Total: 700 lbs)
874. 23 December 1999, 4:55 a.m. Rio de Janeiro, Brazil. Before using bench press machine.
875. 23 December 1999, Rio de Janeiro, Brazil. Before using seated double-arm machine up to 150 lbs with both arms simultaneously.

876. 23 December 1999, Rio de Janeiro, Brazil. Before lifting 350 lbs with both arms simultaneously twice. (Total: 700 lbs)
877. 23 December 1999, Rio de Janeiro, Brazil. Before doing 59 one-arm pushes with 500 lbs (27 right, 32 left).
878. 25 December 1999, 6:30 a.m. Curitiba, Brazil. Before using seated double-arm machine up to 140 lbs with both arms simultaneously.
879. 25 December 1999, 6:47 a.m. Curitiba, Brazil. Before lifting 400 lbs with both arms simultaneously three times. (Total: 800 lbs) New record.
880. 25 December 1999, Curitiba, Brazil. Before doing fifty-nine one-arm pushes with 500 lbs (28 right, 31 left).
881. 25 December 1999, 7:11 a.m. Curitiba, Brazil. Before using bench press machine up to 100 lbs with both arms simultaneously.
882. 27 December 1999, 7:09 a.m. Curitiba, Brazil. Before using seated double-arm machine up to 140 lbs with both arms simultaneously.
883. 27 December 1999, 7:23 a.m. Curitiba, Brazil. Before lifting 400 lbs with both arms simultaneously twice. (Total: 800 lbs)
884. 27 December 1999, 7:37 a.m. Curitiba, Brazil. Before doing fifty-nine one-arm pushes with 500 lbs (29 right, 30 left).
885. 27 December 1999, 7:50 a.m. Curitiba, Brazil. Before using bench press machine up to 120 lbs with both arms simultaneously.
886. 28 December 1999, 7:44 a.m. Curitiba, Brazil. Before using seated double-arm machine up to 150 lbs with both arms simultaneously.
887. 28 December 1999, 7:56 a.m. Curitiba, Brazil. Before lifting 400 lbs with both arms simultaneously. (Total: 800 lbs)
888. 28 December 1999, 8:06 a.m. Curitiba, Brazil. Before doing fifty-six one-arm pushes with 500 lbs (27 right, 29 left).
889. 28 December 1999, 8:20 a.m. Curitiba, Brazil. Before using bench press machine up to 120 lbs with both arms simultaneously.
890. 31 December 1999, 6:01 a.m. Curitiba, Brazil. Before using seated double-arm machine.
891. 31 December 1999, 6:13 a.m. Curitiba, Brazil. Before lifting 400 lbs with both arms simultaneously. (Total: 800 lbs)
892. 31 December 1999, 6:23 a.m. Curitiba, Brazil. Before doing fifty-six one-arm pushes with 500 lbs (27 right, 29 left).
893. 1 January 2000, 8:04 a.m. Curitiba, Brazil. Before using seated double-arm machine up to 120 lbs with both arms simultaneously and 160 lbs with each arm separately.
894. 1 January 2000, 8:22 a.m. Curitiba, Brazil. Before lifting 400 lbs with both arms simultaneously. (Total: 800 lbs)
895. 1 January 2000, 8:31 a.m. Curitiba, Brazil. Before doing fifty-seven one-arm pushes with 500 lbs (28 right, 29 left).
896. 1 January 2000, 8:45 a.m. Curitiba, Brazil. Before using bench press machine up to 100 lbs with both arms simultaneously.
897. 2 January 2000, 8:05 a.m. Curitiba, Brazil. Before using seated double-arm machine up to 140 lbs with both arms simultaneously and 160 lbs with each arm separately.
898. 2 January 2000, 8:19 a.m. Curitiba, Brazil. Before lifting 400 lbs with both arms simultaneously three times. (Total: 800 lbs)
899. 2 January 2000, 8:29 a.m. Curitiba, Brazil. Before doing fifty-seven one-arm pushes with 500 lbs (28 right, 29 left).
900. 3 January 2000, 8:38 a.m. Curitiba, Brazil. Before using seated double-arm machine up to 150 lbs with both arms simultaneously and 170 lbs with each arm separately.
901. 3 January 2000, 8:54 a.m. Curitiba, Brazil. Before lifting 400 lbs with both arms simultaneously. (Total: 800 lbs)
902. 3 January 2000, 9:05 a.m. Curitiba, Brazil. Before doing fifty-six one-arm pushes with 500 lbs (26 right, 30 left).

903. 5 January 2000, 9:48 a.m. Curitiba, Brazil. Before using seated double-arm machine up to 140 lbs with both arms simultaneously.
904. 5 January 2000, 9:59 a.m. Curitiba, Brazil. Before lifting 400 lbs with both arms simultaneously. (Total: 800 lbs)
905. 5 January 2000, 10:12 a.m. Curitiba, Brazil. Before doing fifty-seven one-arm pushes with 500 lbs (28 right, 29 left).
906. 5 January 2000, 10:35 a.m. Curitiba, Brazil. Before using bench press machine (standing position).
907. 7 January 2000, 8:53 a.m. Foz do Iguaçu, Brazil. Before using seated double-arm machine up to 140 lbs with both arms simultaneously.
908. 7 January 2000, 9:07 a.m. Foz do Iguaçu, Brazil. Before lifting 400 lbs with both arms simultaneously twice. (Total: 800 lbs)
909. 8 January 2000, 5:47 a.m. Foz do Iguaçu, Brazil. Before using seated double-arm machine up to 150 lbs with both arms simultaneously.
910. 8 January 2000, 5:58 a.m. Foz do Iguaçu, Brazil. Before lifting 400 lbs with both arms simultaneously. (Total: 800 lbs)
911. 8 January 2000, 6:08 a.m. Foz do Iguaçu, Brazil. Before doing sixty-one one-arm pushes with 500 lbs (30 right, 31 left).
912. 9 January 2000, 8:28 a.m. Foz do Iguaçu, Brazil. Before using seated double-arm machine up to 140 lbs with both arms simultaneously.
913. 9 January 2000, 8:51 a.m. Foz do Iguaçu, Brazil. Before doing fifty-five one-arm pushes with 500 lbs (26 right, 29 left).
914. 9 January 2000, 9:03 a.m. Foz do Iguaçu, Brazil. Before lifting 400 lbs with both arms simultaneously four times. (Total: 800 lbs)
915. 9 January 2000, 9:20 a.m. Foz do Iguaçu, Brazil. Before using bench press machine up to 100 lbs with both arms simultaneously.
916. 11 January 2000, 8:46 a.m. Foz do Iguaçu, Brazil. Before using seated double-arm machine up to 140 lbs with both arms simultaneously.
917. 11 January 2000, 8:58 a.m. Foz do Iguaçu, Brazil. Before doing fifty one-arm pushes with 500 lbs (25 right, 25 left).
918. 11 January 2000, 9:05 a.m. Foz do Iguaçu, Brazil. Before lifting 400 lbs with both arms simultaneously three times. (Total: 800 lbs)
919. 13 January 2000, 7:33 a.m. Foz do Iguaçu, Brazil. Before using seated double-arm machine up to 140 lbs with both arms simultaneously.
920. 13 January 2000, 7:45 a.m. Foz do Iguaçu, Brazil. Before doing sixty-two one-arm pushes with 500 lbs (27 right, 35 left).
921. 13 January 2000, 7:59 a.m. Foz do Iguaçu, Brazil. Before lifting 400 lbs with both arms simultaneously three times. (Total: 800 lbs)
922. 14 January 2000, 8:11 a.m. Foz do Iguaçu, Brazil. Before using seated double-arm machine up to 140 lbs with both arms simultaneously.
923. 14 January 2000, 8:26 a.m. Foz do Iguaçu, Brazil. Before doing fifty-seven one-arm pushes with 500 lbs (28 right, 29 left).
924. 14 January 2000, 8:39 a.m. Foz do Iguaçu, Brazil. Before lifting 400 lbs with both arms simultaneously twice. (Total: 800 lbs)
925. 14 January 2000, 8:53 a.m. Foz do Iguaçu, Brazil. Before using bench press machine up to 110 lbs with both arms simultaneously.
926. 15 January 2000, 8:53 a.m. Foz do Iguaçu, Brazil. Before using seated double-arm machine up to 150 lbs with both arms simultaneously.
927. 15 January 2000, 9:05 a.m. Foz do Iguaçu, Brazil. Before doing fifty-three one-arm pushes with 500 lbs (26 right, 27 left).
928. 18 January 2000, 6:31 a.m. Asunción, Paraguay. Before using seated double-arm machine up to 140 lbs with both arms simultaneously.
929. 18 January 2000, 7:02 a.m. Asunción, Paraguay. Before doing fifty-two one-arm pushes with 500 lbs (25 right, 27 left).

930. 18 January 2000, 7:18 a.m. Asunción, Paraguay. Before lifting 400 lbs with both arms simultaneously five times. (Total: 800 lbs)
931. 18 January 2000, 9:19 a.m. Asunción, Paraguay. Before using bench press machine up to 90 lbs with both arms simultaneously.
932. 20 January 2000, 6:14 a.m. Asunción, Paraguay. Before using seated double-arm machine up to 140 lbs with both arms simultaneously.
933. 20 January 2000, 7:21 a.m. Asunción, Paraguay. Before using bench press machine up to 90 lbs with both arms simultaneously.
934. 20 January 2000, 6:48 a.m. Asunción, Paraguay. Before doing fifty-three one-arm pushes with 500 lbs (26 right, 27 left).
935. 20 January 2000, 6:57 a.m. Asunción, Paraguay. Before lifting 400 lbs with both arms simultaneously four times. (Total: 800 lbs)
936. 21 January 2000, 7:08 a.m. Asunción, Paraguay. Before using seated double-arm machine.
937. 21 January 2000, 7:16 a.m. Asunción, Paraguay. Before lifting 400 lbs with both arms simultaneously five times. (Total: 800 lbs)
938. 23 January 2000, 7:00 a.m. Asunción, Paraguay. Before using seated double-arm machine up to 150 lbs with both arms simultaneously.
939. 23 January 2000, 7:11 a.m. Asunción, Paraguay. Before lifting 400 lbs with both arms simultaneously three times. (Total: 800 lbs)
940. 26 January 2000, 8:31 a.m. Brasilia, Brazil. Before using seated double-arm machine up to 140 lbs with both arms simultaneously.
941. 26 January 2000, 8:45 a.m. Brasilia, Brazil. Before lifting 400 lbs with both arms simultaneously four times. (Total: 800 lbs)
942. 26 January 2000, 9:03 a.m. Brasilia, Brazil. Before doing sixty one-arm pushes with 500 lbs (23 right, 37 left).
943. 27 January 2000, 5:49 a.m. Brasilia, Brazil. Before using seated double-arm machine up to 140 lbs with both arms simultaneously.
944. 27 January 2000, 6:03 a.m. Brasilia, Brazil. Before lifting 400 lbs with both arms simultaneously four times. (Total: 800 lbs)
945. 27 January 2000, 6:22 a.m. Brasilia, Brazil. Before doing forty-three one-arm pushes with 500 lbs (23 right, 20 left).
946. 27 January 2000, 8:56 a.m. Brasilia, Brazil. Before using bench press machine up to 100 lbs with both arms simultaneously.
947. 28 January 2000, 7:51 a.m. Brasilia, Brazil. Before using seated double-arm machine up to 150 lbs with both arms simultaneously.
948. 28 January 2000, 8:07 a.m. Brasilia, Brazil. Before lifting 400 lbs with both arms simultaneously five times. (Total: 800 lbs)
949. 3 February 2000, 7:10 a.m. Before using seated double-arm machine up to 140 lbs with both arms simultaneously.
950. 3 February 2000, 7:24 a.m. Before lifting 400 lbs with both arms simultaneously six times. (Total: 800 lbs)
951. 3 February 2000, 7:36 a.m. Before doing multiple one-arm pushes with 500 lbs.
952. 5 February 2000, 8:02 a.m. Before using seated double-arm machine up to 150 lbs with both arms simultaneously.
953. 5 February 2000, 8:24 a.m. Before lifting 400 lbs with both arms simultaneously. (Total: 800 lbs)
954. 5 February 2000, 8:36 a.m. Before doing multiple one-arm pushes with 500 lbs.
955. 7 February 2000, 8:06 a.m. Before using seated double-arm machine up to 140 lbs with both arms simultaneously.
956. 7 February 2000, 8:18 a.m. Before lifting 400 lbs with both arms simultaneously six times. (Total: 800 lbs)
957. 7 February 2000, 8:31 a.m. Before doing one-arm pushes with 500 lbs.
958. 8 February 2000, 7:15 a.m. Before using seated double-arm machine up to 140 lbs with both arms simultaneously.

MY MORNING SOUL-BODY PRAYERS

959. 8 February 2000, 7:29 a.m. Before lifting 450 lbs with both arms simultaneously. (Total: 900 lbs) New record.
960. 8 February 2000, 7:38 a.m. Before doing sixty one-arm pushes with 600 lbs.
961. 10 February 2000, 8:01 a.m. Before using seated double-arm machine up to 150 lbs with both arms simultaneously.
962. 10 February 2000, 8:17 a.m. Before lifting 450 lbs with both arms simultaneously six times. (Total: 900 lbs)
963. 10 February 2000, 8:33 a.m. Before doing multiple one-arm pushes with 600 lbs.
964. 12 February 2000, 8:23 a.m. Before using seated double-arm machine up to 140 lbs with both arms simultaneously.
965. 12 February 2000, 8:41 a.m. Before lifting 450 lbs with both arms simultaneously five times. (Total: 900 lbs)
966. 12 February 2000, 8:58 a.m. Before doing sixty one-arm pushes with 700 lbs.
967. 14 February 2000, 8:48 a.m. Before using seated double-arm machine up to 120 lbs with both arms simultaneously.
968. 14 February 2000, 9:02 a.m. Before lifting 450 lbs with both arms simultaneously three times. (Total: 900 lbs)
969. 14 February 2000, 9:17 a.m. Before doing fifty-nine one-arm pushes with 700 lbs.
970. 16 February 2000, 7:45 a.m. Before using seated double-arm machine up to 120 lbs with both arms simultaneously.
971. 16 February 2000, 7:53 a.m. Before doing sixty-two one-arm pushes with 700 lbs.
972. 16 February 2000, 8:06 a.m. Before lifting 500 lbs with both arms simultaneously seven times. (Total: 1,000 lbs) New record.
973. 18 February 2000 8:35 a.m. Before using seated double-arm machine up to 140 lbs with both arms simultaneously.
974. 18 February 2000, 8:48 a.m. Before doing multiple one-arm pushes with 700 lbs.
975. 18 February 2000, 9:05 a.m. Before lifting 500 lbs with both arms simultaneously seven times. (Total: 1,000 lbs)
976. 19 February 2000, 8:37 a.m. Before lifting 650 lbs with both arms simultaneously six times. (Total: 1,300 lbs) New record.
977. 19 February 2000, 8:56 a.m. After successfully lifting 1,300 lbs.
978. 21 February 2000, 9:17 a.m. Before lifting 650 lbs with both arms simultaneously. (Total: 1,300 lbs)
979. 23 February 2000, 7:05 a.m. Before using seated double-arm machine up to 140 lbs with both arms simultaneously.
980. 23 February 2000, 7:25 a.m. Before lifting 650 lbs with both arms simultaneously. (Total: 1,300 lbs)
981. 24 February 2000, 9:03 a.m. Before using seated double-arm machine up to 140 lbs with both arms simultaneously.
982. 24 February 2000, 9:15 a.m. Before lifting 650 lbs with both arms simultaneously three times. (Total: 1,300 lbs)
983. 24 February 2000, 9:30 a.m. Before doing multiple one-arm pushes with 700 lbs.
984. 25 February 2000, 8:39 a.m. Before lifting 650 lbs with both arms simultaneously. (Total: 1,300 lbs)
985. 25 February 2000, 8:57 a.m. Before doing multiple one-arm pushes with 700 lbs.
986. 25 February 2000, 9:01 a.m. Before using seated double-arm machine up to 140 lbs with both arms simultaneously.
987. 26 February 2000, 6:26 a.m. Before lifting 650 lbs with both arms simultaneously five times. (Total: 1,300 lbs)
988. 26 February 2000, 6:42 a.m. Before doing multiple one-arm pushes with 700 lbs.
989. 26 February 2000, 6:51 a.m. Before using seated double-arm machine.
990. 28 February 2000, 8:51 a.m. Before using seated double-arm machine up to 140 lbs with both arms simultaneously.
991. 28 February 2000, 9:02 a.m. Before lifting 650 lbs with both arms simultaneously seven times. (Total: 1,300 lbs)

992. 28 February 2000, 9:19 a.m. Before doing sixty-one one-arm pushes with 700 lbs (27 right, 34 left).
993. 1 March 2000, 8:04 a.m. Before using seated double-arm machine up to 140 lbs with both arms simultaneously.
994. 1 March 2000, 8:20 a.m. Before lifting 650 lbs with both arms simultaneously seven times. (Total: 1,300 lbs)
995. 1 March 2000, 8:37 a.m. Before doing sixty-four one-arm pushes with 700 lbs (29 right, 35 left).
996. 2 March 2000. Before using bench press machine up to 80 lbs with both arms simultaneously.
997. 2 March 2000. Before doing clean and press from the ground up to 30 lbs with both arms simultaneously and 40 lbs with one arm.
998. 2 March 2000. Before using seated double-arm machine up to 140 lbs with both arms simultaneously.
999. 2 March 2000, Before doing 60 one-arm pushes with 700 lbs 1000th prayer.
1000. 3 March 2000, 8:53 a.m. Before using seated double-arm machine up to 140 lbs with both arms simultaneously.
1001. 3 March 2000, 9:04 a.m. Before lifting 650 lbs with both arms simultaneously seven times. (Total: 1,300 lbs)
1002. 3 March 2000, 9:22 a.m. Before doing 59 one-arm pushes with 700 lbs (26 right, 33 left).
1003. 5 March 2000, 8:16 a.m. Before using seated double-arm machine up to 140 lbs with both arms simultaneously and 160 lbs with each arm separately.
1004. 5 March 2000, 8:34 a.m. Before lifting 650 lbs with both arms simultaneously six times. (Total: 1,300 lbs)
1005. 5 March 2000, 8:49 a.m. Before doing sixty-five one-arm pushes with 700 lbs (29 right, 36 left).
1006. 6 March 2000, 12:32 a.m. Before lifting 650 lbs with both arms simultaneously six times. (Total: 1,300 lbs)
1007. 6 March 2000, 12:49 a.m. Before doing sixty-two one-arm pushes with 700 lbs (29 right, 33 left).
1008. 6 March 2000, 12:56 a.m. Before using seated double-arm machine up to 150 lbs with both arms simultaneously.
1009. 7 March 2000, 8:44 a.m. Before using seated double-arm machine up to 140 lbs with both arms simultaneously.
1010. 7 March 2000, 8:59 a.m. Before lifting 650 lbs with both arms simultaneously six times. (Total: 1,300 lbs)
1011. 7 March 2000, 9:15 a.m. Before doing ninety-one one-arm pushes with 700 lbs (44 right, 47 left).
1012. 9 March 2000, 8:50 a.m. Before using seated double-arm machine up to 140 lbs with both arms simultaneously.
1013. 9 March 2000, 9:02 a.m. Before lifting 650 lbs with both arms simultaneously six times. (Total: 1,300 lbs)
1014. 9 March 2000, 9:20 a.m. Before doing sixty-seven one-arm pushes with 700 lbs (31 right, 36 left).
1015. 11 March 2000, 4:37 a.m. Before lifting 650 lbs with both arms simultaneously seven times. (Total: 1,300 lbs)
1016. 11 March 2000, 4:58 a.m. Before using seated double-arm machine up to 150 lbs with both arms simultaneously.
1017. 11 March 2000, 5:04 a.m. Before doing fifty-nine one-arm pushes with 700 lbs (29 right, 30 left).
1018. 12 March 2000, 9:00 a.m. Before lifting 650 lbs with both arms simultaneously five times. (Total: 1,300 lbs)
1019. 12 March 2000, 9:14 a.m. Before doing fifty-seven one-arm pushes with 700 lbs (28 right, 29 left).

MY MORNING SOUL-BODY PRAYERS

1020. 12 March 2000, 9:31 a.m. Before using seated double-arm machine up to 140 lbs with both arms simultaneously.
1021. 16 March 2000, 8:39 a.m. Before using seated double-arm machine up to 140 lbs with both arms simultaneously.
1022. 16 March 2000, 9:03 a.m. Before lifting 650 lbs with both arms simultaneously five times. (Total: 1,300 lbs)
1023. 16 March 2000, 9:06 a.m. Before doing sixty-two one-arm pushes with 700 lbs (30 right, 32 left).
1024. 18 March 2000. Before lifting 650 lbs with both arms simultaneously five times. (Total: 1,300 lbs)
1025. 20 March 2000, 9:12 a.m. Before lifting 650 lbs with both arms simultaneously five times. (Total: 1,300 lbs)
1026. 20 March 2000, 9:26 a.m. Before doing sixty-eight one-arm pushes with 700 lbs (35 right, 33 left).
1027. 20 March 2000, 9:34 a.m. Before using seated double-arm machine up to 140 lbs with both arms simultaneously.
1028. 21 March 2000, 7:46 a.m. Before lifting 650 lbs with both arms simultaneously three times. (Total: 1,300 lbs)
1029. 21 March 2000, 8:05 a.m. Before doing fifty-seven one-arm pushes with 700 lbs (25 right, 32 left).
1030. 21 March 2000, 8:11 a.m. Before using seated double-arm machine up to 160 lbs with both arms simultaneously.
1031. 23 March 2000, 8:40 a.m. Before lifting 650 lbs with both arms simultaneously three times. (Total: 1,300 lbs)
1032. 23 March 2000, 9:09 a.m. Before doing fifty-four one-arm pushes with 700 lbs (28 right, 26 left).
1033. 23 March 2000, 9:14. Before using seated double-arm machine up to 140 lbs with both arms simultaneously.
1034. 25 March 2000, 6:18 a.m. Before lifting 650 lbs with both arms simultaneously four times. (Total: 1,300 lbs)
1035. 25 March 2000, 6:40 a.m. Before doing 51 one-arm pushes with 700 lbs (23 right, 28 left).
1036. 25 March 2000, 6:47 a.m. Before using seated double-arm machine up to 160 lbs with both arms simultaneously.
1037. 27 March 2000, 8:38 a.m. Before lifting 650 lbs with both arms simultaneously four times. (Total: 1,300 lbs)
1038. 29 March 2000, 8:10 a.m. Before lifting 650 lbs with both arms simultaneously four times. (Total: 1,300 lbs)
1039. 29 March 2000, 8:23 a.m. Before doing sixty-two one-arm pushes with 700 lbs (36 right, 26 left).
1040. 29 March 2000, 8:39 a.m. Before using seated double-arm machine up to 160 lbs with both arms simultaneously.
1041. 29 March 2000, 9:34 a.m. Before using seated calf raise machine up to 1,000 lbs.
1042. 31 March 2000, 6:34 a.m. Before lifting 650 lbs with both arms simultaneously four times. (Total: 1,300 lbs)
1043. 31 March 2000, 6:55 a.m. Before doing sixty-eight one-arm pushes with 700 lbs (29 right, 39 left).
1044. 31 March 2000, 7:07 a.m. Before using seated double-arm machine up to 140 lbs with both arms simultaneously.
1045. 2 April 2000, 9:23 a.m. Before lifting 650 lbs with both arms simultaneously four times. (Total: 1,300 lbs)
1046. 3 April 2000, 9:39 a.m. Before doing fifty-two one-arm pushes with 700 lbs (33 right, 19 left).
1047. 3 April 2000, 9:45 a.m. Before lifting 140 lbs with both arms simultaneously from a seated position.

1048. 4 April 2000, 7:10 a.m. Before lifting 650 lbs with both arms simultaneously five times. (Total: 1,300 lbs)
1049. 4 April 2000, 7:40 a.m. Before using seated double-arm machine up to 140 lbs with both arms simultaneously.
1050. 4 April 2000, 7:51 a.m. Before doing fifty-two one-arm pushes with 700 lbs (36 right, 16 left).
1051. 6 April 2000, 7:53 a.m. Before lifting 650 lbs with both arms simultaneously four times. (Total: 1,300 lbs)
1052. 6 April 2000, 8:15 a.m. Before doing fifty-three one-arm pushes with 700 lbs (23 right, 30 left).
1053. 6 April 2000, 8:22 a.m. Before lifting 170 lbs with both arms simultaneously from a seated position.
1054. 10 April 2000, 8:52 a.m. Before lifting 650 lbs with both arms simultaneously five times. (Total: 1,300 lbs)
1055. 10 April 2000, 9:08 a.m. Before lifting 140 lbs with both arms simultaneously from a seated position.
1056. 10 April 2000, 9:16 a.m. Before doing sixty one-arm pushes with 700 lbs (31 right, 29 left).
1057. 12 April 2000, 7:56 a.m. Before lifting 650 lbs with both arms simultaneously four times. (Total: 1,300 lbs)
1058. 12 April 2000, 8:14 a.m. Before doing fifty-seven one-arm pushes with 700 lbs (25 right, 32 left).
1059. 12 April 2000, 8:20 a.m. Before using seated double-arm machine.
1060. 14 April 2000, 8:15 a.m. Before lifting 650 lbs with both arms simultaneously four times. (Total: 1,300 lbs)
1061. 14 April 2000, 8:34 a.m. Before using seated double-arm machine up to 140 lbs with both arms simultaneously.
1062. 20 April 2000, 7:54 a.m. Before lifting 650 lbs with both arms simultaneously five times. (Total: 1,300 lbs)
1063. 20 April 2000, 7:36 a.m. Before using seated double-arm machine up to 140 lbs with both arms simultaneously.
1064. 20 April 2000, 8:11 a.m. Before doing fifty-three one-arm pushes with 700 lbs (24 right, 29 left).
1065. 22 April 2000, 8:05 a.m. Before lifting 650 lbs with both arms simultaneously four times. (Total: 1,300 lbs)
1066. 22 April 2000, 8:26 a.m. Before using seated double-arm machine up to 140 lbs with both arms simultaneously.
1067. 22 April 2000, 8:37 a.m. Before doing fifty-two one-arm pushes with 700 lbs (25 right, 27 left).
1068. 28 April 2000, 7:54 a.m. Before lifting 650 lbs with both arms simultaneously four times. (Total: 1,300 lbs)
1069. 28 April 2000, 8:07 a.m. Before doing thirty-seven one-arm pushes with 700 lbs (17 right, 20 left).
1070. 28 April 2000, 8:15 a.m. Before using seated double-arm machine up to 140 lbs with both arms simultaneously.
1071. 1 May 2000, 7:23 a.m. Before doing standing double-dumbbell lift with 1,300 lbs four times.
1072. 1 May 2000, 7:40 a.m. Before using seated double-arm machine up to 300 lbs.
1073. 1 May 2000, 7:50 a.m. Before doing fifty-two one-arm pushes with 700 lbs (23 right, 29 left).
1074. 3 May 2000, 8:08 a.m. Before doing standing double-dumbbell lift with 1,300 lbs five times.
1075. 3 May 2000, 8:22 a.m. Before using seated double-arm machine up to 280 lbs.
1076. 4 May 2000, 8:45 a.m. Before doing standing double-dumbbell lift with 1,300 lbs five times.

1077. 4 May 2000, 8:58 a.m. Before doing fifty one-arm pushes with 700 lbs (22 right, 28 left).
1078. 4 May 2000, 9:03 a.m. Before using seated double-arm machine up to 320 lbs.
1079. 4 May 2000, 9:20 a.m. Before using seated calf raise machine up to 1,050 lbs.
1080. 9 May 2000, 1:45 p.m. Before doing standing double-dumbbell lift with 1,300 lbs four times.
1081. 11 May 2000, 8:44 p.m. Before using seated double-arm machine.
1082. 11 May 2000, 8:57 p.m. Before doing standing double-dumbbell lift with 1,300 lbs four times.
1083. 13 May 2000, 7:33 a.m. Before doing standing double-dumbbell lift with 1,300 lbs four times.
1084. 13 May 2000, 7:49 a.m. Before using seated double-arm machine.
1085. 13 May 2000, 7:59 a.m. Before doing multiple one-arm pushes with 700 lbs.
1086. 15 May 2000, 7:27 a.m. Before doing seated double-dumbbell lift with 200 lbs.
1087. 15 May 2000, 7:33 a.m. Before doing standing double-dumbbell lift with 1,300 lbs four times.
1088. 18 May 2000, 8:25 a.m. Before using seated double-arm machine up to 280 lbs.
1089. 18 May 2000, 8:35 a.m. Before doing seated double-dumbbell lift with 240 lbs.
1090. 18 May 2000, 8:51 a.m. Before doing standing double-dumbbell lift with 1,300 lbs four times.
1091. 18 May 2000, 9:24 p.m. Before doing seated double-dumbbell lifts with 260 lbs, 280 lbs and 300 lbs.
1092. 20 May 2000, 7:55 a.m. Before using seated double-arm machine.
1093. 20 May 2000, 8:06 a.m. Before doing seated double-dumbbell lift with 310 lbs.
1094. 20 May 2000, 8:42 a.m. Before using seated calf raise machine up to 1,150 lbs New record.
1095. 22 May 2000, 8:45 a.m. Before using seated double-arm machine.
1096. 22 May 2000, 8:51 a.m. Before doing standing double-dumbbell lift with 1,300 lbs four times.
1097. 23 May 2000, 3:40 p.m. Before using seated double-arm machine.
1098. 23 May 2000, 3:52 p.m. Before doing seated double-dumbbell lift with 350 lbs New record.
1099. 23 May 2000, 4:03 p.m. Before doing standing double-dumbbell lift with 1,300 lbs four times.
1100. 24 May 2000, 6:02 p.m. Before doing seated double-dumbbell lift with 360 lbs New record.
1101. 24 May 2000, 6:09 p.m. Before doing standing double-dumbbell lift with 1,300 lbs four times.
1102. 25 May 2000, 7:24 p.m. Before doing seated double-dumbbell lift.
1103. 25 May 2000, 7:46 p.m. Before doing standing double-dumbbell lift with 1,300 lbs four times.
1104. 26 May 2000, 7:51 p.m. Before doing seated double-dumbbell lift with 380 lbs New record.
1105. 26 May 2000, 8:00 p.m. Before doing standing double-dumbbell lift with 1,300 lbs four times.
1106. 26 May 2000, 8:37 p.m. Before doing seated double-dumbbell lift with 400 lbs New record.
1107. 30 May 2000, 6:04 a.m. Before using seated double-arm machine.
1108. 30 May 2000, 6:19 a.m. Before doing standing double-dumbbell lift with 1,300 lbs four times.
1109. 1 June 2000, 9:31 a.m. Before using seated calf raise machine up to 1,200 lbs.
1110. 1 June 2000, 7:14 p.m. Before doing standing double-dumbbell lift with 1,300 lbs four times.
1111. 4 June 2000, 6:08 p.m. Before doing standing double-dumbbell lift with 1,300 lbs four times.

SRI CHINMOY

1112. 4 June 2000, 6:16 p.m. Before doing 240 lbs dumbbell bench press.
1113. 5 June 2000, 11:31 a.m. Before doing 260 lbs dumbbell bench press.
1114. 13 June 2000, 4:20 p.m. Before doing 300 lbs dumbbell bench press.
1115. 18 June 2000, 7:54 a.m. Before doing standing double-dumbbell lift with 1,300 lbs four times.
1116. 18 June 2000, 8:09 a.m. Before doing 310 lbs dumbbell bench press.
1117. 18 June 2000, 9:46 a.m. Before doing 330 lbs dumbbell bench press.
1118. 19 June 2000, 9:25 a.m. Before doing 350 lbs dumbbell bench press.
1119. 19 June 2000, 9:32 a.m. Before doing standing double-dumbbell lift with 1,300 lbs four times.
1120. 20 June 2000, 9:45 a.m. Before doing 360 lbs dumbbell bench press.
1121. 20 June 2000, 10:56 a.m. Before doing 370 lbs dumbbell bench press.
1122. 20 June 2000, 11:08 a.m. Before doing 380 lbs dumbbell bench press.
1123. 20 June 2000, 11:33 a.m. Before doing 400 lbs dumbbell bench press.
1124. 21 June 2000, 8:30 a.m. Before using seated double-arm machine up to 140 lbs.
1125. 21 June 2000, 8:55 a.m. Before doing standing double-arm lift with 1,300 lbs four times.
1126. 22 June 2000, 9:16 a.m. Before doing 420 lbs dumbbell bench press.
1127. 22 June 2000, 9:28 a.m. Before doing seated double-dumbbell lift with 420 lbs.
1128. 23 June 2000, 12:10 a.m. Before doing seated double-dumbbell lift with 430 lbs.
1129. 23 June 2000, 12:14 a.m. Before doing 430 lbs dumbbell bench press.
1130. 24 June 2000, 8:52 a.m. Before using seated double-arm machine.
1131. 24 June 2000, 9:08 a.m. Before doing 440 lbs dumbbell bench press.
1132. 24 June 2000, 9:32 a.m. Before doing standing double-dumbbell lift with 1,300 lbs four times.
1133. 26 June 2000, 9:09 a.m. Before doing 450 lbs dumbbell bench press.
1134. 26 June 2000, 9:18 a.m. Before doing standing double-dumbbell lift with 1,300 lbs four times.
1135. 26 June 2000, 7:08 p.m. Before doing 470 lbs dumbbell bench press.
1136. 26 June 2000, 7:30 p.m. Before doing 480 lbs dumbbell bench press.
1137. 26 June 2000, 7:47 p.m. Before doing 500 lbs dumbbell bench press.
1138. 27 June 2000, 5:45 p.m. Before doing 510 lbs dumbbell bench press.
1139. 27 June 2000, 6:02 p.m. Before doing 520 lbs dumbbell bench press.
1140. 27 June 2000, 7:22 p.m. Before doing 530 lbs dumbbell bench press.
1141. 27 June 2000, 7:34 p.m. Before doing 540 lbs dumbbell bench press.
1142. 28 June 2000, 12:25 a.m. Before doing 550 lbs dumbbell bench press.
1143. 28 June 2000, 8:58 a.m. Before doing 560 lbs dumbbell bench press.
1144. 28 June 2000, 9:03 a.m. Before doing standing double-arm lift with 1,300 lbs four times.
1145. 28 June 2000, 5:29 p.m. Before doing 570 lbs dumbbell bench press.
1146. 28 June 2000, 5:54 p.m. Before doing 580 lbs dumbbell bench press.
1147. 28 June 2000, 6:18 p.m. Before doing 600 lbs dumbbell bench press.
1148. 30 June 2000, 9:10 a.m. Before doing standing double-dumbbell lift with 1,300 lbs four times.
1149. 3 July 2000, 8:59 a.m. Before doing 1,300 lbs standing double-dumbbell lift four times.
1150. 5 July 2000, 6:54 a.m. Before doing 1,300 lbs standing double-dumbbell lift four times.
1151. 6 July 2000, 7:39 p.m. Before doing 440 lbs seated double-dumbbell lift.
1152. 7 July 2000, 8:24 a.m. Before doing 1,300 lbs standing double-dumbbell lift four times.
1153. 8 July 2000, 6:54 a.m. Before practising for 700 lbs dumbbell bench press.
1154. 9 July 2000, 7:35 a.m. Before practising for 700 lbs dumbbell bench press.
1155. 9 July 2000, 7:56 a.m. Before doing 450 lbs seated double-dumbbell lift.
1156. 10 July 2000, 7:54 a.m. Before practising for 700 lbs dumbbell bench press.

MY MORNING SOUL-BODY PRAYERS

1157. 10 July 2000, 8:15 a.m. Before doing 1,300 lbs standing double-dumbbell lift four times.
1158. 10 July 2000, 2:43 p.m. Before doing 460 lbs seated double-dumbbell lift.
1159. 11 July 2000, 7:22 a.m. Before doing 700 lbs dumbbell bench press.
1160. 13 July 2000, 8:22 a.m. Before doing 1,300 lbs standing double-dumbbell lift four times.
1161. 14 July 2000, 7:16 a.m. Before practising for 730 lbs dumbbell bench press.
1162. 14 July 2000, 7:29 a.m. Before practising for 730 lbs dumbbell bench press.
1163. 16 July 2000, 7:50 a.m. Before practising for 740 lbs dumbbell bench press.
1164. 16 July 2000, 8:07 a.m. Before doing 470 lbs seated double-dumbbell lift.
1165. 17 July 2000, 7:39 a.m. Before practising for 750 lbs dumbbell bench press.
1166. 17 July 2000, 8:00 a.m. Before doing 1,300 lbs standing double-dumbbell lift four times.
1167. 17 July 2000, 8:13 a.m. Before practising for 480 lbs seated double-dumbbell lift.
1168. 18 July 2000, 9:13 a.m. Before practising for 760 lbs dumbbell bench press.
1169. 18 July 2000, 9:30 a.m. Before practising for 480 lbs seated double-dumbbell lift.
1170. 19 July 2000, 8:21 a.m. Before practising for 770 lbs dumbbell bench press.
1171. 19 July 2000, 8:42 a.m. Before doing 1,300 lbs standing double-dumbbell lift four times.
1172. 19 July 2000, 8:56 a.m. Before doing 480 lbs seated double-dumbbell lift. New record.
1173. 19 July 2000. Aspiration-Ground. After doing 2,100 lbs standing calf raise. New record.
1174. 21 July 2000, 9:13 a.m. Before practising for 800 lbs dumbbell bench press.
1175. 21 July 2000, 9:35 a.m. Before doing 1,300 lbs standing double-dumbbell lift five times.
1176. 21 July 2000, 5:35 p.m. Before practising for 800 lbs dumbbell bench press.
1177. 21 July 2000, 5:50 p.m. Before practising for 500 lbs seated double-dumbbell lift.
1178. 22 July 2000, 8:11 a.m. Before practising for 800 lbs dumbbell bench press.
1179. 22 July 2000, 8:58 a.m. Before practising for 500 lbs seated double-dumbbell lift.
1180. 23 July 2000, 6:44 p.m. Before practising for 800 lbs dumbbell bench press.
1181. 23 July 2000, 6:59 p.m. Before practising for 500 lbs seated double-dumbbell lift.
1182. 24 July 2000, 8:38 a.m. Before practising for 800 lbs dumbbell bench press.
1183. 24 July 2000, 8:54 a.m. Before doing 1,300 lbs standing double-dumbbell lift four times.
1184. 24 July 2000, 9:09 a.m. Before practising for 500 lbs seated double-dumbbell lift.
1185. 25 July 2000, 5:12 p.m. Before practising for 800 lbs dumbbell bench press.
1186. 25 July 2000, 5:28 p.m. Before practising for 500 lbs seated double-dumbbell lift.
1187. 26 July 2000, 6:03 p.m. Before practising for 800 lbs dumbbell bench press.
1188. 26 July 2000, 6:22 p.m. Before doing 1,300 lbs standing double-dumbbell lift four times.
1189. 26 July 2000, 6:34 p.m. Before practising for 500 lbs seated double-dumbbell lift.
1190. 27 July 2000, 7:03 p.m. Before practising for 800 lbs dumbbell bench press.
1191. 27 July 2000, 7:17 p.m. Before practising for 500 lbs seated double-dumbbell lift.
1192. 28 July 2000, 4:07 p.m. Before doing 1,300 lbs standing double-dumbbell lift four times.
1193. 28 July 2000, 4:22 p.m. Before practising for 800 lbs dumbbell bench press.
1194. 28 July 2000, 4:38 p.m. Before practising for 500 lbs seated double-dumbbell lift.
1195. 31 July 2000, 8:11 a.m. Before practising for 800 lbs dumbbell bench press.
1196. 31 July 2000, 8:36 a.m. Before doing 1,300 lbs standing double-dumbbell lift five times.
1197. 31 July 2000, 8:49 a.m. Before practising for 500 lbs seated double-dumbbell lift.
1198. 5 August 2000, 10:42 p.m. Before practising for 800 lbs dumbbell bench press.
1199. 5 August 2000, 10:59 p.m. Before practising for 500 lbs seated double-dumbbell lift.
1200. 6 August 2000. Before doing 1,300 lbs seated calf raise. New record.
1201. 7 August 2000, 9:28 a.m. Before practising for 800 lbs dumbbell bench press.
1202. 7 August 2000, 9:47 a.m. Before practising for 500 lbs seated double-dumbbell lift.

1203. 8 August 2000, 9:19 a.m. Before practising for 800 lbs dumbbell bench press.
1204. 8 August 2000, 9:37 a.m. Before practising for 500 lbs seated double-dumbbell lift.
1205. 9 August 2000, 8:45 a.m. Before practising for 800 lbs dumbbell bench press.
1206. 9 August 2000, 9:03 a.m. Before doing 1,300 lbs standing double-dumbbell lift four times.
1207. 9 August 2000, 9:16 a.m. Before practising for 500 lbs seated double-dumbbell lift.
1208. 10 August 2000, 7:54 p.m. Before practising for 800 lbs dumbbell bench press.
1209. 10 August 2000, 8:19 p.m. Before doing 1,300 lbs standing double-dumbbell lift two times.
1210. 10 August 2000, 8:28 p.m. Before practising for 500 lbs seated double-dumbbell lift.
1211. 12 August 2000, 9:05 a.m. Before practising for 800 lbs dumbbell bench press.
1212. 12 August 2000, 9:21 a.m. Before practising for 500 lbs seated double-dumbbell lift.
1213. 12 August 2000, 9:34 a.m. Before doing 1,300 lbs standing double-dumbbell lift three times.
1214. 13 August 2000, 5:12 p.m. and 5:44 p.m. Same prayer before practising for 800 lbs dumbbell bench press and before practising for 500 lbs seated double-dumbbell lift.
1215. 14 August 2000, 9:34 a.m. Before practising for 800 lbs dumbbell bench press.
1216. 14 August 2000, 9:52 a.m. Before practising for 500 lbs seated double-dumbbell lift.
1217. 15 August 2000, 9:31 a.m. Before doing 500 lbs seated double-dumbbell lift. New record.
1218. 15 August 2000, 9:42 a.m. Before doing 800 lbs dumbbell bench press. New record.
1219. 16 August 2000, 8:48 a.m. Before doing 500 lbs seated double-dumbbell lift.
1220. 16 August 2000, 9:00 a.m. Before doing 800 lbs dumbbell bench press.
1221. 17 August 2000, 9:50 a.m. Before doing 500 lbs seated double-dumbbell lift.
1222. 17 August 2000, 10:01 a.m. Before doing 800 lbs dumbbell bench press.
1223. 19 August 2000, 7:20 a.m. Before doing 800 lbs dumbbell bench press.
1224. 19 August 2000, 7:37 a.m. Before doing 1,300 lbs standing double-dumbbell lift three times.
1225. 21 August 2000, 8:09 a.m. Before doing 510 lbs seated double-dumbbell lift. New record.
1226. 21 August 2000, 8:19 a.m. Before doing 800 lbs dumbbell bench press.
1227. 22 August 2000, 7:58 p.m. Before doing 530 lbs seated double-dumbbell lift. New record.
1228. 22 August 2000, 8:08 p.m. Before doing 800 lbs dumbbell bench press.
1229. 22 August 2000, 8:25 p.m. Before doing 1,300 lbs standing double-dumbbell lift three times.
1230. 23 August 2000, 9:19 a.m. Before doing 540 lbs seated double-dumbbell lift. New record.
1231. 23 August 2000, 9:29 a.m. Before doing 800 lbs dumbbell bench press.
1232. 24 August 2000, 9:57 a.m. Before doing 540 lbs seated double-dumbbell lift.
1233. 24 August 2000, 10:10 a.m. Before doing 800 lbs dumbbell bench press.
1234. 25 August 2000, 8:11 a.m. Before doing 550 lbs seated double-dumbbell lift. New record.
1235. 25 August 2000, 8:21 a.m. Before doing 800 lbs dumbbell bench press.
1236. 25 August 2000, 8:37 a.m. Before doing 1,300 lbs standing double-dumbbell lift three times.
1237. 31 August 2000, 9:03 a.m. Before doing 570 lbs seated double-dumbbell lift. New record.
1238. 31 August 2000, 9:13 a.m. Before doing 800 lbs dumbbell bench press.
1239. 31 August 2000, 11:33 p.m. Before doing 580 lbs seated double-dumbbell lift. New record.
1240. 1 September 2000, 10:18 a.m. Before doing 600 lbs seated double-dumbbell lift. New record.
1241. 3 September 2000, 7:30 a.m. Before doing 600 lbs seated double-dumbbell lift.
1242. 3 September 2000, 7:51 a.m. Before doing 800 lbs dumbbell bench press.

MY MORNING SOUL-BODY PRAYERS

1243. 3 September 2000, 7:40 a.m. Before doing 1,300 lbs standing double-dumbbell lift three times.
1244. 4 September 2000, 10:51 p.m. Before doing 610 lbs seated double-dumbbell lift. New record.
1245. 5 September 2000, 5:55 p.m. Before doing 610 lbs seated double-dumbbell lift.
1246. 5 September 2000, 6:06 p.m. Before doing 800 lbs dumbbell bench press.
1247. 5 September 2000, 6:23 p.m. Before doing 1,300 lbs standing double-dumbbell lift three times.
1248. 8 September 2000, 9:13 a.m. Before doing 620 lbs seated double-dumbbell lift. New record.
1249. 8 September 2000, 9:22 a.m. Before doing 800 lbs dumbbell bench press.
1250. 8 September 2000, 11:07 a.m. A prayerful message for television.
1251. 8 September 2000, 9:36 a.m. Before doing 1,300 lbs standing double-dumbbell lift three times.
1252. 8 September 2000, 8:32 p.m. Before doing 630 lbs seated double-dumbbell lift. New record.
1253. 8 September 2000, 8:44 p.m. Before doing 820 lbs dumbbell bench press. New record.
1254. 9 September 2000, 6:14 a.m. Before doing 640 lbs seated double-dumbbell lift. New record.
1255. 9 September 2000, 6:23 a.m. Before doing 840 lbs dumbbell bench press. New record.
1256. 9 September 2000, 6:39 a.m. Before doing 1,300 lbs standing double-dumbbell lift.
1257. 10 September 2000, 6:43 a.m. Before doing 650 lbs seated double-dumbbell lift. New record.
1258. 10 September 2000, 6:49 a.m. Before doing 850 lbs dumbbell bench press. New record.
1259. 10 September 2000, 7:01 a.m. Before doing 1,300 lbs standing double-dumbbell lift three times.
1260. 12 September 2000, 11:16 p.m. Before doing 660 lbs seated double-dumbbell lift. New record.
1261. 12 September 2000, 11:29 p.m. Before doing 860 lbs dumbbell bench press. New record.
1262. 13 September 2000, 8:45 a.m. Before doing 660 lbs seated double-dumbbell lift.
1263. 13 September 2000, 8:54 a.m. Before doing 860 lbs dumbbell bench press.
1264. 14 September 2000, 8:39 a.m. Before doing 670 lbs seated double-dumbbell lift. New record.
1265. 14 September 2000, 8:50 a.m. Before doing 870 lbs dumbbell bench press. New record.
1266. 14 September 2000, 9:03 a.m. Before doing 1,300 lbs standing double-dumbbell lift three times.
1267. 15 September 2000, 1:21 a.m. Before doing 680 lbs seated double-dumbbell lift. New record.
1268. 15 September 2000, 1:32 a.m. Before doing 880 lbs dumbbell bench press. New record.
1269. 16 September 2000, 12:08 a.m. Before doing 700 lbs seated double-dumbbell lift. New record.
1270. 16 September 2000, 12:27 a.m. Before doing 900 lbs dumbbell bench press. New record.
1271. 20 September 2000, 6:35 p.m. Before doing 710 lbs seated double-dumbbell lift. New record.
1272. 20 September 2000, 6:49 p.m. Before doing 910 lbs dumbbell bench press. New record.
1273. 20 September 2000, 7:06 p.m. Before doing 1,300 lbs standing double-dumbbell lift three times.
1274. 21 September 2000, 2:17 p.m. Before doing 720 lbs seated double-dumbbell lift. New record.
1275. 21 September 2000, 2:31 p.m. Before doing 920 lbs dumbbell bench press. New record.
1276. 22 September 2000, 10:02 a.m. Before doing 730 lbs seated double-dumbbell lift. New record.

1277. 22 September 2000, 10:12 a.m. Before doing 930 lbs dumbbell bench press. New record.
1278. 25 September 2000, 9:28 a.m. Before doing 740 lbs seated double-dumbbell lift. New record.
1279. 25 September 2000, 9:41 a.m. Before doing 940 lbs dumbbell bench press. New record.
1280. 26 September 2000, 9:50 a.m. Before doing 740 lbs seated double-dumbbell lift.
1281. 28 September 2000, 8:51 a.m. Before doing 1,300 lbs standing double-dumbbell lift three times.
1282. 28 September 2000, 9:03 a.m. Before doing 950 lbs dumbbell bench press. New record.
1283. 28 September 2000, 9:15 a.m. Before doing 750 lbs seated double-dumbbell lift. New record.
1284. 29 September 2000, 6:05 p.m. Before doing 760 lbs seated double-dumbbell lift. New record.
1285. 29 September 2000, 6:12 p.m. Before doing 960 lbs dumbbell bench press. New record.
1286. 30 September 2000, 9:43 p.m. Before doing 770 lbs seated double-dumbbell lift. New record.
1287. 30 September 2000, 9:56 p.m. Before doing 970 lbs dumbbell bench press. New record.
1288. 1 October 2000, 9:03 p.m. Before doing 780 lbs seated double-dumbbell lift. New record.
1289. 1 October 2000, 9:13 p.m. Before doing 980 lbs dumbbell bench press. New record.
1290. 2 October 2000, 1:56 p.m. Before doing 800 lbs seated double-dumbbell lift. New record and ultimate goal.
1291. 2 October 2000, 2:09 p.m. Before doing 1,000 lbs dumbbell bench press. New record and ultimate goal.
1292. 3 October 2000, 8:31 a.m. Before doing 1,300 lbs standing double-dumbbell lift three times.
1293. 3 October 2000, 10:40 a.m. Before doing 800 lbs seated double-dumbbell lift.
1294. 4 October 2000, 7:21 p.m. Before doing 800 lbs seated double-dumbbell lift.
1295. 4 October 2000, 7:37 p.m. Before doing 1,000 lbs dumbbell bench press.
1296. 5 October 2000, 7:33 p.m. Before doing 1,300 lbs standing double-dumbbell lift three times.
1297. 5 October 2000, 7:47 p.m. Before doing 1,000 lbs dumbbell bench press.
1298. 5 October 2000, 8:01 p.m. Before doing 800 lbs seated double-dumbbell lift.
1299. 7 October 2000, 2:26 p.m. Before doing 800 lbs seated double-dumbbell lift. 1,300th prayer.
1300. 7 October 2000, 2:31 p.m. Before doing 1,000 lbs dumbbell bench press. 1,301st prayer.
1301. 9 October 2000, 10:20 a.m. Before doing 800 lbs seated double-dumbbell lift.
1302. 9 October 2000, 10:29 a.m. Before doing 1,000 lbs dumbbell bench press.
1303. 9 October 2000, 10:54 a.m. Before doing 1,300 lbs standing double-dumbbell lift three times.
1304. 14 October 2000, 9:46 a.m. Before doing 800 lbs seated double-dumbbell lift.
1305. 14 October 2000, 10:04 a.m. Before doing 1,000 lbs dumbbell bench press.
1306. 14 October 2000. Sri Chinmoy offered this final prayerful message as he concluded his weightlifting endeavours since resuming weightlifting on 29 September 1998. During this period of two years and fifteen days, he has offered 1,307 prayers.
1307–1308. 12 December 2004, 4:18 a.m. Xiamen, China. Seated double-dumbbell lift: 809 lbs.
　SONGS:
　　1. *Janani Mirar*
　　2. *Sri Aurobindo*
1309–1310. 13 December 2004, 4:10 a.m. Xiamen, China. Seated double-dumbbell lift: 809 lbs.
　SONGS:

MY MORNING SOUL-BODY PRAYERS

       1. *Hiya pakhi*
       2. *Sundara madhumoy*
1311–1312. 15 December 2004, 3:48 a.m. Xiamen, China. Seated double-dumbbell lift: 809 lbs.
SONGS:
       1. *Nrityer tale tale tumi aso*
       2. *Chalo chalo chalo chalo*
1313–1314. 16 December 2004, 3:45 a.m. Xiamen, China. Seated double-dumbbell lift: 809 lbs.
SONGS:
       1. *Alpa kathar manush ami alpa katha koy*
       2. *Nidra bihin sangi bihin amar kanna chali ami eka*
       The Eternal Beginner (Blue violin – first day): *Bishwa janani amar janani joy hok taba joy*
1315–1316. 16 December 2004, 11:23 p.m. Xiamen, China. Seated double-dumbbell lift: 809 lbs.
SONGS:
       1. *Ami bholanath srishtir tras*
       2. *Ami bhalobasi sudur desher Japaner antar*
       The Eternal Beginner (Blue violin): *I Came to Your Lotus Feet*
1317–1318. 18 December 2004, 3:43 a.m. Xiamen, China. Seated double-dumbbell lift: 809 lbs.
SONGS:
       1. *Eso eso mor jiban majhare*
       2. *Hiyar duar khulte giye*
       The Eternal Beginner (Blue violin): *Hao aguan hao aguan*
1319–1320. 20 December 2004, 4:38 a.m. Xiamen, China. Seated double-dumbbell lift: 809 lbs.
SONGS:
       1. *Kali ma amar Kali ma amar*
       2. *Hasite hasite duhate amare*
       The Eternal Beginner (Blue violin): *Jedike phirai ankhi*
1321–1322. 22 December 2004, 6:19 a.m. Qingdao, China. Seated double-dumbbell lift: 809 lbs.
SONGS:
       1. *Bangalir gan abangali aji*
       2. *Surjya thakur chanda mama*
       The Eternal Beginner (Blue violin): *Tomai dite rishta chite*
1323–1324. 23 December 2004, 6:09 a.m. Qingdao, China. Seated double-dumbbell lift: 809 lbs.
SONGS:
       1. *Amar jiban amar maran*
       2. *Pranam janate karibona deri*
       The Eternal Beginner (Blue violin): *Jatri chale jatri chale*
1325–1326. 25 December 2004, 4:03 a.m. Qingdao, China. Non-lifting day.
SONGS:
       1. *Khule dao ankhi khule dao hiya*
       Sri Chinmoy played *The Invocation* on his synthesizer and read aloud in Sanskrit from the first chapter of the *Bhagavad Gita*.
       2. *Ogo bholanath ogo mahadev*
       The Eternal Beginner (Blue violin): *Akarane prabhu chitte tomar*
1327–1328. 26 December 2004, 5:24 a.m. Qingdao, China. Seated double-dumbbell lift: 809 lbs.
SONGS:
       1. *Mandire mandire*
       2. *Age nahi bale jadi ghare ele*
       The Eternal Beginner (Blue violin): *Bharater kabi bharater rishi*
1329–1330. 27 December 2004, 4:20 a.m. Seated double-dumbbell lift: 809 lbs.
SONGS:
       1. *Come, come, come, come*
       2. *Hiyar duar khulte giye*
       The Eternal Beginner (Blue violin): *Paper bojha bahan kare*
1331–1332. 28 December 2004, 6:24 a.m. Qingdao, China. Seated double-dumbbell lift: 809 lbs.
SONGS:

1. *Sri Ramachandra adi Avatar*
2. *Krishna bhagaban Krishna bhagaban*
The Eternal Beginner (Blue violin): *Debata eseche ruddha hiyar dare*

1333–1334. 29 December 2004, 3:53 a.m. Qingdao, China. Seated double-dumbbell lift: 809 lbs.
SONGS:
1. *Namo namo namo Buddha deber*
2. *Sachimata dake Nimai Nimai*
The Eternal Beginner (Blue violin): *Bharater kabi bharater rishi*

1335–1336. 31 December 2004, 5:49 a.m. Qingdao, China. Seated double-dumbbell lift: 1,006 lbs (first day).
SONGS:
1. *Sri Ramakrishna Sri Ramakrishna joy hok taba joy*
2. *Sri Aurobindo Sri Aurobindo kandari tumi bhava tarani*
The Eternal Beginner (Blue violin): *Khunjechi khunjechi dekechi peyechi....mata Bhavani*

1337–1338. 1 January 2005, 6:18 a.m. Qingdao, China. Seated double-dumbbell lift: 1,006 lbs.
SONGS:
1. *Jatri chal jatri chal*
2. *Ghumer rani ghumer rani*
The Eternal Beginner (Blue violin): *Bhitir ratrir habe samapti*

1339–1340. 2 January 2005, 3:58 a.m. Qingdao, China. Seated double-dumbbell lift: 1,006 lbs.
SONGS:
1. *Chinta jagate ami asohai*
2. *He Shiva Shankara namami Shankara*
The Eternal Beginner (Blue violin):
1. *Abar asibo phire*
2. *Buddham saranam gachhami*

1341–1342. 3 January 2005, 4:03 a.m. Qingdao, China. Seated double-dumbbell lift: 1,006 lbs.
SONGS:
1. *Bahudin dhare sei ek bhul*
2. *Kemane balibo kemane chalibo*
The Eternal Beginner (Blue violin): *E jibane kabhu nahi hate chahi*

1343–1344. 4 January 2005, 4:05 a.m. Qingdao, China. Seated double-dumbbell lift: 1,006 lbs.
SONGS:
1. *Brindabane Brindabane kheli nachi*
2. *Khunjite chahigo tomar nayan*
The Eternal Beginner (Blue violin): *Aghatir gati e dharar pati*

1345–1346. 6 January 2005, 3:15 a.m. Qingdao, China. Seated double-dumbbell lift: 1,006 lbs.
SONGS:
1. *Bahudin dhare sei ek bhul*
2. *Kemane balibo kemane chalibo*
The Eternal Beginner (Blue violin): *Chinta jagate ami asohai*

1347–1348. 7 January 2005, 5:31 a.m. Qingdao, China. Seated double-dumbbell lift: 1,006 lbs.
SONGS:
1. *Ghumer rani ghumer rani*
2. *Ami habo paramer jyotir nandan*
The Eternal Beginner (Blue violin) *Ogo Bholanath ogo Mahadev*

1349–1350. 8 January 2005, 6:11 a.m. Qingdao, China. Seated double-dumbbell lift: 1,006 lbs.
SONGS:
1. Sri Chinmoy spontaneously set tune to the first weightlifting prayer.
2. *Ajike amar hridaya duar*
3. Sri Chinmoy spontaneously set tune to the second weightlifting prayer.
4. *Jiban debata daki animesh*
The Eternal Beginner (Blue violin): *I came to Your Lotus-Feet*

1351–1352. 9 January 2005, 4:12 a.m. Qingdao, China. Seated double-dumbbell lift: 1,006 lbs.
SONGS:

MY MORNING SOUL-BODY PRAYERS

              1. Sri Chinmoy spontaneously set tune to the first weightlifting prayer.
              2. *Joy joy joy joy Sri Ma Mira joy*
              3. Sri Chinmoy spontaneously set tune to the second weightlifting prayer.
              4. *Jaya jaya jaya Sri Aurobindo jagat gurur joy*
              The Eternal Beginner (Blue violin): *Jedike phirai ankhi*

1353–1354. 10 January 2005, 7:04 a.m. Qingdao, China. Non-lifting day.
            SONGS:
              1. *Swapane aso swapane hasho*
              2. *Gana tana sabrita*
              The Eternal Beginner (Blue violin): *Khule dao ankhi khule dao hiya*

1355–1356. 14 January 2005, 6:35 a.m. Xian, China. Seated double-dumbbell lift: 1,006 lbs.
            SONGS:
              1. *Bahudin dhare sei ek bhul*
              2. Sri Chinmoy spontaneously set tune to the first weightlifting prayer.
              3. *Aghatir gati he dharar pati*
              4. Sri Chinmoy spontaneously set tune to the second weightlifting prayer.
              The Eternal Beginner (Blue violin): *Thakbona ar maner baner*

1357–1358. 15 January 2005, 7:40 a.m. Xian, China. Seated double-dumbbell lift: 1,006 lbs.
            SONGS:
              1. *Dibya premik hate chahi aji*
              2. *Dipti kothai shanti kothai*
              The Eternal Beginner (Blue violin): *He dharani pal he dharani pal*

1359–1360. 16 January 2005, 6:09 a.m. Xian, China. Seated double-dumbbell lift: 1,006 lbs.
            SONGS:
              1. *Srastha amar jagater jyoti*
              2. *Jiban swapan maran swapan*
              The Eternal Beginner (Blue violin): *Bela jai bela jai bela jai*

1361–1362. 17 January 2005, 11:43 p.m. Xian, China. Seated double-dumbbell lift: 1,006 lbs.
            SONGS:
              1. *Hiyar duar khulte giye*
              2. *Hasite hasite duhate amare*
              The Eternal Beginner (Blue violin): *Gurudev tumi amar lagiya*

1363–1364. 19 January 2005, 6:10 a.m. Xian, China. Seated double-dumbbell lift: 1,006 lbs.
            SONGS:
              1. *Dheyane nehari janani tomar*
              2. *Sri Aurobindo....prabhur nimeshe*
              The Eternal Beginner (Blue violin): *Dhol dhol sor gol bhalo lagena*

1365–1366. 25 January 2005, 6:48 a.m. Huangshan, China. Non-lifting day.
            SONGS:
              1. *Surjya thakur chanda mama*
              2. *Ghumer rani ghumer rani*
              The Eternal Beginner (Blue violin): *Khule dao ankhi khule dao hiya*

1367–1368. 26 January 2005, 6:01 a.m. Huangshan, China. Non-lifting day.
            SONGS:
              1. *Aghatir gati he dharar pati*
              2. *Dibya premik hate chahi aji*
              The Eternal Beginner (Blue violin): *Ogo Bholanath ogo Mahadev*

1369–1370. 28 January 2005, 7:02 p.m. Huangshan, China. Seated double-dumbbell lift: 1,006 lbs.
            SONGS:
              1. *Amar jiban amar maran*
              2. *E jibane jadi tomare harai*
              The Eternal Beginner (Blue violin): *Akashe phutilo chand*

1371–1372. 31 January 2005, 5:40 a.m. Nanjing, China. Seated double-dumbbell lift: 1,006 lbs.
            SONGS:

    1. *Hari nam balo hari nam balo*
    2. *Amar hiyar ruddha duar*
   The Eternal Beginner (Blue violin):
    1. *Ami phire ogo* (traditional)
    2. *Shanti pabo tripti pabo*
1373–1374. 7 February 2005, 7:09 a.m. Nanjing, China. Seated double-dumbbell lift: 1,006 lbs.
   SONGS:
    1. *Hari nam balo hari nam balo*
    2. *Amar hiyar ruddha duar*
   The Eternal Beginner (Blue violin):
    1. *Ami phire ogo* (traditional)
    2. *Chinta dhara ashru dhara*
1375–1376. 8 February 2005, 7:11 a.m. Nanjing, China. Non-lifting day.
   SONGS:
    1. *Madhur madhur nidra madhur*
    2. *Bhalobasi ami chira nutanere*
   The Eternal Beginner (Blue violin): *Bela jai bela jai bela jai*
1377–1378. 9 February 2005, 4:17 a.m. Nanjing, China. Seated double-dumbbell lift: 1,006 lbs.
   SONGS:
    1. *Jiban debata daki animesh*
    2. *Gurudev tumi amar lagiya*
   The Eternal Beginner (Blue violin): *Aruna swapan*
1379–1380. 10 February 2005, 4:02 a.m. Nanjing, China. Non-lifting day.
   SONGS:
    1. *Dheyane nehari janani tomar*
    2. *Hiyar duar khulte giye*
   The Eternal Beginner (Blue violin):
    1. *Ami phire ogo* (traditional)
    2. *Pranam janate karibona deri*
1381–1382. 13 February 2005, 6:02 a.m. Nanjing, China. Non-lifting day.
   SONGS:
    1. *Bishwa janani amar janani*
    2. *Jago jago jago jago....mayer kripa*
   The Eternal Beginner (Blue violin):
    1. *Ami phire ogo* (traditional)
    2. *Langhiya chali*
1383–1384. 15 February 2005, 8:55 a.m. Nanjing, China. Non-lifting day.
   SONGS:
    1. *Hiya pakhi egiye chalo*
    2. *Sundara madhumoy*
   The Eternal Beginner (Blue violin):
    1. *Satranga rabi eso eso prane*
    2. *Spontaneous improvisation*
   After performing the songs, Sri Chinmoy commented: "This is the end of our journey, possibly because it was the last day of that Christmas Trip."
  1385. 26 November 2005, 4:12 a.m. Pangkor Island, Perak, Malaysia. Seated double-dumbbell lift: 400 lbs.
   Sri Chinmoy the Eternal Beginner (Blue violin):
    1. *Ami phire ogo* (traditional – hereinafter referred to as *proem*)
    2. *Jedike phirai ankhi*
  1386. 27 November 2005, 4:31 a.m. Pangkor Island, Perak, Malaysia. Seated double-dumbbell lift: 400 lbs.
   Sri Chinmoy the Eternal Beginner (Blue violin):
    1. *Proem*
    2. *Satyam shivam sundaram*

1387. 28 November 2005, 4:13 a.m. Pangkor Island, Perak, Malaysia. Seated double-dumbbell lift: 400 lbs.
Sri Chinmoy the Eternal Beginner (Blue violin):
1. Proem
2. *Ami asimer kalpana gara*

1388. 29 November 2005, 4:06 a.m. Pangkor Island, Perak, Malaysia. Seated double-dumbbell lift: 400 lbs.
Sri Chinmoy the Eternal Beginner (Blue violin):
1. Proem
2. *Gurudev tumi amar lagiya*

1389. 30 November 2005, 4:17 a.m. Pangkor Island, Perak, Malaysia. Non-lifting day.
Sri Chinmoy the Eternal Beginner (Blue violin):
1. Proem
2. *He dharani pal*

1390. 1 December 2005, 4:14 a.m. Pangkor Island, Perak, Malaysia. Non-lifting day.
Sri Chinmoy the Eternal Beginner (Blue violin):
1. Proem
2. *Bela jai bela jai....jiban katai*

1391. 2 December 2005, 4:23 a.m. Pangkor Island, Perak, Malaysia. Non-lifting day.
Sri Chinmoy the Eternal Beginner (Blue violin):
Ami jagibona ami kandibona

1392. 3 December 2005, 4:26 a.m. Pangkor Island, Perak, Malaysia. Non-lifting day.
Sri Chinmoy the Eternal Beginner (Blue violin):
1. Proem
2. *Hasite hasite duhate amare*

1393. 4 December 2005, 4:11 a.m. Pangkor Island, Perak, Malaysia. Non-lifting day.
Sri Chinmoy the Eternal Beginner (Blue violin):
1. Proem
2. *Jishu Jishu nam*

1394. 5 December 2005, 4:16 a.m. Pangkor Island, Perak, Malaysia. Seated double-dumbbell lift: 400 lbs.
Sri Chinmoy the Eternal Beginner (Blue violin):
Abar asibo phire janani sneha nire

1395. 6 December 2005, 4:18 a.m. Pangkor Island, Perak, Malaysia. Non-lifting day.
Sri Chinmoy the Eternal Beginner (Blue violin):
1. Proem
2. *Debata eseche ruddha hiyar duare*

1396. 7 December 2005, 4:10 a.m. Pangkor Island, Perak, Malaysia. Seated double-dumbbell lift: 500 lbs.
Sri Chinmoy the Eternal Beginner (Blue violin):
Buddham saranam gacchami

1397. 8 December 2005, 3:58 a.m. Pangkor Island, Perak, Malaysia. Seated double-dumbbell lift: 500 lbs.
Sri Chinmoy the Eternal Beginner (Blue violin):
1. Proem
2. *I came to Your Lotus-Feet*

1398. 9 December 2005, 4:04 a.m. Pangkor Island, Perak, Malaysia. Seated double-dumbbell lift: 500 lbs.
Sri Chinmoy the Eternal Beginner (Blue violin):
1. Proem
2. *Jatri chal jatri chal*

1399. 13 December 2005, 3:35 a.m. Kuantan, Pahang Darul Makmur, Malaysia. Seated double-dumbbell lift: 500 lbs.
Sri Chinmoy the Eternal Beginner (Blue violin):

1. Proem
2. Anka banka jibaner path

1400. 14 December 2005, 3:56 a.m. Kuantan, Pahang Darul Makmur, Malaysia. Seated double-dumbbell lift: 500 lbs.
Sri Chinmoy the Eternal Beginner (Blue violin):
1. Proem
2. He dharani pal

1401. 15 December 2005, 3:44 a.m. Kuantan Pahang Darul Makmur, Malaysia. Non-lifting day.
Sri Chinmoy the Eternal Beginner (Blue violin):
1. Proem
2. Eso eso mor jiban majhare

1402. 16 December 2005, 3:48 a.m. Kuantan, Pahang Darul Makmur, Malaysia. Non-lifting day.
Sri Chinmoy the Eternal Beginner (Blue violin):
1. Proem
2. Bela jai bela jai bela jai

1403. 17 December 2005, 3:55 a.m. Kuantan, Pahang Darul Makmur, Malaysia. Seated double-dumbbell lift: 500 lbs.
Sri Chinmoy the Eternal Beginner (Blue violin):
Gurudev tumi amar lagiya

1404. 18 December 2005, 3:51 a.m. Kuantan, Pahang Darul Makmur, Malaysia. Seated double-dumbbell lift: 500 lbs.
Sri Chinmoy the Eternal Beginner (Blue violin):
1. Proem
2. Amar jibana bariya

1405. 19 December 2005, 3:56 a.m. Kuantan, Pahang Darul Makmur, Malaysia. Non-lifting day.
Sri Chinmoy the Eternal Beginner (Blue violin):
1. Proem
2. Hao aguan

1406. 20 December 2005, 4:08 a.m. Kuantan, Pahang Darul Makmur, Malaysia. Seated double-dumbbell lift: 600 lbs.
Sri Chinmoy the Eternal Beginner (Blue violin):
1. Proem
2. Amar jiban amar maran
3. My Life, My Death

1407. 21 December 2005, Kuantan, Pahang Darul Makmur, Malaysia. Non-lifting day.
Sri Chinmoy the Eternal Beginner (Blue violin):
1. Proem
2. Swapane aso swapane haso

1408. 22 December 2005, 3:25 a.m. Kuantan, Pahang Darul Makmur, Malaysia. Seated double-dumbbell lift: 600 lbs. Sri Chinmoy sang this prayer as he offered it.
Sri Chinmoy the Eternal Beginner (Blue violin):
1. Proem
2. Ami jagibona ami kandibona

1409. 23 December 2005, 3:48 a.m. Kuantan, Pahang Darul Makmur, Malaysia. Non-lifting day.
Sri Chinmoy the Eternal Beginner (Blue violin):
1. Proem
2. Ami bholanath sristir tras

1410. 24 December 2005, 4:01 a.m. Kuantan, Pahang Darul Makmur, Malaysia. Seated double-dumbbell lift: 600 lbs.
Sri Chinmoy the Eternal Beginner (Blue violin):

MY MORNING SOUL-BODY PRAYERS

    1. *Proem*
    2. *Jishu Jishu nam* (Sri Chinmoy sang this song after playing it.)
1411. 25 December 2005, 4:10 a.m. Kuantan, Pahang Darul Makmur, Malaysia. Seated double-dumbbell lift: 999 lbs.
    Sri Chinmoy the Eternal Beginner (Blue violin):
    1. *Proem*
    2. *Tomare pujite esechi dharai* (Sri Chinmoy sang this new composition as he played it.)
1412. 26 December 2005, 3:57 a.m. Kuantan, Pahang Darul Makmur, Malaysia. Seated double-dumbbell lift: 999 lbs.
    Sri Chinmoy the Eternal Beginner (Blue violin):
    1. *Proem*
    2. *Dak dak dak dak maner praner* (Sri Chinmoy sang this new composition as he played it.)
1413. 27 December 2005, 4:12 a.m. Kuantan, Pahang Darul Makmur, Malaysia. Non-lifting day.
    Sri Chinmoy the Eternal Beginner (Blue violin):
    1. *Proem*
    2. *Tomar sathe chalbo ami* (Sri Chinmoy played and sang this new song.)
1414. 28 December 2005, 3:40 a.m. Kuantan, Pahang Darul Makmur, Malaysia. Seated double-dumbbell lift: 1,004 lbs.
    Sri Chinmoy the Eternal Beginner (Blue violin):
    1. *Proem*
    2. *Tomar madhur nayan dekhe* (Sri Chinmoy played and sang this new song.)
1415. 29 December 2005, 4:13 a.m. Kuantan, Pahang Darul Makmur, Malaysia. Non-lifting day.
    Sri Chinmoy the Eternal Beginner (Blue violin):
    1. *Proem*
    2. *Chaowar paowar kanna hashi tomar rahe* (Sri Chinmoy played and sang this new song.)
1416. 30 December 2005, 3:54 a.m. Kuantan, Pahang Darul Makmur, Malaysia. Non-lifting day.
    Sri Chinmoy the Eternal Beginner (Blue violin):
    1. *Proem*
    2. *Jatri ami jatri ami asim khudha* (Sri Chinmoy played and sang this new song.)
1417. 31 December 2005, 3:54 a.m. Kuantan, Pahang Darul Makmur, Malaysia. Non-lifting day.
    Sri Chinmoy the Eternal Beginner (Blue violin):
    1. *Proem*
    2. *Eso eso mor jiban majhare*
1418. 1 January 2006, 4:00 a.m. Kuantan, Pahang Darul Makmur, Malaysia. Non-lifting day.
    Sri Chinmoy the Eternal Beginner (Blue violin):
    1. *Proem*
    2. *Hasite hasite duhate amare*
1419. 2 January 2006, 4:15 a.m. Kuantan, Pahang Darul Makmur, Malaysia. Non-lifting day.
    Sri Chinmoy the Eternal Beginner (Blue violin):
    1. *Proem*
    2. *He dharani pal*
1420. 3 January 2006. Kuantan, Pahang Darul Makmur, Malaysia. Non-lifting day.
    Sri Chinmoy the Eternal Beginner (Blue violin):
    1. *Akarane prabhu*
    2. *E jibane jadi*
    3. *Jibaner sheshe maraner deshe*
1421. 4 January 2006, 4:19 a.m. Kijal, Kemaman, Terengganu Darul Iman, Malaysia. Non-lifting day.
    Sri Chinmoy the Eternal Beginner (Blue violin):

1. *Proem*
   2. *Jishu Jishu nam*
1422. 5 January 2006, 4:26 a.m. Kijal, Kemaman, Terengganu Darul Iman, Malaysia. Non-lifting day.
   Sri Chinmoy the Eternal Beginner (Blue violin):
   1. *Proem*
   2. *Gurudev tumi amar lagiya*
1423. 6 January 2006, 4:16 a.m. Kijal, Kemaman, Terengganu Darul Iman, Malaysia. Seated double-dumbbell lift: 1,002 lbs.
   Sri Chinmoy the Eternal Beginner (Blue violin):
   1. *Proem*
   2. *Janani Mirar sneha bara ankhi*
1424. 7 January 2006, 4:22 a.m. Kijal, Kemaman, Terengganu Darul Iman, Malaysia. Non-lifting day.
   Sri Chinmoy the Eternal Beginner (Blue violin):
   1. *Proem*
   2. *I came to Your Lotus-Feet*
1425. 8 January 2006, 4:21 a.m. Kijal, Kemaman, Terengganu Darul Iman, Malaysia. Seated double-dumbbell lift: 1,002 lbs.
   Sri Chinmoy the Eternal Beginner (Blue violin):
   1. *Proem*
   2. *Amar jiban amar maran*
   3. *My life, my death*
1426. 9 January 2006, 4:16 a.m. Kijal, Kemaman, Terengganu Darul Iman, Malaysia. Non-lifting day.
   Sri Chinmoy the Eternal Beginner (Blue violin):
   1. *Proem*
   2. *Ar sab jai jak*
1427. 10 January 2006, 4:17 a.m. Kijal, Kemaman, Terengganu Darul Iman, Malaysia. Non-lifting day. Sri Chinmoy also made this prayer into a song.
   Sri Chinmoy the Eternal Beginner (Blue violin):
   1. *Proem*
   2. *Abar asibo phire*
1428. 11 January 2006, 3:17 a.m. Kijal, Kemaman, Terengganu Darul Iman, Malaysia. Non-lifting day.
   Sri Chinmoy the Eternal Beginner (Blue violin):
   1. *Proem*
   2. *Hao aguan*
   3. *Improvisation*
1429. 12 January 2006, 3:23 a.m. Kijal, Kemaman, Terengganu Darul Iman, Malaysia. Non-lifting day.
   Sri Chinmoy the Eternal Beginner (Blue violin):
   1. *Proem*
   2. *Gurudev tumi amar lagiya* (Sri Chinmoy played and sang this song.)
1430. 13 January 2006, 4:36 a.m. Kijal, Kemaman, Terengganu Darul Iman, Malaysia. Non-lifting day.
   Sri Chinmoy the Eternal Beginner (Blue violin):
   1. *Proem*
   2. *Ami bholanath sristir tras*
1431. 14 January 2006, 4:13 a.m. Kijal, Kemaman, Terengganu Darul Iman, Malaysia. Non-lifting day.
   Sri Chinmoy the Eternal Beginner (Blue violin):
   1. *Proem*
   2. *I came to Your Lotus-Feet* (Sri Chinmoy played and sang this song.)

1432. 15 January 2006, 4:14 a.m. Kijal, Kemaman, Terengganu Darul Iman, Malaysia. Non-lifting day.
Sri Chinmoy the Eternal Beginner (Blue violin):
1. Proem
2. *Jishu Jishu nam* (Sri Chinmoy played and sang this song.)

1433. 16 January 2006, 4:27 a.m. Kijal, Kemaman, Terengganu Darul Iman, Malaysia. Non-lifting day.
Sri Chinmoy the Eternal Beginner (Blue violin):
1. Proem
2. *Buddham saranam gacchami* (Sri Chinmoy played and sang this song.)

1434. 17 January 2006, 5:08 a.m. Kijal, Kemaman, Terengganu Darul Iman, Malaysia. Non-lifting day. Sri Chinmoy also made this prayer into a song.
Sri Chinmoy the Eternal Beginner (Blue violin):
1. Proem
2. *Eso eso mor jiban majhare* (Sri Chinmoy played and sang this song.)

1435. 18 January 2006, 4:29 a.m. Kijal, Kemaman, Terengganu Darul Iman, Malaysia. Non-lifting day.
Sri Chinmoy the Eternal Beginner (Blue violin):
1. Proem
2. *Debata eseche ruddha hiyar duare* (Sri Chinmoy played and sang this song.)

1436. 19 January 2006, 4:38 a.m. Kijal, Kemaman, Terengganu Darul Iman, Malaysia. Non-lifting day.
Sri Chinmoy the Eternal Beginner (Blue violin):
1. Proem
2. *Satranga rabi eso eso prane* (Sri Chinmoy played and sang this song.)

1437. 20 January 2006, 4:13 a.m. Kijal, Kemaman, Terengganu Darul Iman, Malaysia. Non-lifting day.
Sri Chinmoy the Eternal Beginner (Blue violin):
1. Proem
2. *Sri Ramachandra adi Avatar* (Sri Chinmoy played and sang this song.)

1438. 21 January 2006, 4:32 a.m. Kijal, Kemaman, Terengganu Darul Iman, Malaysia. Non-lifting day.
Sri Chinmoy the Eternal Beginner (Blue violin):
1. Proem
2. *I came to Your Lotus-Feet* (Sri Chinmoy played and sang this song.)

1439–1440. 23 January 2006, 4:25 a.m. Kijal, Kemaman, Terengganu Darul Iman, Malaysia. Non-lifting day.
Sri Chinmoy the Eternal Beginner (Blue violin):1. Proem
2. *He dharani pal* (Sri Chinmoy played and then sang this song.)
Sri Chinmoy offered two prayers on this day, the second at 9:15 a.m.

1441. 24 January 2006, Kijal, Kemaman, Terengganu Darul Iman, Malaysia. Non-lifting day (no video taken).

1442. 26 January 2006, 4:26 a.m. Kijal, Kemaman, Terengganu Darul Iman, Malaysia. Non-lifting day.
Sri Chinmoy the Eternal Beginner (Blue violin):
1. Proem
2. *Satyam shivam sundaram* (Sri Chinmoy played and then sang this song.)

1443. 28 January 2006, 3:56 a.m. Penang, Malaysia. Non-lifting day.

1444. 29 January 2006, 3:46 a.m. Penang, Malaysia. Non-lifting day.
Sri Chinmoy the Eternal Beginner (Blue violin):
1. Proem
2. *Akarane prabhu* (Sri Chinmoy played and then sang this song.)

1445. 30 January 2006, 4:07 a.m. Penang, Malaysia. Seated double-dumbbell lift: 600 lbs.
Sri Chinmoy the Eternal Beginner (Blue violin):

1. *Proem*
2. *Ami bholanath sristir tras* (Sri Chinmoy played and then sang this song.)
1446. 31 January 2006, Penang, Malaysia. 5:03 a.m. – Non-lifting day.
   PUSH-UPS – first day: 4:36 a.m.
   1st set: 47 (slight dips)
   2nd set: 30 (a little deeper)
   3rd set: 19 (medium dips)
   4th set: 10 (deep dips)
   Total 106 repetitions
1447. 1 February 2006, 3:40 a.m. Penang, Malaysia. Non-lifting day.
   Sri Chinmoy the Eternal Beginner (Blue violin):
   1. *Proem*
   2. *Gurudev tumi* (Sri Chinmoy played and then sang this song.)
   PUSH-UPS: 4:26 a.m.
   1st set: 49 (slight dips)
   2nd set: 27 (medium dips)
   3rd set: 18 (deep dips)
   Total 94 repetitions
1448. 2 February 2006. Penang, Malaysia. Non-lifting day.
   Sri Chinmoy the Eternal Beginner (Blue violin):
   1. *Proem*
   2. *Bela jai bela jai bela jai* (Sri Chinmoy played and then sang this song.)
1449. 3 February 2006, 3:50 a.m. Penang, Malaysia. Non-lifting day.
   Sri Chinmoy the Eternal Beginner (Blue violin):
   1. *Proem*
   2. *I came to Your Lotus-Feet* (Sri Chinmoy played and then sang this song.)
   PUSH-UPS: 4:21 a.m.
   1st set: 49 (slight dips)
   2nd set: 31 (a little deeper)
   3rd set: 21 (medium dips)
   4th set: 12 (deep dips)
   Total 113 repetitions
   PUSH-UPS: 4:28 a.m.
   1st set: 49 (slight dips)
   2nd set: 31 (a little deeper)
   3rd set: 23 (medium dips)
   4th set: 12 (deep dips)
   Total 115 repetitions
1450. 5 February 2006, 3:43 a.m. Penang, Malaysia. Non-lifting day.
   Sri Chinmoy the Eternal Beginner (Blue violin):
   1. *Proem*
   2. *Hasite hasite duhate amare* (Sri Chinmoy played and then sang this song.)
1451. 6 February 2006, 3:44 a.m. Penang, Malaysia. Non-lifting day.
   Sri Chinmoy the Eternal Beginner (Blue violin):
   1. *Proem*
   2. *Amar jiban amar maran* (Sri Chinmoy played and then sang this song.)
   PUSH-UPS: 4:09 a.m.
   1st set: 34 (slight dips)
   2nd set: 28 (a little deeper)
   3rd set: 22 (medium dips)
   4th set: 12 (deep dips)
   Total 96 repetitions
1452. 7 February 2006, 3:45 a.m. Penang, Malaysia. Non-lifting day.
   Sri Chinmoy the Eternal Beginner (Blue violin):
   1. *Proem*

MY MORNING SOUL-BODY PRAYERS

        2. *Savita savita savita* (Sri Chinmoy played and then sang this song. Later he also whistled it.)

1453. 8 February 2006. Penang, Malaysia. Non-lifting day.
Sri Chinmoy the Eternal Beginner (Blue violin):
1. Proem
2. *Ami bholanath* (Sri Chinmoy played and then sang this song.)

1454–1455. 9 February 2006, 7:27 a.m. Penang, Malaysia. Non-lifting day. The second prayer was offered later that morning.
Sri Chinmoy the Eternal Beginner (Blue violin):
1. Proem
2. *Debata eseche ruddha hiyar dware* (Sri Chinmoy played and then sang this song.)

1456. 10 February 2006. Penang, Malaysia. Non-lifting day.

1457–1458. 12 February 2006, 4:17 a.m. Langkawi, Kedah Darul Aman, Malaysia. Seated double-dumbbell lift: 600 lbs. The second prayer was offered later that morning.
Sri Chinmoy played the alto flute:
1. Proem
2. *Brindabane brindabane*
3. *Abar asibo phire*
4. *Buddham saranam gacchami* (Sri Chinmoy played and then sang each song.)

1459. 13 February 2006, 3:55 a.m. Langkawi, Kedah Darul Aman, Malaysia. Non-lifting day.
Sri Chinmoy the Eternal Beginner (Blue violin):
1. Proem
2. *Hao aguan hao aguan* (Sri Chinmoy played and then sang this song.)
PUSH-UPS: 4:56 a.m.
1st set: 28 (slight dips)
2nd set: 18 (a little deeper)
3rd set: 18 (medium dips)
4th set: 10 (deep dips)
Total 74 repetitions

1460–1461. 14 February 2006, 4:11 a.m. Langkawi, Kedah Darul Aman, Malaysia. Seated double-dumbbell lift: 600 lbs. The second prayer was offered later that morning.
Sri Chinmoy the Eternal Beginner (Blue violin):
1. Proem
2. *Ami bholanath* (Sri Chinmoy played and then sang this song.)

1462. 15 February 2006, 4:02 a.m. Langkawi, Kedah Darul Aman, Malaysia. Non-lifting day.
Sri Chinmoy the Eternal Beginner (Blue violin):
1. Proem
2. *Hasite hasite duhate amare* (Sri Chinmoy played and then sang this song.)
PUSH-UPS: 4:25 a.m.
1st set: 40 (slight dips)
2nd set: 24 (a little deeper)
3rd set: 21 (medium dips)
4th set: 12 (deep dips)
Total 97 repetitions

1463. 16 February 2006, Langkawi, Kedah Darul Aman, Malaysia. Non-lifting day.

1464. 17 February 2006, Langkawi, Kedah Darul Aman, Malaysia. Non-lifting day.

1465. 18 February 2006, 3:52 a.m. Langkawi, Kedah Darul Aman, Malaysia. Seated double-dumbbell lift: 600 lbs.
Sri Chinmoy played the alto flute:
1. *Abar asibo phire*
2. *Satyam shivam sundaram*
3. *My Own Gratitude-Heart*
4. *Brindabane brindabane*
PUSH-UPS: 4:09 a.m.
1st set: 46 (slight dips)

2nd set: 27 (a little deeper)
3rd set: 23 (medium dips)
4th set: 13 (deep dips)
Total 109 repetitions

1466. 19 February 2006, 3:58 a.m. Langkawi, Kedah Darul Aman, Malaysia. Non-lifting day. Sri Chinmoy played the viola:
1. *Jishu Jishu nam*
2. *Jedike phirai ankhi* (Sri Chinmoy sang each song as he played it.)

1467. 20 February 2006, 4:04 a.m. Langkawi, Kedah Darul Aman, Malaysia. Seated double-dumbbell lift: 600 lbs.
Sri Chinmoy played the viola:
1. *Namo namo namo buddha deber* (Sri Chinmoy sang as he played the song and then again after playing it.)

1468. 21 February 2006, 4:04 a.m. Langkawi, Kedah Darul Aman, Malaysia. Non-lifting day. Sri Chinmoy played the horn ocarina:
1. *Satyam shivam sundaram*
2. *Ami bholanath*

Sri Chinmoy played the unisphere:
1. *Amar jiban amar maran*
2. *My life, my death*
3. *Bela jai bela jai bela jai*
4. *Hao aguan hao aguan*

1469. 22 February 2006, 4:07 a.m. Langkawi, Kedah Darul Aman, Malaysia. Non-lifting day.
Sri Chinmoy the Eternal Beginner (Blue violin):
1. *Proem*
2. *Debata eseche ruddha hiyar dware* (Sri Chinmoy played and then sang this song.)

1470. 23 February 2006, Langkawi, Kedah Darul Aman, Malaysia. Non-lifting day.

1471. 24 February 2006, Langkawi, Kedah Darul Aman, Malaysia. Non-lifting day.

APPENDIX

NOTES TO CURRENT EDITION

NOTES TO CURRENT EDITION

My morning Soul-Body prayers includes several notes with dates, lifting, songs and other annotations for the numbered prayers. Respecting the Author's wish, they have been grouped at the end of the current edition.

Proem indicates the traditional song *Ami phire ogo*.

PREFACES TO ORIGINAL EDITION

PREFACES TO ORIGINAL EDITION OF
MY MORNING SOUL-BODY PRAYERS

Part 1
The prayers in this volume were offered by Sri Chinmoy during his early-morning weightlifting workouts between 30 September 1998 and 2 December 1998 in New York.

Part 2
On 4 December 1998, Sri Chinmoy left New York for his annual Christmas trip. During the following two months, he travelled to Hawaii, Singapore, Malaysia, Indonesia, India and Nepal. He took with him some of his main pieces of exercise equipment and thus was able to continue his early morning workouts in each new venue, with the exception of India and Nepal.

This book contains the prayers that Sri Chinmoy offered daily before beginning each new lift. Speaking about the prayers, Sri Chinmoy has said, "Every day, with folded hands, I give these prayers for you, for humanity. I do this not for myself. I do it for all my spiritual children. I do not think about what I am going to say on any particular day. I just throw myself into the Universal Consciousness and identify myself with this person or that person. It is like plucking a flower from a garden. The flower that I like most, I take. I see that one particular prayer is most appropriate for that person on that day. Tomorrow I will identify with someone else. It is all oneness, oneness, oneness. Where my spiritual children are, I also am there. If you take me to hell, even there I will go, but with the hope that one day I will be able to bring you to Heaven."

Part 3
These morning prayers were offered by Sri Chinmoy during his weightlifting sessions at his home in New York in February and March 1999.

   Note to cover photo: Sri Chinmoy lifts South African President Nelson Mandela overhead with one arm on 9 March 1999 at the President's official residence in Johannesburg. President Mandela became the 2,000th person to be lifted as part of Sri Chinmoy's "Lifting Up the World with a Oneness-Heart" programme.

Part 4
These morning prayers were offered by Sri Chinmoy during his weightlifting sessions at his home in New York in April 1999.

Part 5
These morning prayers were offered by Sri Chinmoy during his weightlifting sessions at his home in New York in May 1999.

Part 6
These morning prayers were offered by Sri Chinmoy during his weightlifting sessions at his home in New York in June 1999.

Part 7
These morning prayers were offered by Sri Chinmoy during his weightlifting sessions at his home in New York in July 1999.

Part 8
These morning prayers were offered by Sri Chinmoy during his weightlifting sessions at his home in New York in August 1999.

Part 9
These morning prayers were offered by Sri Chinmoy during his weightlifting sessions at his home in New York in September 1999.

Part 10
These morning prayers were offered by Sri Chinmoy during his weightlifting sessions at his home in New York in October 1999.

Part 11
These morning prayers were offered by Sri Chinmoy during his weightlifting sessions at his home in New York in November and during his visit to various cities in Brazil in December 1999.

Part 12
These morning prayers were offered by Sri Chinmoy as part of his weightlifting sessions during his visit to various cities in Brazil and Paraguay in January and at his home in New York in February 2000.

Part 13
These morning prayers were offered by Sri Chinmoy as part of his weightlifting sessions at his home in New York in March and April 2000.

Part 14
These prayers were offered by Sri Chinmoy as part of his weightlifting sessions at his home in New York in May and June 2000.

Part 15
These prayers were offered by Sri Chinmoy as part of his weightlifting sessions at his home in New York in July and August 2000.

Part 16
These prayers were offered by Sri Chinmoy as part of his weightlifting sessions at his home in New York in September and October 2000.

Part 17
During Sri Chinmoy's trip to China – where he visited eight cities between 24 November 2004 and 15 February 2005 – he would often practise his heavy weightlifting in his hotel room in the small hours of the morning. He concentrated on the seated double-dumbbell lift – beginning with 809 pounds and advancing to 1,006 pounds on 31 December.

At these practice sessions, Sri Chinmoy evolved a pattern of prayers, singing, lifting and meditation. He also included a segment which he called *The Eternal Beginner*. Here he played a song on his blue violin. Many times these songs had been composed by him during his trip.

For the first two weeks, Sri Chinmoy concluded each practice session with a humorous joke. But he later mentioned that he found it hard to come down from his meditative state in order to enter into the sweet, joking consciousness and, after 31 December, he told jokes during the evening functions with his disciples.

On the days when Sri Chinmoy's equipment had not arrived from the previous location, or when he was not feeling well, he often continued the same pattern of prayers, singing, meditation and blue violin.

Each day, during the regular morning prayers with his disciples, Sri Chinmoy would replay the video of his soulful workout, pausing frequently so that they could repeat the prayers and sing each song after him. These precious moments became a highlight of the Christmas trip for all who were present.

Part 18
During Sri Chinmoy's trip to China – where he visited eight cities between 24 November 2004 and 15 February 2005 – he would often practise his heavy weightlifting in his hotel room in the small hours of the morning. He concentrated on the seated double-dumbbell lift – beginning with 809 pounds and advancing to 1,006 pounds on 31 December.

At these practice sessions, Sri Chinmoy evolved a pattern of prayers, singing, lifting and meditation. He also included a segment which he called *The Eternal Beginner*. Here he played a song on his blue violin. Many times these songs had been composed by him during his trip.

For the first two weeks, Sri Chinmoy concluded each practice session with a humorous joke. But he later mentioned that he found it hard to come down from his meditative state in order to enter into the sweet, joking consciousness and, after 31 December, he told jokes during the evening functions with his disciples.

Part 19
During Sri Chinmoy's Christmas-New Year trip to Malaysia from 23 November 2005 to 25 February 2006, he visited six locations: Kuala Lumpur, Pangkor Island, Kuantan, Kijal, Penang and Langkawi Island.

As on previous Christmas trips, Sri Chinmoy often practised his heavy weightlifting in his hotel room in the small hours of the morning. In addition to his regular exercises, he concentrated on the seated double-dumbbell lift, using varying weights, ranging from 400 pounds to 1,004 pounds.

At these sessions, which were recorded on video, Sri Chinmoy continued his pattern established in previous years of offering an early morning prayer and performing one of his compositions on his blue violin – a segment which he calls *Sri Chinmoy the Eternal Beginner.* He would frequently sing these songs after playing them. Towards the end of the trip, Sri Chinmoy also played songs on the alto flute, viola, horn ocarina and unisphere.

Part 20
During Sri Chinmoy's Christmas/New Year trip to Malaysia from 23 November 2005 to 25 February 2006, he visited six locations. They were Kuala Lumpur, Pangkor Island, Kuantan, Kijal, Penang and Langkawi Island.

As in previous Christmas trips, Sri Chinmoy often practised his heavy weightlifting in his hotel room in the small hours of the morning. In addition to his regular exercises, he concentrated on the seated double-dumbbell lift, using varying weights ranging from 400 pounds to 1,004 pounds.

At these sessions, which were recorded on video, Sri Chinmoy continued his pattern established in previous years, offering an early morning prayer and performing one of his compositions on his blue violin – a segment which he calls *Sri Chinmoy the Eternal Beginner.* He would frequently sing these songs after playing them. Towards the end of the trip, Sri Chinmoy also played songs on the alto flute, viola, horn ocarina and unisphere.

Each day Sri Chinmoy showed the video of his early morning workouts to his students. On 6 December 2005, Sri Chinmoy formed a new group of girls under 25 years of age to recite his early morning prayers.

On 31 January 2006 – the day after lifting 270 pounds in the wrist curl – Sri Chinmoy introduced push-ups into his morning sessions. This was the first time he had done push-ups on a Christmas trip since 7 January 1986 in Kyoto, Japan, where he performed 2,230 push-ups continuously in 59 minutes and 50 seconds.

This year, Sri Chinmoy's push-ups were mostly done in four sets, beginning with rapid, slight dips and progressing to full, deep dips.

Part 21
During Sri Chinmoy's Christmas/New Year trip to Malaysia from 23 November 2005 to 25 February 2006, he visited six locations. They were Kuala Lumpur, Pangkor Island, Kuantan, Kijal, Penang and Langkawi Island.

As in previous Christmas trips, Sri Chinmoy often practised his heavy weightlifting in his hotel room in the small hours of the morning. In addition to his regular exercises, he concentrated on the seated double-dumbbell lift, using varying weights ranging from 400 pounds to 1,004 pounds.

At these sessions, which were recorded on video, Sri Chinmoy continued his pattern established in previous years, offering an early morning prayer and performing one of his compositions on his blue violin – a segment which he calls *Sri Chinmoy the Eternal Beginner*. He would frequently sing these songs after playing them. Towards the end of the trip, Sri Chinmoy also played songs on the alto flute, viola, horn ocarina and unisphere.

Each day Sri Chinmoy showed the video of his early morning workouts to his students. On 6 December 2005, Sri Chinmoy formed a new group of girls under 25 years of age to recite his early morning prayers.

On 31 January 2006 – the day after lifting 270 pounds in the wrist curl – Sri Chinmoy introduced push-ups into his morning sessions. This was the first time he had done push-ups on a Christmas trip since 7 January 1986 in Kyoto, Japan, where he performed 2,230 push-ups continuously in 59 minutes and 50 seconds.

This year, Sri Chinmoy's push-ups were mostly done in four sets, beginning with rapid, slight dips and progressing to full, deep dips.

BIBLIOGRAPHY

MY MORNING SOUL-BODY PRAYERS (21 VOLUMES)

SRI CHINMOY:
–*My Morning Soul-Body Prayers, part 1*, New York, Agni Press, 1999.
–*My Morning Soul-Body Prayers, part 2*, New York, Agni Press, 1999.
–*My Morning Soul-Body Prayers, part 3*, New York, Agni Press, 1999.
–*My Morning Soul-Body Prayers, part 4*, New York, Agni Press, 1999.
–*My Morning Soul-Body Prayers, part 5*, New York, Agni Press, 1999.
–*My Morning Soul-Body Prayers, part 6*, New York, Agni Press, 1999.
–*My Morning Soul-Body Prayers, part 7*, New York, Agni Press, 1999.
–*My Morning Soul-Body Prayers, part 8*, New York, Agni Press, 1999.
–*My Morning Soul-Body Prayers, part 9*, New York, Agni Press, 1999.
–*My Morning Soul-Body Prayers, part 10*, New York, Agni Press, 2000.
–*My Morning Soul-Body Prayers, part 11*, New York, Agni Press, 2000.
–*My Morning Soul-Body Prayers, part 12*, New York, Agni Press, 2000.
–*My Morning Soul-Body Prayers, part 13*, New York, Agni Press, 2000.
–*My Morning Soul-Body Prayers, part 14*, New York, Agni Press, 2000.
–*My Morning Soul-Body Prayers, part 15*, New York, Agni Press, 2000.

—*My Morning Soul-Body Prayers, part 16*, New York, Agni Press, 2000.
—*My Morning Soul-Body Prayers, part 17*, New York, Agni Press, 2005.
—*My Morning Soul-Body Prayers, part 18*, New York, Agni Press, 2005.
—*My Morning Soul-Body Prayers, part 19*, New York, Agni Press, 2006.
—*My Morning Soul-Body Prayers, part 20*, New York, Agni Press, 2006.
—*My Morning Soul-Body Prayers, part 21*, New York, Agni Press, 2006.

Suggested citation key is MP.

POSTFACE

PUBLISHING PRINCIPLES

This edition of *The works of Sri Chinmoy* aims to obey the Author's wish: scrupulous fidelity to his original words, use of typographical style by him selected, specific spelling choices, end placement of any editorial content (i.e. not written by Sri Chinmoy himself), particular treatment of some personal nouns in special cases, etc.

TEXTUAL ACCURACY

This edition has been checked to ensure faithful accuracy to the originals. Although much effort has been put in proofreading and comparing different versions of the text, this print may still present lingering errors. The Publisher would be grateful to be apprised of any mistypes via postal mail or facsimile, possibly with scan of the original page where the text is different. Please use original books only, specifying the year of publication, as no online version can be considered authoritative.

Ongoing reprints will include any revised text from these errata.

ACKNOWLEDGEMENTS

The Publisher is very grateful to the late Professor Lambert and his équipe for his invaluable advice. For many decades Prof. Lambert conducted a small publishing house specialising in hand-made prints of philological edition of the classics. The standard of this edition would not have been the same without his scholarly advice.

The Publisher is also grateful to the international team of collaborators that spent countless hours proofreading and checking the current text against the originals.

Our deepest gratitude to Sri Chinmoy. His living presence can be felt breathing throughout his writings. It is a privilege to be involved with his works, in any form.

CITATION KEYS

Citation keys are used throughout *The works of Sri Chinmoy* to allow accurate cross-reference of texts across titles and editions. Examples: EA 13, ST 50000, UPA 7.

SRI CHINMOY CANON

We could not use better words than Professor Lambert's, who kindly offered the name *Sri Chinmoy Canon*:

«By defining Sri Chinmoy's first editions as *editio princeps* we chose to follow classical scholarship criteria, not because we consider Sri Chinmoy's work antique, but because we believe it is among the few post ‹classical antiquity› works to rightly deserve to be considered a *classicus*, designating by that term *superiority, authority* and *perfection*.

«The monumental work Sri Chinmoy is offering to mankind is awe-inspiring and supremely pre-eminent in proportions and quality. It is manifest that Sri Chinmoy's work — which we feel right to call *The Sri Chinmoy Canon* — will be of profound help and source of enlightenment to anyone seeking a higher wisdom, truth and reality supreme.»

[Translated from French by M. G.S.]

TABLE OF CONTENTS

MY MORNING SOUL-BODY PRAYERS	3
APPENDIX	671
NOTES TO CURRENT EDITION	673
PREFACES TO ORIGINAL EDITION	677
BIBLIOGRAPHY	687
POSTFACE	691
TABLE OF CONTENTS	695

*Composition typographique par imprimerie
Ab Academia Aoidon, Paris & Lyon.*

*Un grand merci à Prof Knuth pour
l'utilisation avancée de TeX.*

A LYON, LE 7 FÉVRIER LXXXIX Æ.G.